Autism Intervention in the iEra

The Socially Speaking™ Program

Practical Social Communication Strategies for Integrating Toys and Tech in Treatment

Penina Rybak MA/CCC-SLP

authorHOUSE®

AuthorHouse™
1663 Liberty Drive
Bloomington, IN 47403
www.authorhouse.com
Phone: 1 (800) 839-8640

Published by AuthorHouse   04/23/2015

ISBN: 978-1-5049-0708-8 (sc)
ISBN: 978-1-5049-0707-1 (e)

Print information available on the last page.

Table of Contents

Advance Praise

I am amazed at the abundant resources this book has to offer! Penina Rybak provides a rich source of fresh ideas, original techniques, references, and information with tried and true approaches to help your child or student reach their potential. This book should be on the bookshelf every parent or educator who touches the lives of individuals on the autism spectrum!

Lois Jean Brady, MA/CCC-SLP, CAS
Speech-Language Pathologist and Author, *Apps for Autism*

Penina Rybak digs deep to address the root causes of specific learning challenges that are unique to children on the autism spectrum. Teachers and therapists will love her extensive lists of educational goals and teaching resources that reflect the visual learning strengths of these students. Her innovative ideas for developing "digital citizenship" capture the most up-to-date uses for iPad® and apps for ASD.

Linda Hodgdon M.Ed., CCC-SLP
Speech-Language Pathologist, Autism Consultant,
Author: *Visual Strategies for Improving Communication*

I have traveled both nationally and internationally as a speaker who addresses multiple pediatric neurological topics and I have met some interesting people. However, Penina Rybak is one who stands out; with her enthusiastic, brilliant mind, and her unique educational seminars. Penina has produced some amazing work here! She has created a historical pathway for social skills intervention using groundbreaking educational tools for those who treat and teach children with social skill deficits.

I know many avid readers have read books, only to be left, with the thought of, "Yes, but why?" Many books explain the problems with great detail. However, the solutions are limited. I am extremely excited to say that Penina Rybak's book is one of the most descriptive and detailed educational books of our decade!

Penina has provided the reader with a step by step format for understanding why social deficits exist for children with Autism. She clearly identifies what happens developmentally to create social skills in the first place. One aspect of Penina's book that I found most intriguing was the fact that she defines and makes detailed lists, graphs and pictures as descriptors of what is taking place, and what should be taking place, as a child develops socially. Most often in health care and education we tend to get the cart before the horse.

Penina displays a clear, concise understanding of the sequential process for socio-emotional development. More importantly, Penina gives us tools to remediate the national epidemic of social decline. This book is geared toward Autism. However, I do believe that this is one book that will touch the lives of readers and facilitate their desire to become more aware of their own social powers.

Charlene Young, OTR/L, CEAS
Occupational Therapist and Founder, CharBrian Foundation Inc.

As a developer of apps for autistic children, I have collaborated with Penina Rybak on and off for the last 4 years. Her insights into the minds of autistic children has made her an invaluable resource. I have consulted with her on everything from small changes to existing apps to creating new apps from scratch. It's wonderful to see her put all of her knowledge into a single text for all to benefit. A must read for educators and parents alike who interact with children on the autism spectrum.

Kyle Tomson
President and Founder of Mobile Education Store

You will find this book to be a valuable resource! Jam-packed with information, this book is designed to educate the reader about the social difficulties children with Autism and special needs face. More importantly, it is overflowing with practical strategies which take the abstractness out of social skills intervention. Anecdotes allow for the understanding of specific social difficulties common to many children with Autism. But the real strength in this book, is the ability to provide a wealth of intervention techniques on how to achieve social success! Conceptual strategies, clinical implications, You Tube™ video suggestions for lessons, suggested apps, narrative descriptions, hierarchies of intervention, references to other authors' works, and links to informative sites, are just some of the many components Penina Rybak provides. Learn what to add to your toolbox, and improve your ability to make a positive change for children with Autism struggling with social difficulties at home and in school.

Timothy P. Kowalski, MA/CCC-SLP
Speech-Language Pathologist and President at Professional Communication Services Inc.

Penina delivers a plethora of information and resources! There is something here for every age and every stage on the Autism Spectrum. Penina methodically and humanely approaches childhood social skills development, reminding us of the importance of viewing the person as a whole, existing within a community. She understands that all children have their own inner unique landscape, and suggests solutions appropriate for different learning styles and ability levels. The developmental implementation of technology makes this book a welcome, cutting edge read!

Erin Wilson
Co-Founder: If I Need Help

The Socially Speaking™ Program by Penina Rybak is a **must have** for parents, teachers and therapists alike! The Socially Speaking™ program is a powerful instructional guide that takes you from fostering compliance to actual implementation with a child with Autism. Penina has given us an eye-opening look at the need for orientation to time, person, and place, and how to assist the child with Autism in developing these important skills.

We can all learn from Penina's expertise, especially in the field of educational technology. This book shows how to be "best" citizens in the iEra we live in. It provides a wonderful step by step approach to integrating iOS technology in the educational and clinical setting.

The numerous list of suggested Apps, suggested materials, and resources, are the most comprehensive I have ever seen. At The Vine School, we apply The Socially Speaking™ Program and Protocols with each one of our students! It has been the perfect tool to implement, so that our unique students can learn and progress.

Erin Hatley
Executive Director: The Vine School, Victoria, Texas

Having a curiously extensive background in education, the medical model, childhood development, and neuropsychology, I've collected amazing amounts of information (useful to absurd) while attempting to understand some of the childhood-related dilemmas such as autism spectrum, and other developmental disorders. At this belated time in my life education and practice, I have been gratefully introduced to a an original collection of work by Penina Rybak that elucidates core principles of child development through the rocky path of *sensory-executive functioning-communication* difficulties experienced by so many of our children today.

While an expert in speech-language development and therapeutic techniques, Ms. Rybak shares much more. She could have bound her research, writings, teaching, and social media to speech-language borders, yet she understood the importance of an integrative approach to collective domains with social norms, psychological expansion, multiple forms of learning, and just plain 'getting along' in this world. She reminds us that these children have underdeveloped, not absent skills, thus changing our approach to helping them learn and process information. Her approach is thus always positive!

This book has a comfortable, engaging flow of information. It is written in colloquial human-speak rather than bewildering techno-jargon so often used in works disguised as therapeutic guides. Where appropriate, technical terms are succinctly described. The anecdotes starting each chapter prove that Ms. Rybak has thought deeply, connecting questions to strategies that work for individuals and also have more global applications. The problems are real, as is her Socratic method to uncover where the human glitch occurs, then formulate the strategies to use for optimal outcomes. Strategies are laid out in clear language with just enough integrated redundancy to aid clarity. Case studies are poignant, often delineating gaps in biopsychosocial development. The glory of this book is that there are step-by-step methods to actually assist the child in the moment and for the future.

Penina uses props, toys, games, pictures, video, and social media, to incorporate real-world experiences for young individuals who do not experiences their sensory worlds as 'typical' individuals. Ms. Rybak breaks down the organization of learning into a manageable hierarchy of steps anyone can follow, both figuratively and literally taking cues from *Theory of Mind, Applied Behavioral* approaches, and various play therapies.

Penina shares her practice revelations with the reader as a comrade in care for children with autism and other developmental disorders, be it parents, classroom teacher, therapist, school psychologist, or the community of peers and others in the child's life. Her effort is exhaustive, attaching seminal discoveries in human development and education to new findings; low tech transforming into high tech for today's problem solving methods.

Anyone involved with a child who has an IEP needs this book! It's the all-inclusive guide to discerning the multi-layered dilemma of autism spectrum disorders and other childhood communication problems. The discussion of *Digital Citizenship in the iEra,* is spot on! Appropriate! Integrative! Necessary in 2015! Kudos to Ms. Rybak for having the intelligence and grace to take a serious, yet informal approach to help us wade through the voluminous explosion of advances that can be adapted for our current and future digital age. Kudos to Penina for providing therapeutic stratagems for various levels of development, thus assisting a core problem as it appears and how may manifest in the future with chronological age/social maturity. References, citations, and links are exhaustive. This book has it all! I will use this information with all new students, clients, and families.

Dr. Susan Fralick-Ball, PsyD, MSN, CLNC, CH

Acknowledgements

I want to thank the following people whose digital footprint and virtual mentorship have contributed to this book, and greatly impacted my own Theory of Mind. Thank you fellow iPad® Evangelists Lauren S. Enders and Matt Gomez, and for being such awesome pinners on Pinterest! Thank you ed-tech gurus and bloggers Med Kharbach and Tony Vincent, whose posts fill up whole notebooks in Evernote! Thank you fellow Autism advocate and woman entrepreneur, Erin Wilson, who founded If I Need Help, to help those who wander. Thank you CLASP International, especially Shannon Benton and Elisabeth Miller for allowing me to be a part of your wonderful work. Thank you to my mentors and fellow speakers on the lecture circuit, for leaving me a great bread crumb trail to follow: Linda Hodgdon, Lois Jean Brady, Susan Fralick-Ball, Jay Berk, Charlene Young, and Tim Kowalski.

Thank you to these educators and rainmakers for your consistent support: Susan Gartenberg, Zita Moses, Prestine Parten and Karina Barley. Finally, thank you to my family and friends, and all my seminar attendees who believed in me, and in this book. This one's the result of my parents' influence and grace.

Dedication

"TEAM: Together Everyone Achieves More"

This book is dedicated to the memory of my best friend, first and most treasured mentor, Apple™ Techie/fellow Mac Girl from way back when, Mary Poppins pal, Mrs. Piggle Wiggle buddy, and all around hero, Dr. Natalie "Nechah" Hochstein PsyD. She was a true scholar, lady, and a brilliant analyst of human behavior. She effortlessly and elegantly taught me so much, from the time I met her in late childhood, until she lost her valiant battle to breast cancer, in December 2012. Most of all, she taught me to work hard, think like a child, laugh often, and readily share information with others in need. She was a terrific child psychologist, my sister in arms, my cheerleader and my muse. She is sorely missed, but echoes of her vast wisdom live on; in my work and actions, on a daily basis, and in the words found on these pages. Any misinformation or poor choices of word are my fault alone. I humbly ask for the reader's understanding.

I also humbly dedicate this book to the myriad of children whom I treat, and have treated, especially those who have passed on like YE, the very first student entrusted to my care in Camp HASC in 1990. They continuously teach me more than I can ever teach them. You all have each enriched my life for having known you, even if it was sometimes for a short period of time. I am a better person, and certainly a much better educator and therapist than I would have been, had I not been introduced to your inner landscapes, at pivotal moments in my life. Thank you for letting me see the world through your eyes, and experience childhood all over again, through your play.

This book is also dedicated to all the special education teachers, paras, fellow speech therapists, social workers, psychologists, physical therapists, and occupational therapists, all of whom have crossed my path, deliberately or randomly, and worked so tirelessly with me to co-treat, care for, and create such meaningful "teachable moments" for our students in need. Your depth of knowledge, sense of humor, and collaborative spirit are much appreciated!

I would like to conclude that I could not have professionally grown and written this book without my Creator, who instilled in me a passion and talent for education and communication. I give profound thanks to You, for putting me on this road. I am grateful for having been given the drive to unlock the doors keeping me out of my students' worlds and letting them visit me in mine every day. It has been and continues to be a wonderful journey. As one of my mentors Dr. Susan Fralick Ball says, "the journey *is* the blessing!"

About Me and My Digital Footprint

Penina Rybak, MA/CCC-SLP, TSHH, CEO Socially Speaking LLC, is an educational technology consultant and an Autism specialist. She is also a practicing, pediatric speech-language pathologist, who earned her master's degree from New York University. She has been practicing for two decades, and has provided treatment to young children with Autism/special needs, in home-based early intervention, center-based preschool intervention, self- contained school-age classrooms, and private practice. Penina participated in the 1995-2000 *NY TRAID Project*, in conjunction with the Westchester Institute for Human Development. She worked to integrate Apple™ technology into special education classrooms and therapy sessions. She also spearheaded *The Boardmaker™ Initiative*, from 2008-2010, which worked on customizing curriculum needs and implementing behavior management strategies at a charter school in New York. It resulted in her launch of her copyrighted and trademarked **Socially Speaking™ Social Skills Curriculum**, seminars and iPad® App. Penina has lectured nationally and internationally on the topic of customizing social communication strategies, the developmental integration of iPad® apps into treatment of Autism/Special Needs and early childhood play based assessment and intervention. She advocates the use of an eclectic, multi-sensory treatment approach, using customized lesson plans involving toys and tech. For more information, please visit her social media sites below:

Email: Penina.SociallySpeaking@gmail.com
LinkedIn: Penina Rybak http://www.linkedin.com/pub/penina-rybak/37/900/191
About.Me Page: http://about.me/sociallyspeakingwithpenina
Website: http://sociallyspeakingLLC.com
Facebook: Socially Speaking LLC http://www.facebook.com/pages/Socially-Speaking-LLC/142172065830783
YouTube Channel: socialslp http://www.youtube.com/user/socialslp
Google+: Socially Speaking LLC https://plus.google.com/107696934832037278182/posts
Pinterest: Peninaslp pinterest.com/Peninaslp
Twitter: @PopGoesPenina

Disclaimer: This book's content is not authorized by Apple™ Inc. The author independently discusses/recommends iOS apps for educational/therapeutic purposes only.

Preface

Growing up, my favorite children's books were actually part of a series; the Mary Poppins Series by P.L. Travers, and the Mrs. Piggle Wiggle series, by Betty MacDonald. I loved both the humor and inherent lessons of both books. I appreciated the conveyed messages about the importance of educating children, and that each child is special, with a unique inner landscape that should be cherished and honored. As I grew older, I was deeply moved by reading about Helen Keller, and equally moved by observing the interactions several friends had with their siblings with special needs, some of whom had hearing loss or Autism. Before college, I spent the summer as a counselor in Camp HASC, a camp for children with special needs. I realized that I wanted to become a speech-language pathologist specializing in treatment of young children with Autism and other special needs. I wanted to honor, cherish, nurture, and traverse the inner landscape of these unique children, and help them traverse mine. I wanted to educate them, educate others about them, and make a difference.

So I started my "journey for change", as I called it, by first becoming a special education teacher, then a pediatric speech therapist who regularly co-treated with my colleagues, especially occupational therapists, and then an educational technology consultant. It gave me a crash course in teamwork and "whole body learning" which I value to this day. It also gave me a greater understanding of child development and the importance of play. Along the way I got to play with toys, play with Apple™ technology and play with children; on the floor, at the sink, at the table, and on the playground. Not a bad way to spend a day at work! As years passed, I assessed, treated, discussed, and discharged, many different children with special needs. I found myself steadily gravitating towards the children with Autism-- the children with behavioral and social communication challenges. The children whose IEP goals were repeated 3, 4, and sometimes 5 years in a row, before the 2004 revisions to the IDEA, made it a federal mandate to include a Behavior Intervention Plan as part of the IEP.

With echoes of Mrs. Piggle Wiggle and Mary Poppins in my mind, and whispers of parental warnings in my ears, I began to change the trajectory of my therapy regimen with these children. I began to prioritize compliance over the other goals I was addressing. I began to methodically research and implement ways to bridge the gap between readiness to learn and actual performance, to help these children become less "situation specific" learners, and more "tuned in" when engaging with peers, family, and community. I did so by actively fostering compliance, proactively modifying the environment with and without the child's participation and teaching carefully chosen cognitive based language skills in a specific order. This was all geared to facilitate self regulation, orientation to person/place/time, Theory of Mind, Executive Functioning, and social communication proficiency.

Armed with knowledge I gleaned from reading books and attending conferences about therapeutic approaches such as Cognitive Behavioral Therapy, Positive Behavioral Support, Functional Behavioral Analysis, Applied Behavioral Analysis, TEACCH, PECS, Visual Strategies™, Floortime™, REPLAYS™, and RTI, I began to recreate my personal credo, mission statement, plan of action, and philosophy. I started to change how I provided intervention for young children with Autism and behavioral challenges. The outcome was a new therapy regimen which stressed Emotional Attunement, play skills development, pre-literacy skills and language development, as well as social communication development, in that order. The outcome was the development and deployment of my trademarked *Socially Speaking™ Social Skills Curriculum* and subsequent national/international seminars and iPad® App, which launched my career as an entrepreneur in the educational arena.

This book was written in response to the many questions from parents and educators I have met over the years. There are countless caring, devoted, creative, and frustrated people who work with preschoolers having issues with behavior and social skills. This book is a response to the many requests I have had to share my techniques and rationales for specific behavioral and language goals I target in therapy. So many of us have learned about Autism intervention, but not how to formulate goals and practically treat the social difficulties that these children face every day. I hope this book proves to be helpful in that regard. I have written this book as a means of bringing together parents, educators and therapists to collaborate more effectively in addressing the needs of these special children. It would have been nice to have found a book like this and read some of this content when I was a graduate student, and then a beginning speech therapist, looking for lesson plan guidance and information about where to start and why.

Since I was a child, I have enjoyed cooking and have been a voracious reader. I have an ongoing fascination with science fiction stories and cookbooks in particular. I have been enamored by the visual imagery, the simple step by step directions and the glossy photographs. I have been awed by the ability both genres have, to be used as portals to a whole new world, wherein one's five senses could indulge. This is especially true today, thanks to 3D movies such as *Avatar* and The Food Network, especially my favorite show, "Chopped!"

As a pediatric speech-language pathologist working in a school setting for two decades, my fondness for cookbooks of all natures has steadily grown. I have increasingly used cookbook type formats when writing memos to parents and teachers, to succinctly get my points across. Cookbook style therapy was reviled when I was in graduate school. However, in today's fast moving times, where the Internet provides a steady stream of "sound bytes", short and sweet is the new order of the day. The idea behind cookbook style therapy is making a comeback. These books are deceptively simple to navigate, yet are crammed with invaluable information that can really help with time management. As any busy parent and/or educator knows, successful lesson planning, be it for life or learning to read, involves three elements. They are: a presentation of materials that wows, a time frame that is compatible with the child involved, and opportunities to internalize the lesson. It is my sincere hope that this book will do all three.

"Successful lesson planning involves three elements:
  1. *a presentation of material that wows*
  2. *a time frame that is compatible with the child involved*
  3. *opportunities to internalize the lesson."*

That is what this book is about. It is a primer, a handbook, about aligning baseline data, best practices, and behavior management, to foster the ability to transition from being a Me to a We as needed. It is a succinct field guide for busy educators and service providers "in the trenches" who have asked me for strategies. It is for those who have asked me about integrating toys and tech in treatment, to facilitate Theory of Mind, executive functioning, and pre-literacy skills; all of which are needed to develop play, language, and social communication proficiency. All of these are needed to master and generalize self regulation across space and time.

Come take a train ride with me and see how the *Socially Speaking™ Curriculum* works. The Train Tracks= Behavior Management Strategies, Train Cars= My Trifecta of Goals: Body Awareness, Expressing Feelings, and Problem Solving, and the Train's Bins= Toys and Tech i.e. Materials for Suggested "Social Skills Kits" to promote play and pre-literacy skills.

I know many of you are familiar with these goals, but let me give you an analogy. Imagine baking your favorite brownies. You may have a set recipe that works for you, but what if I suggested you change ingredients? Or change the order of pouring the ingredients into the bowl? Or mix the ingredients separately in different bowls and then add them together to create a batter? That is what my *Socially Speaking™ Curriculum* is all about. It is about taking the script, the recipe, the toolbox, and revising how it used. It is about paring down your best practices for better time management and productivity. It's about tweaking your inner dialogue as an educator and heeding the one the child has in his/her head. It is about reconfiguring the brownie, the outcome, the performance, the end-product, we all so diligently work on, with these children. Come into my kitchen and see what develops.

Having been a pediatric speech-language pathologist before the Digital Age i.e. Tech Revolution, the 2001 No Child Left Behind Act, and the 2004 revisions to the IDEA, I have seen the futility of working on mandated IEP goals that the child is not psycho-socially ready for. I have seen the struggle these children engage in, to make sense of their surroundings, to establish rapport with those in it, and to learn. For years I was increasingly seeing splintered acquisition of skills, fluctuating carryover of learned material and situation specific performance. I saw the value in visual supports and implemented it into treatment. I saw the benefits of Assistive Technology, especially Apple™ technology integration into lessons, and made it part of my therapy regimen. I even educated others how to do the same and "reboot" their goals and methodology. I saw the value of consistent, collaborative behavior management to address self regulation issues, and incorporated best practices into my therapy plans and IEP goals.

But it wasn't enough. These were all pieces of the puzzle, ingredients in my recipe, to effect change. But there was something missing. I realized that it was time to change the collective mindset, to shift from a crisis intervention paradigm to one that promotes proactive intervention to teach social communication proficiency more naturally, more developmentally and more enjoyably. It was time to foster self motivation to complete tasks, and self evaluation of behavior while doing so, in a different way. The *Socially Speaking™ Way*. One that fosters compliance and social communication development through play. Through bridging the gap between readiness to learn and actual performance, by early detection of "red flags", readiness indicators, and specific cognitive based language skills, taught in a multi-sensory manner, emphasizing the visual modality.

So I tweaked my recipe for therapy, and created something new from the sum of its parts. Something familiar yet unique, with powerful implications. Something profoundly simple yet difficult to ignore; a child-centric approach to treatment, dubbed the *Socially Speaking™ Social Skills Curriculum for Early Childhood Special Education*. Take a look inside my pantry, inside my mixing bowls. Come see what I see. This book, a cookbook of sorts, was created with the busy educator in mind, with time sensitive responsibilities, sometimes limited resources and a love for the bottom line. I thus designed it to contain a mixture of lists, memos, and graphs, utilizing a unique outline in each chapter which includes techniques and explanations of the Socially Speaking™ philosophy, suggested resources and even final words. Let the recipe tweaking begin!

Socially Speaking™ Part I - Fostering Compliance
Bridging the Gap Between
Readiness to Learn and Actual Performance

**Understanding the Roots of the Problematic Behaviors and How
to Counteract Them: Disorientation to Person/Place/Time and
Clinical Implications**

Chapter 1
Disorientation to <u>Person</u>
Socially Speaking™ Social Skills Curriculum: Level I
<u>Body Awareness</u>: Address Rapport and Who? Questions

Anecdote

Lexie is a sweet, gentle, and passive girl with Autism. She is reportedly nonverbal and has self-stimulation behaviors, causing her to "tune out". She was assigned to my caseload and presented as a cognitively challenged preschooler who loves music, hates touching things with her hands and is unresponsive in many of her therapy sessions, especially in OT. I decided to co-treat with the OT on a weekly basis, to work on establishing crossover rapport, patterns of behavior and preferences, and Body Awareness, through sensory brushing, feeding, and play based activities. Lexie initially resisted all attempts to win her over and enter her world. She did indeed seem reluctant to enter my world and frequently "tuned out", but not my music. I learned that singing, humming, turning on a musical toy, or the computer screen, had her craning her neck and even scanning for the source of that sound. I decided to let her gorge on music for the first part of every session, no strings attached. I slowly paired music with tasks, and slowly created a bridge between our worlds. My work with Lexie in particular is the inspiration for many of the strategies and materials written in this book.

Strategy and Technique

Disorientation: The Root of the Behavior Issues

Neuro-typical children follow an extensively documented progression, which needs to be duly considered before deciding which social skills to target therapeutically with children with Autism. These children follow similar patterns, although the circuit may not be as linear, and the time tables for each milestone may be longer or shorter. Nonetheless, I have found that most children of varying abilities exhibit three initial psycho-social phases of development:

1. Making inferences about feelings-The "Terrible Twos" Stage, age 18 months-3
2. Making inferences about events-The "Police man" Stage, age 3-5
3. Understanding Causality (sequencing, predicting outcomes)- The "Indian Giver" Stage, age 5-7

I have observed and learned that these are early indicators of the later acquisition of the ability to play cooperatively, display a sense of humor and problem solve. All of these are the outcomes of being socially appropriate and having pragmatic skills. I have seen that special needs children do not start demonstrating behaviors of these three stages until they have mastered the pre-linguistic and early socio-emotional goals previously discussed.

When working with lower functioning, globally delayed children, it can be easy to forget that the socio-emotional and mental ages, NOT the chronological age, are crucial to consider when planning appropriate social skills goals. Sometimes much time needs to be spent on working towards achieving these prerequisite skills. A working knowledge of developmental milestones for language and play skills is also important to have, to counteract splintered style, nonlinear, situation specific acquisition of the desired skill.

It is necessary that a child achieve these pre-linguistic goals, so that he/she can "live in the moment" and engage in social interactions with others:

1. Joint Attention
2. Object Permanence, and
3. Cause & Effect
4. Visual Scanning: Observation and Curiosity
5. Empathy and Emotional Attunement
6. Play

It is necessary that a child be able to "tune in" and view and wonder about his/her surroundings and those in it, if vision is intact. This can help develop awareness and interest i.e. wanting to further explore the environment and later learn to ask "why?"

questions. As the child's lexicon expands, i.e. the "memory bank" fills, he/she can access the information from semantic and episodic memory, when deciding how to respond in a given social situation. That's why orientation to person and having rapport with others is the first nonverbal skill I address when starting treatment.

It is important that a child learn to "tune in" to how others are feeling. He/she can then ask after their welfare and mimic and/or alter his emotional response to an event that triggers a desirable or undesirable sensation/memory. He/she will start to realize when things are not as they should be, or are an exaggerated manifestation of how the world works. This is the beginning of the understanding of humor. Humor is what separates man from animal, and individual from individual. It is where mental health and emotional health intersect. I will discuss humor more in-depth later on.

I have found that the development of a sense of humor, and the ability to laugh at the absurd; in self and others, is crucial when I target social skills in lessons, especially more advanced skills! It serves the dual purpose of:

• Increasing self awareness of errors and the subsequent ability to take constructive criticism
• Increasing self motivation to learn, practice, and perform the skill.

This is accomplished through the perception that the lesson and the one delivering it, is fun! As we all know, if we are having fun completing a task, be it baking, gardening, or math homework, then we are doing something right! We will obviously want to repeat the behavior and/or the learning experience with the fun person who makes us feel good!

FAQ: What is the child getting by engaging in a specific behavior?

All behavior serves a function, be it positive or negative. We need to remember this, when formulating a social skills plan for all special needs children. We need to analyze the child's actions, when we want to either foster the increased independence of a specific appropriate behavior, or reduce and eliminate an unwanted behavior. It is important to take the time to think what purpose the present behavior serves. What is the child getting by engaging in a specific behavior? Where is the root of the behavior issue, the disorientation coming from? Person? Place? Time?

Orientation to person/place/time is a behavior, an active process that all human beings engage in. Behavior modification is needed when children, especially those with ASD, become disoriented to person/place/time, which can happen because of environmental, biological, sensory, and emotional "triggers". The *Merriam-Webster Dictionary* defines behavior as "a) the manner of conducting oneself, b) anything that an organism does involving action and response to stimulation, and c) the response of an individual, group, or species to its environment". As most educators and parents know, "setting the stage" i.e. structuring the surrounding area where the learning is to take place, (whether in school at a desk, or at home on the couch) is **crucial** to success.

Furthermore, all human beings operate on an "action-reaction" continuum! Special needs children in particular can have strong reactions to various sensory stimuli, resulting in a variety of behaviors; some positive and some negative. Finally, the whole purpose of intervention is to shape an emerging or desired behavior such as requesting help, modify an undesirable behavior such as hitting, and extinguish socially inappropriate or physically unsafe behaviors such as self mutilation (pulling out one's hair).

It is therefore important to understand a child's cognitive and emotional level, his or her Theory of Mind and what is being perceived, and how to navigate through that child's "inner landscape". We can then more accurately analyze the behaviors being demonstrated, and discover if they are a response to disorientation to person/place/time.

What is Disorientation to Person?

It is a disruption in emotional resonance, i.e. rapport with another person, a lack of empathy for what that person feels and/or wants. It's the splintered or absent comprehension of expectations from that person. It is the delayed or absent reaction to "sharing space" which usually leads to being able to connect to others and make inferences about one's own feelings triggered by someone else's emotional/physical response to him/her. Children who are disoriented to person may not even respond to their own face in the mirror, let alone yours, something I check out right away.

Cognitive Symptoms of Disorientation to Person:
Poor/Absent Joint Attention and Object Permanence
Poor/Absent Cause & Effect
Poor/Absent Communicative Intent
Poor/Absent Pronoun/Possessives Use
Poor/Absent Body Awareness: Identifying Body Parts in Self & Others
Poor/Absent Ability to Answer what? and who? questions

CASE STUDY

Lily, who has a developmental age of fifteen months, is a playful, inquisitive girl with Down Syndrome, hearing aids, moderate-severe mental retardation, and "autistic tendencies". Her favorite pastime is to happily bang two balls together, for a long time, without being interrupted. She will be quite vocally unappreciative, if her relatively new babysitter (who started two weeks ago) suddenly swoops in and firmly, even abruptly (without warning) scoops her up and whisks her off for a nap. Lily's senses will raise red flags, and her radar will zoom in on the fact that she is now airborne, by an unfamiliar person. Her babysitter's sudden movement, and displaying of a no nonsense, change in demeanor, requires a "shift in gears" on Lily's part.

Lily may misread the situation and the degree of tension her babysitter is feeling, and/or the nuances of her facial expression. Lily may feel disconnected and confused if her harried babysitter picks her up without any verbal or tactile warning, and without eye contact, and begins removing the balls from her hands. Lily may begin to tantrum, despite reassurance that the balls will be there later. All she knows is that there are no more balls. The sudden disassociation and loss of emotional attunement hampers the realization of Object Permanence about the balls and the babysitter not really being a stranger. This disorientation to person, combined with the developmental egocentricity of being a toddler, can result in a "meltdown" that contributes to the coining of the term "Terrible Twos".

At her level of functioning, Lily's play is perseverative (repetitive), tactile, and self directed, frequently causing her to have "tunnel vision" and to lose sight of her surroundings and those in it. She is therefore not good at transitioning from one activity to another. Lily also does not fully comprehend the idea of time passing, and that familiar, constant people such as this babysitter are meant to be her first anchors in learning to fluidly and smoothly move to a different point in time. She needs to learn to perceive the familiar person in her "inner circle" as a helper in "grounding" her and keeping her on the moving train of time and progress.

SOLUTION

Proactive Attention To Build Rapport

Every human being wants attention and to connect, even children with special needs. *The first rule of good behavior management is to establish rapport with the student and show that you see his or her worth.* Everyone can do one thing well, whether it is menial (ex: washing dishes) or lofty (ex: singing nicely). It is important to make a child the "point man" to do a job using his skill, either as a reinforcer and/or embedded into the daily Visual Schedule, and then publicly acknowledging the child's expertise and prowess (verbal praise). Another idea to consider is to flood the child with attention first by talking about a topic relevant or important to him/her, and THEN doing the task. You can also use attention as a reinforcer in a token economy system, by returning to that conversation/topic etc. in between each completed task. This is the first step of intervention, much like planting is the first step in harvesting a crop.

Building Rapport Means Being Vigilant in the Driver's Seat During a Therapy Session

The first rule of rapport building is to increase awareness; on the part of the student and on the part of the service provider. It is important to get the student's attention and keep it, so that learning can happen. A child's attention to an adult depends on the level of rapport and trust that is established, the level of emotional well being causing that child to want to interact with the adult, and the level of cognition and understanding affecting the child's ability to comprehend what the adult wants from him/her. Building rapport means being vigilant in the driver's seat and noticing everything the student does, while ensuring the student's safety; both emotional and physical. So that he/she thinks you aren't a driver but a passenger. So that he/she thinks you aren't "the boss"; yet!

It is therefore essential that you pay attention to the road you are on with the child. It is crucial to FIRST build trust and appear non-threatening and not in control of the situation, so that you can foster compliance. As stated previously, when I am working with children with ASD, I take the time, as much as needed, at the onset of therapy, to be a vigilant driver through the inner landscape of the child's mind. I spend time navigating through parental and teacher interviews, to find out what the child gravitates towards, and runs away from. I initially follow a child's lead in my therapy office, seeing what he or she explores, and what is considered fun and exciting, or scary and challenging.

"FIRST build trust and appear non-threatening so that you can foster compliance."

In the beginning, I place few demands on my student, allowing spontaneous play and/or initiation of social contact to express wants and needs, to occur naturally. I actually let the student have the run of the room and toys so I can observe and take notes. What am I looking for exactly?
• An idea of what the learning style is, based on the types of toys the child is drawn to
• An idea of preferences so that I can start building my strategy and "ammunition"
• Insight into the child's level of play and cognition, not to mention overall dexterity etc.
• Insight into the child's fears and aversions, and tactile sensitivities, based on which items are avoided or ignored. That will be listed as "future toys to use in therapy if relevant" and "what to mention to the OT or PT"

As the emotional empathy, rapport, and trust grows, so does the structure and demand I place on the student to perform. I begin modifying the environment and letting the student have the run of the room for less time, or after having done something I wanted. Only now, the student is there with me, in my car so to speak, confident that I will heed his or her needs/wants. He or she now knows that I can correctly interpret the road signs and road blocks. As no two people are alike, the time it takes to get the student "into the car" varies. Patience is a virtue they say, and it is especially true for children with ASD. I cannot stress enough how important it is to build trust and camaraderie. It lays the groundwork for future learning to happen.

It is thus imperative that we get to know the "inner landscape" of the child's mind. It prepares the child to interact better with his or her environment and those in it. It also allows us a glimpse into the way the child thinks and perceives the world around him and those in it. We can then know WHY the problematic behavior occurs, and then HOW to counteract it, when it arises. Below are some probable outcomes of the outbursts that children with ASD can experience if they lack emotional attunement with others. This list is not exhaustive, but meant as a starting point, to provide some food for thought about possible "triggers" to keep in mind.

Bridging the Gap Between Rapport & Readiness to Learn and Actual Performance: A "Playpen" vs. a "Floor Mat" Approach to Intervention

Over time, I realized that I had to abandon conventional wisdom and advice about children like Lexie, and follow their lead. I decided to embrace Dr. Stanley Greenspan's *Floortime™ Approach* and combine it with elements of both *Applied Behavioral Analysis* and *Verbal Behavior Therapy*. I decided to adopt the practice of "flooding the reinforcer" while giving Lexie the run of the room, **at the start** of the session. I wanted to see what she would gravitate towards, and what she would avoid. I started taking notes; first by hand, and later using an iOS app on my iPad®, as the years passed.

Have you ever seen babies play in a playpen? How about a Floor Mat with embedded toys? I find it so interesting how much visual scanning and awareness neurotypical babies display for what's outside their range, for what's beyond the confines of that mat! True, they will first explore what's in front of them, but then they inevitably turn to what's not. These same babies are apt to concentrate longer on the toy in their reach, when seated or prone in a playpen. I decided to try an experiment with Lexie, and children like her, on my caseload. I decided to give them freedom to roam within the confines of my therapy room, with free access to all toys, all at once, that I deemed interesting, age appropriate for their cognitive level, and safe. The results were quite surprising. The results spurned my creation of The Reinforcer Roster in Chapter 12 and Body Awareness Protocol, found later in this chapter.

I needed to establish rapport with a child who did not exhibit orientation to person. That meant that the child displayed a lack of rapport and emotional empathy with others. That meant that the child had not yet mastered these prerequisite early social skills:
- Joint Attention and Object Permanence
- Cause & Effect
- Communicative Intent
- Pronoun/Possessives Use
- Identifying Body Parts in Self & Others
- Answering what? and who? questions

These were the goals I wrote for the IEP, the ones I addressed repeatedly over time, and using specific materials and lessons. But first I had to establish rapport, foster compliance, and start teaching self regulation. That meant that my first order of business was to take notes on what Lexie was drawn to. What she gravitated towards. What she shied away from. Those were hidden blueprints for my *Reinforcer Roster*, and for future therapy goals involving oral/tactile desensitization using play and co-treatments with the OT. The *Reinforcer Roster* based upon:
✎ Observations of the child's learning style when given "mirror time" and the "run of the room" to see what is enticing and what seems aversive
✎ Paying the child currency that resonates with his/her "inner landscape" i.e. TOM
✎ Providing "Proactive Attention" at the start of a "teachable moment" to foster rapport

I had to shift from doing crisis intervention, a reaction to every tantrum, "in the moment", with little if any carryover, to preventive intervention. That meant that I proactively provided my attention, by commenting on what Lexie was doing (monologue), and talking about things she liked; music, bread. I also had to proactively provide materials and environmental modifications (seat positioning, flooding the reinforcer, Visual Supports-more on that in Chapter 2), designed to develop, prolong, and generalize periods of self regulation. By doing so, Lexie would slowly start to be ready to learn. Like many special education service providers out there, I started my paradigm shift out of necessity, and later out of a directive. I took my cues from the 2004 Revisions to the IDEA. It federally mandated a Behavior Plan as part of the IEP. It highlighted why Positive Behavioral Support is so crucial. It is beyond the scope of this book to provide an overview of PBS, or Functional Behavioral Analysis for that matter. I refer the reader to my suggested reading list at the end of this chapter, and this book's chapter 4, where I elaborate on:
❖ The ABC Chart
❖ The *Four Crisis Intervention Questions* for Team Meetings when drafting a Behavior Intervention Plan AKA Behavior Plan for the IEP (See Chapter 12)

My overall goal was to help Lexie bridge the gap between readiness to learn and actual performance. That meant that I had to first get her interested in what I was doing and what I had to say. That meant I had to address her disorientation to person. So I had to have a team meeting to educate everyone on readiness indicators and *Theory of Mind*, and the implications for social communication skill acquisition. The outcome was that I produced my *Executive Functioning Memo* to explain some of my methodology. I also created Readiness Indicator Checklists and these lists:

The Clinical Considerations for Social Skills Building
✱ **Understanding Components of Communication:**
1. The Talking Framework: C/F/U (Content-Semantics/Vocabulary, Form/Syntax, and Use/Pragmatics)
    a) Target vocabulary re: Communicative Intent
    b) Target vocabulary re: feelings
    c) Nonverbal communication (gesture, pointing, signing/ASL)

    d) Integration of AAC and ASL (TC) into pragmatic functioning of non speaking or unintelligible children

2. Speech Intelligibility/clarity (dysarthria/muscle weakness vs. apraxia/ neuro-motor planning dysfunction)

3. Prosody (Melody of Speech: inflection, rate, fluency, vocal quality)-connects communication and emotional engagement

✱ **Understanding Components of Emotional Engagement:**

1. Joint Attention with Eye Contact
2. Facial Affect: The Social Smile
3. Communicative Intent
4. Social Referencing of Others Through TOM (Theory of Mind)
5. Play Skills Development integrated with psycho-social development
6. Body Awareness
7. Self Regulation of Behavior-Orientation to person/place and later on, time
a) Proprioception (physical awareness)
b) Joint attention (emotional awareness)
c) Transitioning and self soothing (spatial awareness)

I advocated for permission to regularly (usually once a week) co-treat with the OT, for Lexie's sake and the sake of many other children on my caseload, whose reduced Body Awareness was contributing to their disorientation to person. I introduced the *Socially Speaking™ Toilet Training Protocol* to parents, teachers, therapists, and other team members wondering how to instill the first bodily related social skill in a child with special needs. I advocated for customized lessons, tailored to the child's unique "inner landscape" and learning style, that would appeal to the dominant of the five senses, or decrease the sensitivity/defensiveness seen as well.

I also advocated for speech therapy-occupational therapy co-treatment sessions for another reason. I wanted to facilitate the development of Theory of Mind and other psycho-social and communication pre-requisite skills through play. Play is the vehicle through which children practice the rules and roles they see enacted in their environment. Play is thus the vehicle I had to use, to reorient children like Lexie to person, place, and time, and engage in self regulation when they got disconnected again, resulting in tantrums and "tuning out" behaviors so familiar to so many special education service providers around the globe. The importance of play, and the developmental, methodical, customizable integration of play skills into social communication is so vital to my curriculum that I have devoted an entire chapter on it, which will be provided later in this book. In the meantime, I would like to list some clinical and non-clinical pre-requisites for addressing social communication development.

Clinical Prerequisites For Addressing Social Skills Difficulties: What Needs to Blossom
Fostering Self Awareness and identification of body parts in class/therapy
Understanding "Theory of Mind" and "Mirror Neuron Hypothesis"
Referencing developmental milestones re: neuro-typical language and socio-emotional development

Non-Clinical Prerequisites for Building Social Skills: What Needs to Bloom
Understanding the Five Senses and their effect on learning language and connecting emotionally to others
Understanding the importance of team collaboration for assessment/ treatment purposes
Understanding the child's preferences, learning style, and "inner landscape" which all contribute to Theory of Mind and rapport

The Five Senses in A Nutshell - What You Need to Know About Intervention

Hearing:

A Quick Word On.....Hearing Impairment and Central Auditory Processing Dysfunction (CAPD), Down Syndrome and ASD in Children: Ramifications for Play & Learning Social Skills

Hearing issues affect auditory localization to sound (an early precursor for play skills), both receptive and expressive language (vocabulary, grammar, sentence length), and articulation development. It affects prosody, eye contact, topic maintenance, following directions, and pragmatic (social language and behavior) development.

What You Can Do:
1. Request medical follow up re: ENT/audiological exams as needed
2. Provide VISUAL materials as the main ingredient
3. Consult with the speech therapist re: speech and language skills and the OT re: equilibrium/vestibular functioning
4. Allow student to compensate by hyper-vigilance re: constantly visually scanning the area. Allow for what looks like visual distractibility and reduced eye contact, which really does serve a purpose in this case.

Vision:

A Quick Word On.....Blindness and Visuo-spatial Deficits, ASD, and Genetic Syndromes such as Cornelia de Lange Syndrome in Children: Ramifications for Play & Learning Social Skills

Visual issues affect Object Permanence and exploratory play as a whole. They impede facial affect, eye contact, interpreting feelings, attention span, turn taking, requesting and Communicative Intent (early pointing skills). The understanding of quality (textures, adjectives), quantity (amounts and numbers), space (prepositions), and time (basic orientation to person/place/time, and comprehension of time related vocabulary such as seasons and weather, sequencing first/middle/last) concepts are further exacerbated by visual deficits.

What You Can Do:
1. Request medical follow up re: neurology, developmental optometry, and developmental ophthalmology as needed

2. Provide TACTILE & AUDITORY materials as the main ingredient
3. Consult with the SLP re: play, social, and language skills, the PT re: balance and safety, and the TVI and OT re: visual, fine motor and sensory integration skills
4. Allow student to compensate by constantly "checking in" with you via tangential speech and invasion of personal space-allow for verbal non-sequiturs. Also, use tactile cues to teach the passage of time, reestablish rapport/routine (i.e. reorient) frequently, and positively reinforce attempts using tactile input (ex: hug).

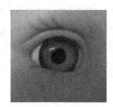

Touch:

A Quick Word On.....Cerebral Palsy (CP), ASD, Genetic Syndromes such as ML Type IV, and SI Dysfunction in Children: Ramifications for Play & Learning Social Skills

Tactile Defensiveness and Sensory Dysfunction affect exploratory play as a whole. They impact upon the ability to build a working vocabulary through the understanding of quality (textures, adjectives) and quantity (amounts, numbers). They also impede oral-motor and articulation skills, facial affect, and social interactions as in general, due to tactile defensiveness and resistance to being touched. They exacerbate the overall ability to self soothe and play with toys independently, thereby leading to issues with self regulation.

What You Can Do:
1. Request medical follow up re: neurology, feeding and swallowing skills, and overall bone structure as needed
2. Provide MULTI-SENSORY materials in unison and desensitize the student slowly to touching and being touched by different textures, degrees, and depth of stimuli (ex: toothbrush versus laundry brush)
3. Consult with the Psychologist/Psychotherapist re: behavior, and the SLP, PT, and OT re: ways to improve overall functional feeding, play, and behavior. Find out if child can be without wheelchair or splint and played with in your lap or embrace for a little at a time to develop further psychosocial and exploratory play skills.
4. Allow student to compensate by pulling away, expressing feelings of displeasure or fear etc. Use the bond (i.e. the rapport) you have to acknowledge and coax (use the "If....Then" Contingent), and then use TACTILE reinforcers that are already tolerated and enjoyed VERY frequently!

Smell:

Note: The perception of smell starts with the sensation of odors, and the experiences and emotions associated with these smells. Our ability to discern various odors increases in the early years and plateaus around age eight in children. Our olfactory receptors are directly sent to the cerebral cortex and then connected to the limbic system, where emotion is processed. Smells can thus evoke strong emotional reactions. When one correctly identifies a specific smell such as pizza, the scent has already started the limbic system, triggering an emotional response, be it negative or positive, depending on one's memory associated with the emotional imprint of that event. Subsequently, a good smell can positively affect a person's mood and social interactions, and vice versa. However, this may not always be beneficial! Pleasant scents can cloud our judgment by triggering positive emotions and memories. Also, children can have their sense of smell affected by being around chronic smokers. This is especially important to keep in mind when teaching social skills!

A Quick Word On.....Down Syndrome, ASD, Bipolar and Psychotic Disorder, ADHD/ ADD, Developmental Apraxia of Speech (lDAS), and Cranio-facial Anomalies in Children: Ramifications for Play & Learning Social Skills

Olfactory Dysfunction can be present in certain syndromes exacerbated by cranio-facial anomalies, has been found in children with psychiatric disorders, and can be a byproduct of medical issues such as chronic sleep apnea and chronic congestion in children. There has been recent research linking sleep apnea and DAS in children, and linking olfactory dysfunction with emotionally disturbed and depressed children. It impedes initiating social contact as a whole, understanding of quality (textures, adjectives) concepts, phrase length/breath support (resulting in "telegraphic" speech), oral-motor, resonance, and articulation skills. It affects facial affect and attention span due to irritability and/or fatigue from not getting enough sleep.

What You Can Do:

1. Request medical follow up re: congestion and hearing status, fatigue, and sleep apnea (ENT) as needed, and a neurologist and/or psychiatrist for children with increasing mood swings and/or distractibility/impulsivity that may be organic in nature
2. Provide TACTILE & VISUAL materials as the main ingredient of the lesson plan
3. Consult with the SLP re: pragmatic, resonance, prosody, and articulation skills, and the Psychologist/Psychotherapist re: communicative and social functioning
4. Allow student to compensate by being sensitive, cautious and/or quiet. Allow student to be an observer first and then join in, after seeing the activity being modeled. Allow for breaks as this type of student will fatigue easily and/or have a low tolerance threshold, thereby needing coaxing and regular intervals of reinforcement (token economy may not work well here).

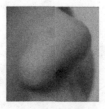

Taste:

A Quick Word On.....Cerebral Palsy (CP), ASD, Down Syndrome, Prematurity, and SI Dysfunction in Children: Ramifications for Play & Learning Social Skills

Oral Defensiveness and Sensory Integration (SI) Dysfunction affect oral-motor, feeding, articulation, and expressive language skills. They also impact upon the understanding of body parts i.e. the different parts that make up the mouth, comprehension of quality (textures, adjectives) concepts, as well as overall play skills and socio-emotional development. These children are usually labeled as "picky eaters" or being "fussy" babies. Oral sensitivity and/or defensiveness can overlap with tactile defensiveness. It can cause a child to miss out on mouthing toys as the first stage in exploratory play, on bonding with caregivers at mealtime and on feeling pleasure from eating. Furthermore, it affects the ability to self soothe, which is the start of self regulation. Reduced oral sensation in the mouth area may also affect nutrition intake, tolerating various temperatures and textures of food, and spillage and drooling when eating or drinking. Sleep cycles and the length of mealtimes may also be affected, in that the child may not tolerate a bottle, pacifier, thumb, or spoon.

What You Can Do
1. Request medical follow up re: neurology, feeding and swallowing skills, and overall nutrition and weight gain/loss issues
2. Provide MULTI-SENSORY materials in unison, desensitize the student slowly to eating and touching and being touched, and remember to use different textures, degrees, and depth of stimuli (ex: yogurt versus pretzel)
3. Make sure you have established rapport with the non-eater and/or "picky" eater before working on social skills goals! Consult with the nutritionist, SLP, Psychologist/ Psychotherapist, and OT re: healthy ways to incorporate eating into social skills play activities. You need to improve socialization and interest and happiness and pleasure in joining in at mealtime later on, which will affect overall functional feeding, play, and pragmatic skills. Use CHOICES and reduced number of trials during a snack time task as part of the Visual Schedule, in a matter of fact way (ex: everyone is eating one piece of fruit and then going outside to play ball). Reinforce attempts and cooperation regularly (do not use delayed gratification). Do NOT use food as the reward! In this case it can be counterproductive and affect your rapport and productivity!

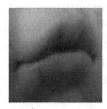

Final Words

One cannot start working on social communication skills with an Autistic child and/or special needs child until baseline data is established re: inner landscape, the five senses and environmental awareness. It is thus crucial to first observe behavior, discern patterns and establish rapport. When deciding to work on social communication skills, one should keep in mind these three factors needed for implementing a successful Social Skills Management Plan. It is important to remember these 3 tips:

☑ *Play* is the first vehicle through which normally developing children gain Self Concept and body/self awareness. It is their portal to learning to empathize and imitate what they see in the world around them. It is their introduction to emotional referencing and self soothing and self regulation; all needed for Body Awareness

☑ When charting a course of action to address social skills building, the child's **cognitive** age is more important than the given **chronological** age. Furthermore, developmental, repetitive, structured, and linear style intervention is encouraged, despite the child's possible splintered, non-sequential development and situation specific mastery of learned social skills.

☑ The "inner landscape" of a special needs child directly affects his/her Body Awareness and ability to process, understand and empathize with another's point of view.

Materials for Your Toolbox

• <u>Key References</u>

Baker, Jed (2008). *No More Meltdowns: Positive Strategies for Managing and Preventing Out of Control Behavior*. Arlington, TX: Future Horizons

Barnes, K. et al (2008). Self- regulation strategies of children with emotional disturbance, *Physical & Occupational* Therapy In Pediatrics, 28 (4), 369-387.

Baron-Cohen, Simon (2002). *Targeting Autism: What We Know, Don't Know, and Can Do to Help Young Children with Autism and Related Disorders*. Berkeley, CA: University of California Press.

Biel, Lindsey, and Peske, Nancy (2005). *Raising a Sensory Smart Child: The Definitive Handbook for Helping Your Child with Sensory Integration Issues*. New York, NY: Penguin Books.

Blimes, Jenna (2004). *Beyond Behavior Management: The Six Life Skills Children Need to Thrive in Today's World*. St. Paul, MN: Red Leaf Press.

Chandler, Lynette, and Dahlquist, Carol (2009). *Functional Assessment: Strategies to Prevent and Remediate Challenging Behavior in School Settings, Third Edition.* Upper Saddle River, NJ: Prentice- Hall/Pearson Education.

Charman, Tony, and Stone, Wendy (2006). *Social and Communication Development in Autism Spectrum Disorders.* New York, NY: Guilford Press.

Christie, Phil et al (2009). *First Steps in Intervention with Your Child with Autism: Frameworks for Communication.* Philadelphia, PA: Jessica Kingsley Publishers.

Fouse, Beth and Wheeler, Maria (1997). *A Treasure Chest of Behavioral Strategies for Individuals with Autism.* Arlington, TX: Future Horizons.

Greenspan, Stanley, and Weider, Serena (1998). *The Child with Special Needs: Encouraging Intellectual and Emotional Growth.* Cambridge, MA: Perseus Books Group.

Greenspan, Stanley (2002). *The Secure Child: Helping Our Children Feel Safe and Confident in an Insecure World.* Cambridge, MA: Perseus Books Group.

Gutstein, Steven (2002). *Relationship Development Intervention with Young Children: Social and Emotional Development Activities for Asperger Syndrome, Autism, PDD, and NLD.* Philadelphia, PA: Jessica Kingsley Publishers.

Hannaford, Carla (1995). *Smart Moves: Why Learning is Not All in Your Head.* Marshall, NC: Great Ocean Books.

Kranowitz, Carol, and Miller, Lucy Jane (2005). *The Out of Sync Child.* New York, NY: Penguin Group Inc.

Notbohm, Ellen (2005). *Ten Things Every Child with Autism Wishes You Knew.* Arlington, TX: Future Horizons

Prizant, Barry et al (2003). The SCERTS Model: A Family Centered, Transactional Approach to Enhancing Communication and Socioemotional Abilities of Young Children with ASD. *Infant and Young Children, (16), 4, 296-316*

Schneider, Catherine (2006). *Sensory Secrets: How to Jump Start Learning in Children.* Siloam Springs, AK: Concerned Communications Inc.

Shellenberger, Sherry, and Williams, Mary Sue (2001). *How Does Your Engine Run? A Leader's Guide to the Alert Program, Take Five: Staying Alert at Home and School.* Albuquerque, NM: Therapy Works Inc.

Thompson, Thomas (2008). *Freedom From Meltdowns: Dr. Thompson's Solutions for Children with Autism.* Baltimore, MD: Paul H. Brookes Publishing

Volkmar, Fred, and Weisner, Lisa (2009). *A Practical Guide to Autism: What Every Parent, Family Member, and Teacher Needs to Know.* Hoboken, NJ: Wiley Press

• Key Links to Peruse

http://1.usa.gov/1zk3xxz

http://bit.ly/1CsVLQW

http://bit.ly/1JvmrTA

http://bit.ly/1yo7C44

http://bit.ly/1DbOOSZ

http://bit.ly/1EnFkaX

http://bit.ly/15MhCH7

http://bit.ly/18lHXg9

http://bit.ly/1uvQ6TN

http://bit.ly/1uTNEMD

• Key Concepts to Address

Body Awareness, Emotional Attunement, Rapport, Theory of Mind (TOM), Executive Functioning, and Beginning Causality-Action/Reaction

A Quick Vocabulary Lesson

Understanding terminology is a way of life in the world of special education. With the creation of the Information Superhighway, also known as The World Wide Web (WWW), it is now easier than ever for parents and educators to speak the same language. The Internet affords people the opportunity to quickly learn new things and new vocabulary from the comfort of one's home. Search engines such as Google and Bing and open source sites such as Wikipedia have become part of everyday life. Content curation from Massive Open Online Courses (MOOCS) such as EdX and Coursera, and mobile technology Apps such as Zite, Evernote, and Pocket, enable both the layman and the expert to find, share and store information "in the cloud".

There are three catch phrases now used in current Autism research: Theory of Mind (TOM), Mirror Neuron Hypothesis, and Executive Functioning. As the fields of neuropsychology and neuroscience advance, much time is being spent on trying to understand what these terms really mean, and what are the practical implications for brain functioning in children with Autism. Let me summarize what these catch phrases mean:

- Theory of Mind is the internal mental state of a human being's perspective. It is gleaned from one's attention **to**, and view **of** his or her environment (Joint Attention and Causality), his or her understanding of and ability to relate to the emotions of another (empathy), and his social interactions with others (pragmatics). A child's TOM helps to decipher another person's intentions, feelings and actions, to make predictions about the behavior of another. One's TOM enables him to perceive, understand, empathize, and respond to the "inner landscape" of another person. It expands the developing child's awareness of self, others, place and time. This increasing orientation results in improved Self Concept and emotional attunement. These two factors are needed for social skills development, which is one of the greatest challenges for children with ASD.

- Mirror Neuron Hypothesis is based on the premise of a neuron that fires both when a person completes an action, and when he sees someone else doing the same thing. It is presumed that the neuron "mirrors" the behavior seen in another person, even if the observer sits still, passively watching. Neuropsychological research has implied that mirror neurons may be important in facilitating the cognitive development of visual imitation skills, and subsequent language and social skills acquisition. These are two areas of difficulty for children with ASD.

- Executive Functioning is a higher level, psychological and cognitive skill which originates in the cerebral cortex. It aides in a person's motor planning, sensory discrimination, and abstract thinking, to make judgement calls to inhibit or execute a specific behavior. It helps one access and extrapolate data from previous or past life experiences. It is the act of the brain's "computer" sizing up and knowing when to do what in any given situation, be it regarding safety or socialization. As stated in the ubiquitously "user friendly" online encyclopedia known as Wikipedia, psychologists Don Norman and Tim Shallice have listed five types of situations where executive functioning affects optimal performance. Let me paraphrase what is written there:

  1. Those that involve making decisions or plans
  2. Those that involve troubleshooting of correcting mistakes
  3. Those that involve executing action sequences that are novel, not rote
  4. Those that involve technically difficult or dangerous feats, and safety precautions
  5. Those that involve overcoming temptation or a strong habitual response

A person's Theory of Mind will affect **when** he uses his or her executive functioning skills to respond to an environmental stimulus. His or her "inner landscape" will affect perceptions of danger, the unknown, and the problematic. Children with ASD in particular are thought to have neuropsychological differences resulting in both impaired Theory of Mind and executive functioning. Furthermore, their mirror neurons may be inhibited, resulting in skewed visual perceptions and subsequent difficulty with visual imitation, two prerequisite neuropsychological skills needed to learn better social skills. Children with ASD often exhibit difficulty in intuitively knowing what is expected of them in group situations involving rules of socialization and play skills.

• Key Toys to Use in Treatment

Toys To Facilitate Rapport and Communicative Intent (because they are repetitive and/or composed of pieces-remember safety, allowing you to draw out the interaction):
  ✦ Musical mobiles and musical cause & effect toys
  ✦ Ball and hammer toys, ball and slider toys
  ✦ Ring stacker toys
  ✦ Soft BIG blocks
  ✦ Stacking cups & nesting toys
  ✦ Chunky knob puzzles with matching photos underneath, chunky bead threading toys
  ✦ Toy bus and/or house/farm with chunky "little people" (e.g. Battatt™, Fisher Price™)
  ✦ Activity centers and mats for the floor, with nooks and crannies to explore
  ✦ Magnetic objects/photos and magnetic board (or cookie sheet) to mount them
  ✦ Push/pull and propelling toys for "cruising" (toy shopping cart, wind-up vehicles)
  ✦ Fisher Price™ See and Say the Farmer Says
  ✦ Early Years Roll & Swirl Ball Ramp
  ✦ Playskool Busy Boppin' Pals Toy
  ✦ Fisher-Price™ Peek-a-Blocks Tumblin' Sounds Giraffe
  ✦ TOMY Push n' Go Truck Baby Toy

Toys To Facilitate Body Awareness and Engage the Five Senses (leading to developing Emotional Attunement)
  ✦ Mirrors of various sizes
  ✦ Bubble play
  ✦ Different homemade textured ribbons tied to a hula hoop
  ✦ Textured blocks, books and small blankets with tags (keep safety in mind)
  ✦ Real looking dolls as well as stuffed animals such as Earlyears Baby Farm Friends Bowling Set
  ✦ Mr. or Mrs. Potato Head™ (child needs supervision when playing with the small pieces)
  ✦ Play dough that is scented and of various colors (keep safety in mind!)
  ✦ Shaving cream with foam blocks hidden within (keep safety in mind!)
  ✦ Beads and stringing toys

♦ Musical instrument toys (Melissa & Doug™)
♦ Dot paint, finger paint, and textured 3D stickers
♦ Learning Resources: Where is Howie's Owie? Game
♦ Learning Resources: Pretend and Play Doctor Set
♦ Thread Heads Family Block Set from Beyond Play Catalog
♦ Fisher-Price Laugh & Learn Love to Play Puppy

• <u>Key iPad® Apps to Use in Treatment</u>

☞ **For the Service Provider**: Orientation to person involves giving the child the "run of the room" initially so that you can determine learning style and preferences. This will help you establish rapport and will thus require apps that can record your impressions, observations, and baseline data. Here's a sampling of suggested Stickies, Voice Recorders, and Note Taking/List Apps:

☞ *Stickies:* Sticky, Sticky Notes Free, BugMe! Concept, Real Sticky HD, lino- Sticky and Photo Sharing, StickMe Notes, Sticky by tewks, Sticky Notes iPad®, Stickies- Todo Note & Task List, and abc Notes Lite and Paid.

☞ *Audio Memos:* Voice Recorder (FREE), Memo, Rec & Player, iVoice, SmartRecord Free, Super Note by Clear Sky Apps Lite and Paid, RecordBox, Recordium, Voicer-Sound Recorder, AudioNote Lite and Paid, Dictaphone, AudioNotebook by Qrayon, Daily Clock: Ringtone Recorder, QuickVoice® Recorder, Dragon Dictation, Notability, and Evernote.

☞ *Note Taking & Lists:* Evernote, Pages (my favorite!), TopNotes, NotesHD Free and Paid, UPad Lite and Paid, Tree Notepad, PlainText 2- Drop Text Editing, Textilus (for PC Users), Documents Pro 7, MyScript Memo, Now What?, TopNotes, INKredible, Notes HD Free, Pencilicious Lite, Notebook Free, 7Notes HD, Paper by FiftyThree, Inkflow Visual Notebook, You Doodle Plus, 30/30 Paperless Lite and Paid, Wunderlist, Memo, Checklist Again, Taskboard, Listastic, Forgetful, Actions Lists Lite, Daily To-Do List, Notifly, To Do List+, Things for iPad®, Circus Ponies Notebook Four, and Microsoft OneNote for iPad®.

☞ **For the Child:** In the initial phase of treatment, the focus in on Self Concept. That means building a sense of self, reinforcing performance, empowering the child, and facilitating Body Awareness. It also means teaching beginning Causality-action/reaction using these types of Apps; Camera, Music, Drawing, and Farm/Animal Apps:

☞ *Camera:* iPhoto and iMovie by Apple™, SPOKEnPHOTO Album, Photo Buttons, Chatterpix, ChatterKid, SonicPics, Popplet Lite and Paid, Shuttersong, MashCAM, Juxtaposer, Family Touch Album Lite, PicJointer, Turbo Collage, PicCollage, Photo Collage Free, Juxtaposer, Caption It, Cooliris, ColorBlast! Lite, Captions, Comic Life, ComicBook! 2: Creative Superpowers, Strip Designer, Story Me, Photo Slide Pro, Bill

Atkinson PhotoCard, iFunFace, CamCool HD, Kidomatic Camera, Photo Grid, Phonto, and Wig It.

☞ *Music:* MusicSparkle, Monsters, aXylophone, PianoBall, Sago Mini Music Box, ZoLO Lite, Music4Babies, Storybots® Tap & Sing, Music Group by Tiny Tap, Abby Musical Puzzle, Kids Music Factory, Twinkle Star, Kidsong Box, Tuneville, KSM2 Free, IfYoureHappy, Croco Band, Seuss Band, Toca Band, Ariel's Musical Surprise, Peg + Cat Big Gig, Cat Doorman's Little Red Wagon, Kidsong, Falling Stars, Old MacDonald All in One, Wheels on the Bus All in One, and Songs for Kids.

☞ *Drawing:* Sago Mini Doodlecast, @Draw, Little Fingers Lite, Paint Sparkles Draw, Paint Melody, Fingerpaint Magic II, Music Group by Tiny Tap, Paint My Cat, Draw Free for iPad®, Draw & Doodle Free, My Drawing Book HD, Doodoo Pad for Kids, Kaleidoscope Drawing Pad, Kids Doodle- Movie Kids Color & Draw, Art of Glow, Doodle Buddy for iPad®, Drawing Box Free, Kid Paint Express, Doodlelicious, Kids Rainbow, Kidpix, SingingFingers, Fingerpaint Magic II, Paint, This Stamper by PhotoUp, Crayola LLC, Zoodle Pad, Drawing With Carl, Canvastic, Drawing Desk, Brush and Smudge Coloring Book, Hello Crayon, Hello Color Pencil, Liquid Sketch, Scribble Press, Scribble My Story, Paint Gallery, Draw with me™, and Drawp.

☞ *Farm/Animal Apps:* Injini Lite and Paid, Peekaboo Barn HD, Peekaboo Friends, Farm Sounds Free, Photo Touch Farm Animals by Grasshopper, Sound Touch Lite, Video Touch Lite, Zoola Animals Lite, Vocal Zoo, Animals Zoo, Zoo Sounds Free, The Farm Noises, Make a Scene: Farmyard, Animal Sounds, PeekabooPets, Animal Sound Buttons, Big Fun Little App- BiFLA, Toddler Animal Sounds and Pictures, Feed Maxi, MatchAnimals, PairAnimals Free, Farm Flip, Memory King, and Nugget's First Day of School.

☞ *Body Awareness:* Disclaimer: I believe in using real time play, mirrors, and manipulatives first. Once achieved, mastery can be addressed using these Apps or similar ones: Baby Face by Tiny Tap, Meebie, Mr. Potato Head Create and Play, Laugh & Learn™ Where's Puppy's Nose? Human Body Parts, Recycling Workshop Free, Cartoon Builder FREE, Faces iMake- Right Brain Creativity, Photo Buttons, and picture collage Apps for body part photo review such as Pic Jointer and Bitsboard.

☞ **Honorable Mention: Suggested AAC Apps Worth Checking Out:**

★ AAC Evaluation Genie:
https://itunes.Apple™.com/us/app/aac-evaluation-genie/id541418407?mt=8
★ SpeakColors HD (I use this App to informally determine readiness for an official AAC evaluation) https://itunes.Apple™.com/us/app/speakcolors/id459123512?mt=8
★ Inner Voice: http://www.innervoiceapp.com
★ Look 2 Learn: https://itunes.Apple™.com/us/app/look2learn-aac/id319600029?mt=8

Note: It is beyond the scope of this book to delve into AAC Apps and related Assistive Technology (AT) for children with Autism and special needs who appear nonverbal or having emerging verbal skills. There are many great and accessible references to choose from today, thanks to the myriad of publications for the special needs community and search engines on the Internet. I especially recommend readers first getting in touch with a certified Assistive Technology Professional (ATP) and occupational therapist, and *together*, looking at these fabulous Pinterest boards by Lauren S. Enders MS/CCC-SLP. One needs to implement a plan based on specific data and collaboration, before proceeding with a course of treatment for a specific student with Augmentative and Alternative Communication needs (AAC).

- http://www.pinterest.com/lasenders/aac-faqs-myths-and-more/
- http://www.pinterest.com/lasenders/aac-evaluation-assessment/
- http://www.pinterest.com/lasenders/aac-writing-goals-objectives/
- http://www.pinterest.com/lasenders/aac-ideasactivitiesapps-for-teaching-how-to-commun/
- http://www.pinterest.com/lasenders/aac-and-literacy-curricular-access/
- http://www.pinterest.com/lasenders/aac-apps/

Anecdote

"The Inner Landscape" of the Mind:

I recall having to write a final paper in college on philosophy and psychology, and how the two, in symbiosis, play a crucial role in real life. I chose to write about one's "inner landscape" and its effect on interpersonal relationships; our expectations of others, ways of perceiving our environment, and our ways of communicating within it. As I began to work with many preschoolers diagnosed with Autism or "on the spectrum" (ASD), and others with a variety of special needs, this phrase, the "inner landscape of the mind", began to really resonate with me. It dramatically changed the way I began viewing my students. It formed the basis of what I would later dub the Socially Speaking™ Philosophy about Theory of Mind (TOM).

I started to imagine myself as an architect of a small villa, whose job it was to please the client with my creation of the "desired space". I would pore over room designs, decorating and furnishings tailored to that client's tastes. We would thus have mutually beneficial transactions from the start, enabling us to build a rapport and a good working relationship. Years later, I applied this idea to my students, and spent time playing detective, finding out the child's likes/dislikes, learning style (auditory, visual, or tactile), and favorite activities/items. I then found common ground between us, where we could meet and eventually communicate. I built trust and a "safety zone" in my therapy sessions, before I ever started to work on the goals I was given. I found that my attempts to get to know a child's "inner landscape" helped me reorient the child to place, and accommodate his or her differences in perception. Understanding their disorientation to place then allowed me to better pinpoint why these children have such difficulty with social skills development.

I began to better understand the inner workings of my student's mind. I was now able to write, implement and justify lesson plans that were truly individualized, effective and clearly delineated with a beginning/middle/end. Progress reports and team meetings, especially with parents, were no longer quite as daunting. My documentation and therapy materials became more "user friendly". Other service providers did not need a map and legend to understand my therapy goals and criteria for achieving those goals. This was especially helpful to one of my "poster children" for disorientation to place: Jake, whom you will meet soon.

Strategy and Technique

What is Disorientation to Place?

It is a noticeable lack of ability to navigate one's surroundings and be anchored to the present location/activity. It is also a sign of reduced ability to make inferences about an occurring event triggered by someone else's physical interference of space and/or alteration of the event's place. It results in difficulty with concentration, attention span, and retention of learned skills due to poor memory transfer re: episodic memory. Episodic memory is used to store impressions of events and the vocabulary related to those events, for later recall. A child who is disorientated to place often displays behavior indicating under-stimulation or over-stimulation resulting in an "environmental disconnect". The child literally shuts down/tunes out, tries to run away, or even has a "sudden" tantrum. In reality, this is due to a buildup of factors which hamper the child's ability to "live in the moment" and adapt/self regulate accordingly. It results in the child having difficulty understanding what is expected, thereby resulting in insufficient anticipation of outcomes, leading to poor transitioning and inadequate problem solving.

Cognitive Symptoms of Disorientation to Place
Reduced Ability to Label and Match Objects/Pictures and Ask What? and Who? Questions
Reduced Ability to Group Like/Unalike Items into categories, Provide Rationales, and Ask/Answer How? Questions re: Object Function
Poor Comprehension of Size and Space Concepts: Spatial Relationships (Prepositions)
Poor Expressive Communication Skills re: Conversations: Asking/Answering Where? Questions, Topic Maintenance
Poor Episodic Memory & Self Regulation Due to These Contributing Factors:
Neurological (MR, ADHD, SPD, ASD, CAPD, visual-spatial deficits etc.)
Biological (sometimes due to fatigue, hunger, illness such as chronic congestion or chronic otitis media)
Environmental (sometimes due to lack of appropriate models, neglect, abuse, poverty, deprivation)

Disorientation to Place Is Neuro-Biological in Nature and Everyone's Issue

Jake came to me for treatment mid year. He presented as an almost 3 year old adorable, strong willed, curious youngster with "fluffy hands", poor verbal and play skills, a visual learning style, and a diagnosis of Sensory Processing Dysfunction and Specific Language Impairment (SLI). I saw right away that his tactile sensitivity and low tolerance threshold contributed to his reduced self regulation, transitioning skills and topic maintenance skills re: the few vocabulary words he had in his lexicon. He seemed to want to learn and interact with others, but became easily distracted, frustrated and fatigued. He displayed some classic symptoms of disorientation to place, including fidgeting, distractibility, and poor Time on Task AKA TOT. This resulted in an "environmental disconnect" due to internal (sensory) and external factors. The busier the room, the more distracted and anxious he became. The noisier the room the less patience Jake had to sustain attention, complete tasks and "keep it together". Suffice it to say, he did not transition well at all, even with hand-over hand assistance and multi-sensory prompting.

Jake had access to specialized services and a terrific support system; supportive parents, a collaborative OT, a creative, caring special education teacher and a curious and competent PT. He was one of the first students on my caseload whose IEP reflected real teamwork, an elimination of the "silo mindset" many special educators unfortunately face and goals that addressed "whole body learning". We all worked together to consistently and carefully address his noticeable disorientation to place; long-term and short term.

Why Does It Matter?

Why was I so concerned? Because for many years, special education operated on a crisis intervention paradigm. It didn't work. Preventive intervention is what's needed to counteract disorientation to place, which leads to splintered skill acquisition, environmental disconnects and confusion, inconsistent performance, situation specific performance, continued tantrums that vary in frequency and duration and fluctuating carryover/generalization. That's why I am a child-centric behaviorist who believes in **teamwork** and collaboration. I want to reduce the child's passive participation in his/ her own learning, and help develop a more active, sequential, holistic approach to learning. That is why I am a big proponent of environmental modifications by addressing positioning, sensory needs and visual supports; all of which will be explained shortly.

 Let's take a closer look at what collaborative teamwork can do to implement proactive environmental modifications for the child in need.

CASE STUDY

Danny is an active, strong willed, immature four year old boy with essentially intact cognition, mild-moderate Sensory Processing Dysfunction and mild Autism. He has a pretty good idea of how his world works, especially family dynamics and family rules. He is told to clean his room and then he can play with his favorite toy, the Wii. Barring any unforeseen circumstances, Danny will obligingly attempt to somewhat tidy up and happily trudge off to find the remote. If Danny finds his older brother already holding the remote and playing, there may or may not be a period of rule reciting and loud warnings, hence the term "Police Man Stage". If the brother ignores him, which can be likely, a fight can erupt, where Danny, frustrated and feeling helpless, can run to a parent for help. More often then not, Danny will try to resolve the matter on his own, and resort to a full out scuffle for ownership of the remote, or fisticuffs with his brother, before his parent realizes what happened. His parent will understandably have an inclination to put Danny in "time out".

The little police man 5 will probably initially act out even more, over the unfairness of it all, and grouse that this is not the way it's supposed to work! He will complain vociferously how he tidied up and was given permission to have the Wii. At this age, a normally developing child's "inner landscape" resembles straight, even roads, where the signs are clearly seen and stated, and police men lurk in the bushes, giving many warnings and tickets for "not following the rules". Danny's play schemas essentially resemble this landscape, and he is likewise fascinated with the idea of everyone having a place and job and/or special chore, especially at home and in class. His conversations and recall of events are also reminiscent of this perception. Topic switches are frequently initiated to point out who "went off track" today and what was the consequence.

The problem is that Danny's Autism may not always allow him to quickly and smoothly access his episodic memory i.e. his mental file cabinet of road maps and rules of engagement. His temper is quick to ignite, due to the internal distractibility. It acts like a flickering light switch, causing an intermittent or full black out of his "inner landscape". Danny's neurological impulsivity overrides his quick yet incomplete and/or inconsistent attempts to self regulate. This then affects his ability to access his semantic memory of what target vocabulary to use in order to influence his brother's compliance. His ability to make inferences about the "here and now" and access episodic memory of what happened last time or what alternative reaction he was supposed to have, is subsequently also compromised. This results in difficulties with expressing displeasure and problem solving. It further contributes to continued anxiety over changes in routine. This leads to a tantrum when he has to wait his turn and/or is challenged, and his continued immature way of handling obstacles.

SOLUTION

1. Implement a Sensory Diet

"The daily total of sensorimotor experiences needed by a person to adaptively interact with the environment." -- Bonnie Hanschu
Reisman, Judith, and Haschu, Bonnie (1992). *Sensory Integration Inventory: Revised for Individuals with Developmental Disabilities-User's Guide.* Hugo, MN: PDP Press

While it is the domain of the OT, best practices re: behavior management today include a working knowledge of Sensory Processing Dysfunction. I listed suggested references at the end of this chapter. What I want to state here is that the *entire* team must make sure that a student with sensory issues has undergone an occupational therapist evaluation and/or has an OT recommending a Sensory Diet. Everyone should know how to "feed the need" (such as the need for touching things, deep pressure, or movement). Also, it's crucial to note that a child who is not feeling well, or is hungry, may appear to have sensory issues and disorientation to place. That child will also have difficulty with attention and Time on Task (TOT). Remember, biological needs must be met *before* sensory needs for intervention can meet with success! Also, the materials you pick should help foster finger isolation and fine motor skills; also usually the domain of the OT.

2. *Implement Visual Supports*

For the most part, I want this book to be a practical, hands-on survival guide for parents and professionals "in the trenches". However, everything has a time and place and this is the place for me to get on my soapbox about visual cues and visual supports as a viable treatment option for children with ASD. This is the time for me to quote research and expound on the virtues of visual learning and instruction.

There has been a noticeable rise in diagnosis of Autism and Autism Spectrum Disorders (ASD), resulting in new guidelines and revisions in the DSM V, which was published in May 2013. There is increasing interest to find evidence about how to effectively treat children with ASD using technology, particularly iOS Apps. Much research has already been done on the benefits of visual supports to treat children with ASD and challenging behaviors. There are now many known and proven benefits and ways to use visual supports for behavior management, starting with Augmentative Alternative Communication (AAC) devices and the Picture Exchange Communication System (PECS), to teach less verbal or nonverbal children to express wants/needs instead of acting out (Communicative Intent).

Recently, there have been a rising number of school wide initiatives to introduce visual supports through eLearning, into curriculums and best practices. The implications of how the very nature of eLearning aligns with the visual learning style seen in so many children with Autism can no longer be ignored. From TEACCH to PECS, from basic visual supports using the old standby "If..Then Contingent", to Linda Hodgdon's *Visual Strategies™ Program*, it has been determined that many children with Autism appear to be visual learners. It has been proposed that the use of the visual modality when implementing IEP goals and lessons, greatly facilitates comprehension, self regulation and generalization of learned skills.

Roa and Gagie (2006) compiled a list of why visual supports are so crucial to support success, in both self contained and mainstreamed/inclusive settings, and self regulation within familiar and unfamiliar or challenging environments. In my *Socially Speaking™ Seminars*, I spend time discussing the benefits of using visual supports, and not fading them, for these purposes:

Benefits of Visual Support Integration Into Treatment of Children with ASD

★ They are part of everyone's communication system (universally understood)

★ They can attract and hold a child's attention (focus and Time on Task-TOT)

★ They enable the child to glean the message and reduce anxiety/fear of the unknown or unexpected (behavior management)

★ They make abstract concepts more concrete for the child (orientation to person/place/time)

According to Hodgdon (2000), visual supports, such as *Visual Schedules*, *Transition Helpers*, and *Rules Reminders*, when implemented correctly, allow children with Autism to more freely navigate and make sense of their environment and those in it. According to Roa and Gagie (2006) "Visual supports help bring in structure, routine, and sequence that many children with Autism require, in order to carry on their daily activities". Dalryaple (1989) found that in addition, visual supports can help children with Autism, many of whom have difficulty understanding social communication cues such as gestures, facial expression, body language and prosody/inflection.

Visual supports thus facilitate better orientation to person/place/time, including transitioning and self regulation. These areas are often challenging for children with Autism, resulting in fluctuating performance, inconsistent carryover of learned skills, situation specific learning and ritualistic behaviors. It is therefore imperative that some type of visual support be introduced into therapeutic regimens for children with ASD, from the beginning, to "set the stage". To provide systematic, static cues to for the child to decipher, retain, and recall, in order to clarify the environment, clarify expectations for how the child needs to perform in said environment and increase comprehension and use of the overall target vocabulary needed to learn about said environment. This will enable the child to develop more age appropriate behaviors and performance; in school, at home and within the confines of the community.

Special education best practices today, include well known programs to help these children with Autism, who tend to be visual learners, and display social communication challenges. The reader is invited to peruse this chapter's bibliography for more information. In a nutshell, here is the basic list of reputable programs:

Therapeutic Techniques Implementing Visual Supports:
1.PECS (Bondy & Frost)
2.TEACCH (Schopler)
3.Social Stories™ (Gray)
4.Visual Strategies™ (Hodgdon)

Addressing Disorientation to Place Improves Episodic Memory

You will recall our discussion of Jake's disorientation to place. Let's examine how we worked through it. addressing what I saw right away, that after implementing a Sensory Diet which was given at regular intervals, the "environmental disconnect" lessened. After implementing visual supports across the board such as building a *Reinforcer Roster*, which the entire team used, the disorientation decreased further. We were able to collaboratively enforce structure and routine, to help anchor Jake to the present. This was an integral component to jump-starting his episodic memory. Episodic memory is crucial, because it pairs the event someone experiences with the relevant vocabulary associated with the event, to formulate language and feelings modules in the brain, which can be extrapolated later on as needed; for carryover of learned skills, and for transitioning to new or unfamiliar environments. Episodic memory is what's honed, when a child "lives in the moment", oriented to place, so that the development of Theory of Mind and Executive Functioning can ensue.

To enable Jake to reorient to **place**, so that he could later learn the vocabulary of feelings and use it instead of "acting out", I first needed to work with the OT, to provide a *Sensory Diet*, in addition to the visual supports I created with a camera, Boardmaker™, and later a digital camera and iPad®. Like Lexie, Jake needed me to first do proactive clinical intervention by "setting the stage" without his active participation, to get his body ready to learn. We chose to use the *ALERT Program*: Shellenberger, Sherry, and Williams, Mary Sue (2001). *How Does Your Engine Run? A Leader's Guide to the Alert Program, Take Five: Staying Alert at Home and School*. Albuquerque, NM: Therapy Works Inc.

We also chose to implement the *Visual Strategies™ Technique* by Linda Hodgdon MEd CCC-SLP, and the *Social Story™ Technique* by Carol Gray MA/CCC-SLP. I created various instructional videos for the team; some of which I later uploaded to my YouTube channel, socialslp. I also created specific visual supports and Social Stories to foster self regulation and transitioning such as this one:

http://bit.ly/19aUDqP

It is beyond the scope of this book to delve into each technique. Suffice it to say, first using proactive Sensory Diet implementation, and then direct clinical intervention through Visual Supports with active participation, really helped Jake reorient to place, formulate episodic memory and Theory of Mind, and start to use the vocabulary of feelings in context. By using a methodical, visually dominant, and "whole body approach", Jake began to "see the forest for the trees". We did too. I'd like to provide another story to hit my point home.

What I Learned From The Movie "Avatar"

"I See You!"
- Neytiri of the Na'avi, Avatar, by James Cameron © 2009

I love the film *Avatar*, as both a special educator and as a science fiction fan. I really love that quote. In the movie, the Na'avi people greet each other with this deceptively simple phrase. It's so eloquent and meaningful to the human experience, especially for the visual learners we all are, not just children with Autism. I try to get this point across at my *Socially Speaking™ Seminars*. I explain that it is easier at first to learn to navigate our students' inner worlds than to bring them into ours, unaware and unprepared. The idea of educating a special needs student on his or her own terms is not new, nor is the practice of providing teachable moments based on a student's preferences and learning styles i.e. "inner landscape".

I am reminded of the "total immersion" technique used by educators such as Dr. Stanley Greenspan MD, who pioneered his Floortime™ approach in treating children with ASD. He emphasizes that the "starting point" with these children is not where you, the instructor, be it a service provider or parent, is at. The key is to see what the child's landscape is at that moment, be it the inner landscape or the outer landscape created by schemas of play. The trick is to join in and live "in the moment" that the child with ASD is experiencing. This leads to improved understanding of where that child is at, and the subsequent establishing of rapport and routine for further learning to continue.

"Join in and live 'in the moment' that the child with ASD is experiencing."

Following the child's lead facilitates Self Concept in the child with ASD. He or she starts to realize that his or her ideas and wants are important. This is the start of understanding what I means, and how a Me can become a We. Everyone knows the importance of seamless transitions from Me to We. It is crucial at home with the family, in school, in the workplace, and in adulthood through interpersonal relationships with others.

Avatar is a wonderful example of this. The film moved so many people on so many levels. It changed the way people view cinematography, and I think it will change the way people view Theory of Mind i.e. differences in viewpoint and Self Concept. It certainly moved me, and took a whole new spin on the adage of learning by "walking in someone else's shoes".

The movie is about an aloof, lonely, sensitive, brave, curious, paraplegic marine named Jake Sully. It is about his epic journey to readjust his thinking, rediscover himself and reaffirm his life. He travels to another planet named Pandora, where he literally begins a new life in a new body. The medically engineered body called an avatar, was originally meant for his deceased twin brother, a scientist. Jake's initial clashes with his scholarly team, his military training and repressed anger over the loss of his legs temporarily blind him when he first lands on Pandora. It takes a series of circumstances, through which his remote controlled body i.e. his avatar, becomes immersed in the tribal life of the native population, in order for his perspective to change. Jake slowly begins to open his eyes and really see. His lessons with Neytiri reshape his "inner landscape" i.e. his Theory of Mind. This allows him to gradually transition from thinking as an I to thinking as a We. He is then able to internalize the ways of The People and bond with them and with his teacher, their leader's daughter.

The movie is rich with symbolism. It is rife with much food for thought for people from all backgrounds, whether they are pragmatists, scholars, environmentalists or special educators. The main lesson I took from this tale is the idea of perspective. This movie reaffirms my belief that to address socialization in children with special needs we need to first learn about the child's perspective, i.e. the "inner landscape". We need to help him or her want to explore his or her environment, and want us to interact with and teach the child. We need to acknowledge the different way these students see the world, as well as respect the power that the visual modality holds for children with ASD. In short, successful intervention begins with us transmitting the message to these children that we see what they see, and that we really see them. This is especially important to keep in mind when the child has to transition tasks.

Addressing Disorientation to Place Helps with Transitioning

FAQ: Why is transitioning so challenging?

It's frequently hard for these children to master because they often need tangible anchoring to the present i.e. orientation to place, in order to:

• Develop Resiliency (the opposite of transitioning difficulty)
• Develop Time on Task i.e. Attention Span

- Develop episodic memory: pairing the event being experienced + target vocabulary for later recall and extrapolation i.e. executive functioning

How to teach transitioning to a child who is disoriented to place

I have two suggestions:

1. Create a <u>Visual Support</u> showing Before/After or Now/Next and also embed the If...Then Contingent with positive reinforcement

2. Use <u>Emotional Attunement</u> to appeal to the child's helpful side. It's not about going to a different place. It's about what the child will get/do once there. a) Have him/her bring something useful to a person in that other place (tissues, water etc.) and notify that person in advance to be very appreciative; vocally and overtly with exaggerated affect, so that the child feels empowered. b) Ask for advance notice/warning of what the child can expect upon return, so that you "prep" him/her and the child knows that he/she is going back to do____.

ⓃⓄⓉⒺ

Visual Supports are crucial to facilitating transitioning, self regulation and orientation to place. All three are connected and must be treated simultaneously. All are offshoots of underdeveloped Sensory Processing and Executive Functioning Skills. This can contribute to the "environmental disconnect".

What does that look like in real life? Here is a wonderful video which I show in all my Socially Speaking™ Seminars. You can find it on Vimeo: The 2012 Autism Project- "Sensory Overload":

http://vimeo.com/52193530

Clinical Implications of Targeting Disorientation to Place in Treatment- Review:

1. Children with Behavioral Challenges Usually "Act Out" to Get Something in Return, Something Missing-Classic Triggers:
- Attention
- Sensory/biological needs
- Avoidance/escape from unwanted activities/environments
- Lack of Structure i.e. clarification re: your expectations of him/her

2. Proactive Measures to Consider Before "The Meltdown"-Since Crisis Intervention Is Not As Helpful As Preventive Intervention:
- Proactive Attention: Every human being craves attention and empowerment!

- Sanitize the Environment: Remove potential distractors
- A Sensory Diet, created by the OT, is integral to treatment of behavioral issues
- Assistive Technology/Visual Supports: Provide clarification (of what you expect of the child using simple, firm verbal instructions, or pictures showing the appropriate response). Structuring your educational activity from the start means reconfiguring the learning environment i.e. the:
  - ❖ Nature of the materials presented (ex: objects AKA manipulatives vs. photos)
  - ❖ Physical surroundings (remove all distractors that can potentially "set off" the child)
  - ❖ Mental framework of the task at hand i.e. the use of Visual Strategies™ such as "Visual Schedules", "Task Organizers", and Social Stories™ about specific routines etc. so that you clearly communicate what you want from the child, and what can be expected

3. Proactive Intervention-Modifying the Structure of Your Activity Means Reconfiguring These Parameters:

- Nature of your demands on the child (ex: tactile manipulatives vs. visual pictures to learn: address learning style!)
- Physical (remove distractors) and mental surroundings (use Visual Strategies™ to negotiate with an "If...Then Contingent" style Visual Schedule, remind child of the rules etc), bring in reinforcers that are *motivating to the particular child, to use ongoing vs. token economy/delayed gratification).*
- Timing of the activity i.e. modify how many discreet trials before stopping (review literature on ABA and VBT), OR time the challenging activity so that it precedes an enjoyable activity, OR trade off between both (ex: First..... do ____ and Then......____)

4. Why Use Visual Supports in Treatment?

- Easier to comprehend. "If I see it I understand it!" (quote by Dr. Temple Grandin)
- Many children with learning difficulties, especially with ASD, are *visua*l learners
- Pictures are motivational, universally deciphered, "attention grabbers"
- Pictures are a physical aide in enabling the child to "live in the moment"
- Pictures facilitate "shifting gears" (transitioning) with less anxiety/confusion
- Visual Supports help the child predict the environment/know expectations
- Visual Supports allow better task completion (timely, independent, sequential)

Tips to Remember About Visual Supports:

▸ It is easier to teach a *NEW* routine than it is to change an *old* behavior (Linda Hodgdon 2003)

▸ Giving *choices* fosters trust and empowerment-which increases compliance and productivity

▸ Set a time limit for each task on the Visual Schedule: Using the AT Link Clips(more on that later) helps child realize *time is passing* (Penina Rybak 2004)

▸ Creating a "time duration map" by manipulating a string of clips which corresponds to each "job" the child completes, helps the child concretely begin to understand before/during/after, and beginning/middle/end.

▸ Break down task into little steps visually, like a comic strip, to help structure the environment-this can be done with objects and/or pictures

▸ Say things ONCE and give child time to process what was said....while simultaneously showing/viewing the picture/object

▸ Reinforcers can be embedded into the Visual Schedule and/or used separately depending on the child's level of cognition and cooperation

▸ Use Visual Supports constantly! Do NOT fade! (Velcro and wall space will become coveted)

▸ Make sure the child understands the objects/pictures being used! Practice identifying and matching pairs of objects/pictures and see if the child can name the items on demand. Only then can they be used within the visual support. PRACTICE OFTEN!

▸ Visual Supports are objective and need to be provided on a case by case basis. It is important to note the mental age of the child, not the chronological. It is important to note the child's cognition, visuo-spatial skills, hand-eye coordination skills and learning style.

3. Implement an Object Function Protocol Through Play and Pre-Literacy Activities

Children need to learn how their world "works" and what the things in it do. That's the essence of object function, which is retained in episodic memory and plays a role in both language and social communication development. Play is the vehicle through which children first learn about their world. Play development is a precursor to pre-literacy acquisition where the groundwork for advanced language comprehension is laid out. We need to ensure that the child with Autism learns to play. This will help with the development of episodic memory while remaining anchored to the present. This will help the child retain learned vocabulary and their meaning. Counteracting disorientation to place leads to mastery of object function, tolerance of delayed gratification, increased resiliency, increased Time on Task, and ultimately improved problem solving and self regulation. How do I achieve all this?

- My first line of defense: Teach Play in a developmental sequence, using my *Formula for Assessing Play Skills Acquisition* (Chapter 8).

- My second line of defense: Teach The "If...Then" Contingent using visual supports, including my dubbed *AT Link Clips* as a "time duration map". I basically embed Lauri™ Math Links (or Boomerings® by Discovery Toy) into the Visual Schedule and into the Reinforcer photo to "count down" to the completion of an activity. I make sure the activities are doable and that the tangible reinforcers are appealing and motivating. The "If...Then Contingent is presented while providing the applicable visual support in conjunction with the structured activities with a clearly delineated beginning/middle/end.

Lauri™ Math Clips   Boardmaker™ Doll Icon
                         ©Mayer-Johnson Inc.

- My third line of defense: Create lessons (implemented using visual supports) based on the *Pre-Reading Readiness Hierarchy Protocol (Chapter 8 and 12).*

Best Practices Roundup: How to Bridge the Gap between Disorientation to Person/ Place/Time, Readiness to Learn, and Actual Performance

FAQ: How can we help children with ASD stay anchored to the present?

I have two suggestions:
- Use replacement behaviors/terminology to help maintain attention and/or help anticipate unwanted/unexpected event (moving, new sibling, doctor's appointment or surgery, going to a family celebration, going to a new school etc.) and repeat. Note: acting out is a cry for help or sign of confusion, so my 2 key phrases I use in treatment are:
1. "I don't understand"
2. "You are not ready yet"

- Don't Reinvent the Wheel: Search Google and YouTube for samples and this website:

http://bit.ly/1wyfWX7

FAQ: How can we foster compliance indirectly and directly, for better outcomes?

▪ Two Indirect Clinical Methods of Intervention to Foster Compliance and Orientation to Person/Place Using Play:

1. Proactive Attention + *Reinforcer Roster*
2. Sensory Diet + "flooding" the reinforcer

▪ Three Direct Clinical Methods of Intervention to Foster Compliance and Orientation to Person/Place Using Visual Supports-An Overview:

• Social Stories™ by Carol Gray

☺ Social Stories are VISUALLY relevant to the actual child:
☺ Child details and/or clip art is incorporated into story
☺ Digital photos of child and surroundings is included in the body of story
☺ Social Stories are written in a POSITIVE manner
☺ Tone is "matter of fact" and states alternate and/or acceptable behaviors to do instead
☺ Text lists various choices and/or possibilities so child can learn what to expect
☺ Writing is simple and phrased in first person

• Visual Strategies™ by Linda Hodgdon with Penina's AT Link Clips (see Chapter 12)

☺ "My Rules" and "Topic Flash Cards" (structure & preventive measures)

☺ "Visual Schedule" (If/Then Board using objects/photos)

☺ "Reinforcer Chart" (rewards i.e. token economy set up with "Linked Clips")

☺ "Task Organizer" (breaking down steps to a task)

☺ "Transition Helper" (fostering compliance re: changes in activity and/or routine)

☺ "Communication From The Trenches": (providing information & clarification for child and the team)

• REPLAYS™ by Karen Levine and Naomi Chedd

1. Reenact the "trigger" event dramatically (ex: avoiding bedtime)
2. Role Play the resolution and/or alternate reaction that should be encouraged
3. Write a Social Story about the "trigger" and the appropriate reaction to it
4. Recreate the "trigger" event on a much smaller scale
5. Swiftly reinforce the child's modified, more "low key" reaction

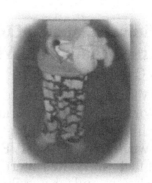

NOTE

This technique can only be used with verbal, higher functioning children whose cognitive level allows for critique, self evaluation (judging) of performance, and pretend play. A child with emerging play skills and/or who does not self monitor verbal output, will not understand this approach yet!

A Word About Digital Resources re: Photos for Lessons

Jake and I got into a routine where we started the session by reviewing our Visual Supports; *Rules in School* and *Visual Schedule*, then got a dose of sensory input by going to the PT/OT room to jump on the trampoline, then did a quick customized why? question worksheet at the table, and then flopped down on the floor with my vintage Fisher Price® dollhouse for a REPLAY™ (his favorite activity for a while). If he cooperated, he got to play on the computer (later the iPad®) at the end, specific games utilizing the target vocabulary and concepts touched on earlier. And so it went. While orienting Jake to person, then place, and eventually time, I was providing carefully orchestrated "teachable moments" to enable him to internalize the vocabulary of feelings and pre-literacy skills (more on that later). I ensured that he was familiar with all my target vocabulary in both object and picture format. I used various resources to find, customize, display, and share photos with Jake in therapy, and with the rest of the IEP team including his parents. This is where mobile technology was so helpful in both finding online photos (see below) and storing them and their links for later reference. Here are my favorite, free, cloud storage i.e. "holding pen" Apps:

• Pocket
• Evernote
• Google Docs
• Sugar Sync
• Pinterest

Here are 5 suggested links re: finding/sharing images and creative common license guidelines:

http://bit.ly/1zQeRB4

http://bit.ly/1BgIWoX

http://bit.ly/1Ct0CBD

http://bit.ly/1yWoY61

http://bit.ly/15DotC2

Where to Find Pictures Online:
Google Images
Pinterest
EduPic
Pics for Learning
The Getty: Open Content Program and Getty Images iPad® App
Welcome Library: http://wellcomeimages.org

A Word About Teaching the Expression of Feelings

How did I really teach Jake to express his feelings instead of "acting out" when he became disoriented to place? I used a combination of music, art, and worksheet based activities, coupled with Cognitive Therapy Techniques (CBT), to increase his self awareness, self motivation, and self evaluation of performance, over time.

I have also found it extremely helpful to consult with both a music therapist and an art therapist when starting to target social skills level 2 in therapy. Both art and music engage the five senses, increase Emotional Attunement, and facilitate self regulation for the creator and the listener/viewer alike. A good social skills treatment plan includes structured arts & crafts and musical activities to facilitate the child's understanding of Emotional and Motoric Tempo/ Rhythm and that:

⊚ Feelings can be experienced on different levels simultaneously, like a collage of various materials, or like different instruments multi- layered for the same song
⊚ Feelings can vary in intensity, like a brushstroke on canvas, or like changing tempos in a song
⊚ Feelings can be expressed in a diverse manner, like different colors of the rainbow, or a solo versus a duet or a lone bagpipe versus a trio of violins. I especially like to explore this imagery with higher functioning students who need to move beyond simply verbalizing the basic four feelings (happy, sad, mad, afraid) by using increasingly rich vocabulary such as 'hopeful, regret, and embarrassed'.
⊚ Feelings can be thus be individualized and interpreted, like any good painting or musical composition. I especially like to discuss an older, higher functioning student's "inner landscape" with both him and his "inner circle" and how it affects his or her ability to perceive emotion, and degrees of emotion, in self and in others, accurately and uniquely. I use arts & crafts projects to help the child measure his or her feelings.

Targeting Disorientation to Place: Justification Wording for Grants

FAQ: Why incorporate music into social skills kits and lessons?
Music facilitates self regulation and orientation
Music facilitates Emotional Attunement, through engaging the brain's ability to perceive the tempo of feelings
Music also facilitates Motoric Tempo through Body Awareness and Proprioception
Music helps the child with ASD perform time sequenced movements (rhythm), which can be an area of real challenge regarding motor, play and communication

FAQ: Why incorporate art into social skills kits and lessons?
Arts & Crafts facilitates Body Awareness and Proprioception
Art is a "whole body experience" using multi-sensory learning to build "muscle memory" through engaging The Five Senses
Arts & Crafts facilitates episodic memory and subsequent recall of concepts/ideas
Art is FUN and fosters Emotional Attunement
Art+worksheet fosters attention (Time on Task) and Causality naturally and in context: has beginning/middle/end

Final Words:

Jake's mother in particular was amazing to work with, with an awesome sense of humor. She understood right away what I was trying to accomplish, and was a very active participant in her son's progress and orientation to person and then place. I frequently joked with her that a speech therapist walks a fine line between being an educator and an ambassador. I had to devise fun "teachable moments" and beguile Jake to join me, interact with me and stay with me "in the moment". It required creativity, an understanding of his inner landscape and diplomacy; three traits ambassadors need.

My joke has never been more true. The revision of the IDEA in 2004 has brought the necessity of self regulation and behavioral appropriateness to the forefront of our collective social and educational consciousness. These areas of performance now need to be documented in the IEP. If a child's behavior is interfering with his or her ability to participate in classroom routines and lessons, it is now a federal law to draft functional goals to address those behavioral issues. In today's school system, many speech therapists are being asked to attend team meetings to discuss and help formulate the Behavior Intervention Plans (BIP). The BIP is then annually included in the child's IEP.

As special educators, we see first hand the impact of problematic behaviors on the student's ability to get his or her needs met, and get along with others. We live in an increasingly diverse society. Cultural differences are now encouraged and even celebrated. This has fostered the belief that individualization is good, and that there are many paths leading to these desired commodities of individualism-- truth, knowledge and success. There are many advantages to being unique and thinking "outside the box". There is a practical application to the idea of individualism. Educators know that there is more than one way to teach, to learn and to address an issue. I have always felt that an eclectic approach in therapy fosters multidimensional thinking. It also alleviates boredom, for both the child and the clinician.

Please keep this in mind when reading this book. Like any good cookbook, some ingredients may be familiar, but the ways in which they are used may vary. Some terminology may have been replaced by new, unfamiliar phrases such as Theory of Mind (TOM). It has been postulated that children with Autism have a different TOM, possibly due to neurological differences. They possess differences in the way they process incoming information and literally how they view the world around them.

Dr. Temple Grandin, one of the premier ambassadors for people with Autism says, "If I see it, I understand it." Many children with ASD have difficulty with auditory processing, making it hard to follow oral directions promptly, sequence a procedure and/or retell a story in the correct order and maintain topic. Multi-sensory learning experiences (visual-auditory-tactile), with an emphasis on the visual, enable these children to "close the loop" and to increase consistency of overall performance. Visual input helps these children with their TOM, or their "inner landscape" as I call it.

"For children with ASD, the visual modality is the key pipeline for getting information in and out."

I like to imagine speech therapy for children with ASD being akin to a drive in a foreign country, where I do not speak the native language. As I drive through my student's "inner landscape" I see road signs that are not written, but depicted as pictures. I therefore try to tailor the therapy materials I use to fit their needs. Some children need real photographs to learn, while others can use icons such as the PCS™ library from Boardmaker™. What is important to remember is that everyone's "inner landscape" is multidimensional, multi-layered, and full of imagery gleaned from memory and learned experiences. What we now know about children with ASD is that their "inner landscape" is rich with visual imagery, and that the visual modality is the key pipeline to getting information in and out. Research has proven this, and those of us "in the trenches" have experienced it firsthand.

The down side of working on orientation to place by structuring the routine/ environment for maximum learning, is that it frequently erodes choice. Children must be empowered to make choices, to express their wants/needs in a safe, caring setting and know they will be heard. It helps with Self Concept and self regulation. Children need to develop *Verbal Rejection* skills so that they express their preferences/choices and their fear, reluctance, anger and pain in a more age appropriate manner. They also need to understand why they feel this way, so that they can move on to developing self protection and verbal problem solving in the future.

So when I am working on orientation to place, being mindful of the need to facilitate expression of feelings, I am mindful of the importance of embedding choices and the ability to decline them, into my lessons and conversation. In the end, honoring a child's TOM and inner landscape means encouraging and abiding by the choices made, within reason of course. The Socially Speaking™ Curriculum is predicated on the need to be child-centric while remaining firm and structured, so that *Verbal Rejection* and *Transitioning* are learned more naturally, contextually, and developmentally.

Materials for Your Toolbox

- <u>Key References</u>

Attwood, Tony (2004). *Exploring Feelings: Anxiety-Cognitive Behavior Therapy to manage Anxiety*. Arlington, TX: Future Horizons.

Bader, Stephanie et al (2010). *Enhancing Communication in Children With Autism Spectrum Disorders: Practical Strategies Series in Autism Education*. Waco, TX: Prufrock Press Inc.

Baker, Jed (2008). *No More Meltdowns: Positive Strategies for Managing and Preventing Out of Control Behavior*. Arlington, TX: Future Horizons.

Barbera, Mary Lynch, and Rassmussen, Tracy (2007). *The Verbal Behavior Approach: How to Teach Children with Autism and Related Disorders*. Philadelphia, PA: Jessica Kingsley Publishers.

Barnes, K. et al (2008). Self- regulation strategies of children with emotional disturbance, *Physical & Occupational* Therapy In Pediatrics, 28 (4), 369-387.

Baron-Cohen, Simon, et al (1985). Does the Autistic Child Have a "Theory of Mind?" *Cognition*, 21, 37-46.

Biel, Lindsey, and Peske, Nancy (2005). *Raising a Sensory Smart Child: The Definitive Handbook for Helping Your Child with Sensory Integration Issues*. New York, NY: Penguin Books.

Bondy, Andy and Frost, Lori (2002). *A Picture's Worth: PECS and Other Visual Communication Strategies in Autism*. Bethesda, MD: Woodbine House

Chiak, D.F., Wright, R., and Ayres, K.M. (2010). Use of Self-Modeling Static- Picture Prompts Via a Handheld Computer to Facilitate Self-Monitoring in the General Education Classroom. *Education and Training in Autism and Developmental Disabilities*, 45(1), 136-149.

Dogoe, M.S. et al (2010). Acquisition and Generalization of the Picture Exchange Communication System Behaviors Across Settings, Persons, and Stimulus Classes with

Three Students with Autism. *Education and Training in Autism and Developmental Disabilities, 45(2), 216-229.*

Gimpel Peacock, Gretchen, and Holland, Melissa (2003). *Emotional and Behavioral Problems of Young Children: Effective Interventions in the Preschool and Kindergarten Years.* New York, NY: Guilford Press.

Grandin, Temple (1996). *Thinking in Pictures and Other Reports From My Life with Autism.* New York, NY: Vintage Books/Random House.

Greenspan, Stanley, and Thorndike-Greenspan, Nancy (1995). *First Feelings.* New York, NY: Penguin Books.

Greenspan, Stanley, and Weider, Serena (1998). *The Child with Special Needs: Encouraging Intellectual and Emotional Growth.* Cambridge, MA: Perseus Books Group.

Greenspan, Stanley (2002). *The Secure Child: Helping Our Children Feel Safe and Confident in an Insecure World.* Cambridge, MA: Perseus Books Group.

Greenspan, Stanley, and Weider, Serena (2006). *Engaging Autism: Using the Floortime Approach to Help Children Relate, Communicate, and Think.* Cambridge, MA: Da Capo Press/Perseus Books Group.

Gray, Carol (2010). *The New Social Story Book: Revised and Expanded Tenth Anniversary Edition.* Arlington, TX: Future Horizons.

Gutstein, Steven (2002). *Relationship Development Intervention with Young Children: Social and Emotional Development Activities for Asperger Syndrome, Autism, PDD, and NLD.* Philadelphia, PA: Jessica Kingsley Publishers.

Hodgdon, Linda (1995). *Visual Strategies for Improving Communication: Practical Supports for School and Home.* Troy, MI: Quirk Roberts Publishing.

Hodgdon, Linda (1999). *Solving Behavior Problems in Autism.* Troy, MI: Quirk Roberts Publishing.

Kranowitz, Carol, and Miller, Lucy Jane (2005). *The Out of Sync Child.* New York, NY: Penguin Group Inc.

Levine, Karen, and Chedd, Naomi (2007). *REPLAYS: Using Play to Enhance Emotional and Behavioral Development for Children with Autism Spectrum Disorders.* Philadelphia, PA: Jessica Kingsley Publishers.

Prelock, Patricia et al (2012). *Treatment of Autism Spectrum Disorders: Evidence-Based Intervention Strategies for Communication and Social Interactions.* Baltimore, MD: Paul H. Brookes Publishing Company.

Prest, J. M., Mirenda, P., and Mercier D. (2010). Using Symbol-Supported Writing Software with Students with Down Syndrome: An Exploratory Study. *Journal of Special Education Technology,* 25(2), 1-12.

Quill, Kathleen Ann (2000). *Do-Watch-Listen-Say: Social and Communication Intervention for Children with Autism.* Baltimore, MD: Paul H. Brookes Publishing Co.

Reisman, Judith, and Haschu, Bonnie (1992). *Sensory Integration Inventory: Revised for Individuals with Developmental Disabilities-User's Guide.* Hugo, MN: PDP Press

Schneider, Catherine (2006). *Sensory Secrets: How to Jump Start Learning in Children.* Siloam Springs, AK: Concerned Communications Inc.

Shellenberger, Sherry, and Williams, Mary Sue (2001). *How Does Your Engine Run? A Leader's Guide to the Alert Program, Take Five: Staying Alert at Home and School.* Albuquerque, NM: Therapy Works Inc.

Steere, Bob (1988). *Becoming an Effective Classroom Manager: A Resource for Teachers.* Albany, NY: State University of New York Press

Weiss, Mary Jane and Harris, Sandra (2001). *Reaching Out, Joining In: Teaching Social Skills to Young Children with Autism.* Bethesda, MD: Woodbine House

Weiss, Mary Jane and Demiri, Valbona (2011). *Jumpstarting Communication Skills in Children with Autism: A Parents' Guide to Applied Verbal Behavior.* Bethesda, MD: Woodbine House.

Willis, Clarissa (2006). *Teaching Young Children with Autism Spectrum Disorder.* Beltsville, MD: Gryphon House Inc.

• Key Concepts to Address

Sensory Processing, Sensory Diet, Visual Supports, Verbal Rejection, Object Function, Episodic Memory, and Transitioning

• Key Links to Peruse

http://bit.ly/1thWkLC

http://bit.ly/1H1vRs1

http://bit.ly/1uTZTZy

http://bit.ly/1yJJbf6

http://bit.ly/15MqLzC

http://usevisualstrategies.com

http://bit.ly/15Dr8f3

http://bit.ly/1z3lrRO

http://bit.ly/1CZYQpW

http://bit.ly/1yJJWog

• Links for Finding/Sharing Images and Creative Common License Guidelines:

http://bit.ly/1zQeRB4

http://bit.ly/1BgIWoX

http://bit.ly/1CtoCBD

http://bit.ly/1yWoY61

http://bit.ly/15DotC2

• Key Toys to Use in Treatment

Toys that facilitate Comprehension of Object Function(because they are replicas of real life objects)
- ✦ Doll and accessories, including dollhouse
- ✦ *Where Does It Go?* Book by Margaret Miller
- ✦ Melissa and Doug™ puzzle assortment
- ✦ Patch Products/Lauri™/Smethport Magnetic Foam Objects
- ✦ Ravensburger What Goes Together? Game
- ✦ What Goes Together? Puzzle by Trend
- ✦ Categories Language Cards by Smethport
- ✦ Name That Category! Fun Deck by Super Duper
- ✦ Webber: Every Day Go Togethers Fun Deck by Super Duper
- ✦ Educational Insights Laundry Jumble Game
- ✦ Hello Sunshine Game by Think Fun
- ✦ Carson-Dellosa Publishing Opposites Attract

- ✦ Carson Dellosa Key Education: What's Missing? Learning Cards
- ✦ Language Games - What Doesn't Belong?
- ✦ Photo What's Wrong? Flashcards by Speechmark

Toys that facilitate Expressing Feelings
- ✦ Mirrors
- ✦ Dot paint, finger paint, crayons, and markers

+ Fisher-Price™ Little People & Accessories
+ Battat™ School Bus
+ Hape - Eggspressions - Game of Feelings
+ Melissa & Doug Expressions Stampers
+ *Lots of Feelings* Book (Shelley Rotner's Early Childhood Library)
+ Crayola Beginnings Color Me A Song
+ Understanding Emotions: Flashcards for Visual Learners
+ Make Your Own Sock Puppets by Faber Castell
+ Doll house and furniture
+ *Today I Feel Silly: And Other Moods That Make My Day* By Jamie Lee Curtis
+ Carson Dellosa Kid-Drawn Emotions Bulletin Board Set
+ Funny Faces Game by International Playthings
+ Webber "What Are They Thinking?" Photo Card Deck from Super Duper

• Key iPad® Apps to Use in Treatment

☞ **For the Service Provider:** Orientation to place involves the use of visual supports to reduce tantrums and anxiety about changes in routines. I thus recommend Timers, Video Recording, Photo, and Social Story Apps. Here's a suggested sampling:

☞ *Timers:* Children's Countdown Timer Free, Timer for Kids and Kids Countdown Free by Idea4e, Time Timer iPad® Edition, Wait Timer by Touch Autism, VisTimer Free, See and Do- Autism Series, Beep Me by Yaniv Kalsky, Giant Timer, Timer+, Self Timer Camera, Countdown!!, Best Sand Timer, 30/30, and Stopwatch%.

☞ *Video Recording:* iMovie by Apple™, iPad®'s Camera App (native), Sago Mini Doodlecast, Explain Everything, Stick Around, Art Maker, Videolicious, ABC Video Pro, Magisto Magical Video Editor, Video Star, Best Video Downloader by Appseed, and Video Tube Free for YouTube.

☞ *Social Story Creators and Pre-Made Social Stories:* Pictello, Stories About Me, My Story, Stories2Learn, StoryMaker, My Daily Schedule and Going to Fireworks by I Get It, LLC, Kids Journal, Story Creator Pro and Little Story by Grasshopper Apps, Social Stories by TouchAutism, StoryBuddy 2, Adobe Voice- Show Your Story, Learn Words, Kid In Story, Story Me, Sago Mini Doodlecast, Shuttersong, Scribble Press and Scribble My Story, Skioory, StoryKit, Getty Images, and SPOKEnPHOTO Album.

☞ **For the Child:** Teaching children the lexicon of their environment helps them interact with those in it, and stay anchored to the present. I therefore recommend vocabulary builders, emotion, and story book Apps to increase episodic memory, attention span, comprehension of object function, self regulation (including verbal rejection) and inferencing skills. Here's a sampling of suggested Apps:

☞ *Object Function:* Bitsboard, Talking Picture Board, Chatterpix, SonicPics, Marcus' Discoveries, Sophie's Discoveries, Touch the Sound, Touch, Look, Listen-My First Words, Baby's First Puzzle with Funny Sounds-Baby App by Happy-Touch®, Music

Color Lite- Baby flash cards by SoundTouch, My First Words- Flashcards by Alligator Apps, Baby Flashcards- Free: Staple Goods, Photo Buttons, My PlayHome Lite and Paid, My PlayHome Stores, Word Slapps, Question Sleuth, Baby Flash Cards FREE, PicCardMaker, Meebie, Speech with Milo: Nouns, Describe It To Me by Smarty Ears, SpeakColors, Knock Knock, Word Slapps by Zorten Apps, Words by iTouchiLearn, My Little Suitcase by Alligator Apps, Receptive Furniture, Put It Away, Shuttersong, Toca House, Toca Kitchen, Toca Store, In the Kitchen, *Fiete* (Book), See. Touch. Learn. Site Edition by Brain Parade, Sounds of the House Lite, Pepi Bath Lite, American Doctor, and Bingo Card Generator Free.

☞ *Expressing Feelings:* Emotions Flashcards by I Can Do Apps, ABA Flashcards and Games- Emotions and Touch & Learn Emotions by Innovative Mobile Apps, Autism Emotions by Model Me Kids, Chatterpix, SonicPics, MashCAM, Meebie, Preschool Feelings by iTouchiLearn, Pepi Doctor, Social Emotional Exchange-S.E.E. by Saym Basheer, EQ for Kids, Feel Electric, What's the Expression by Web Team Corporation, Feelings with Milo, Avokiddo Emotions, Emotions Collections by ItBook, Expressions for Autism, Discovering Emotions with Zeely, Recycling Workshop, Puppet Workshop, American Doctor, Sago Mini Doodlecast, Tellagami, Smiley Booth and Cartoon Builder Free.

Note: I also recommend music Apps which have different tempos, and drawing Apps, which can teach degree and depth. Please see the listings in Chapter 1 for suggestions.

Story Books: StoryMaker Free, Stories About Me, StoryBuddy 2, Book Creator, Toy Story Read Along, Trixie and Jinx by Auryn , I Like Books Series-37 by Grasshopper Apps, Elephant's Bath, Princess Chocolate, A Story B4 Bed, Dr. Seuss Books, Crack the Books Apps, Starring You Books by StoryBots, The Monster at the End of This Book, Christopher Can't Sleep by Hallmark Interactive, and peruse these links for more ideas:

http://bit.ly/1zk0EzR

http://bit.ly/1uvWcnf

http://bit.ly/1uvWg6s

http://bit.ly/1zkqbG1

http://bit.ly/15E3pLB

☞ *Wh? Questions:* Touch the Sound, Sago Mini Doodlecast, My First Words- Flashcards by Alligator Apps, Knock Knock Family, Model Me Going Places 2, I Like Stories, Autism iHelp- WH Questions, Questions2Learn Lite, Autism iHelp- WH SLP Edition, Action Words by Innovative Mobile Apps, Question Sleuth, Kids CARS by Pyjamas Apps, iPractice Verbs by Smarty Ears Apps, Describe It To Me by Smarty Ears Apps, Wh? Questions by Smarty Ears Apps, StoryBuilder, Sentence Builder, and Tense Builder by Mobile Education Apps, QuestionIt, Bag Game, Talking Train, Opposite

Day, Build a Story, Question TherAppy Lite, Scratch Jr., StoryMaker Free, Stories About Me, Build a Story, Abigail and the Balance Beam, and Expanding Language by Special Learning Inc.

Chapter 3: Disorientation to <u>Time</u>:
Socially Speaking™ Social Skills Curriculum: Level III
<u>Problem Solving</u>**: When? questions Re: Past/Present/Future Events,**
Sequencing Events, and/or Expressing Wants/Needs More Age
Appropriately

Anecdote

Have you ever traveled to a different time zone and experienced jet-lag? Did you wake up in the middle of the night hungry for breakfast, or "zone out" in the middle of the day, wanting to take a nap? I remember being a panelist at a symposium about the future of education in a globally and technologically connected world in Silicon Valley in November of 2013. After speaking at the Hack for Big Choices Event, I was invited out to eat with the other panelists at 9:00 PM Palo Alto, CA time. But my jet-lagged, NY time body clock and queasy stomach kept insisting it was midnight and time to sleep! Suffice it to say, I joined the group for a bit, but declined to partake from the menu!

For children with Autism, having different neurological hardwiring can partially account for actually perceiving the passage of time differently. It can also lead to decreased sequencing and problem solving skills and increased vulnerability to sensory overload, which is why changes in routine/environment can be so stressful. It is also why disorientation to place frequently accompanies disorientation to time.

Strategy and Technique

Disorientation to Time: Underdeveloped Causality

Causality involves understanding The If...Then Contingent and the predictions of outcomes. That is, predictions that one makes based on an emotional action or physical action another makes, in his/her environment. The only way to see this action is to "live in the moment" and be oriented to person and place first. Orientation to time occurs later on in child development. It impacts a child's attempts to learn the schedule of the day, make inferences about it, ask and answer "why"? questions about i, and fit in with the group and the group etiquette.

Causality thus results in the child's methodical time sensitive sequencing of a procedure; to internalize and generalize it, to react to it behaviorally, intellectually and emotionally. This is especially evident when a child attempts to make friends. Causality begins to emerge around 18 months of age in neurotypical children. That's the age you can start to reason with them and talk about things in terms of if/then i.e. before/after and now/later. Causality is really mastered through trial and error later on. It coincides with the pre-literacy period where sequencing is mastered. I call this "The Indian Giver" Stage, occurring at ages 5-7, which can be seen in children at play, in the school playground.

Normally developing children at this age and stage understand Causality and time related vocabulary. They can usually verbally sequence a story in order, or give an accurate and lengthy running monologue on each of the steps involved in "baking a pizza just like the pizza store guys". They begin to learn the power of bartering during recess, whether it is a snack, a toy, or a verbal agreement (e.g. to be "taggee" or to have the more coveted role of being the "tagger").

Some children are innately intuitive emotionally. They size up the situation at a glance, and can predict to the nanosecond, how long it will take to make friends and/or have someone warm up to them during recess. Other children, especially children with ASD, can have a strong start, bring something of value "to the table", and still peter out midway through the social interaction. They can lose sight of the passage of time, or the remaining time needed to "clinch the deal" and stay in the game. This results in a social experience that has a weak finish and an emotional letdown, resulting in an aversion to repeating the experience.

These children with ASD have difficulty with orientation to time and the subsequent Causality Loop it entails. They start off with high hopes at the beginning of recess, showing their interest in giving to another, or to the group effort (such as building a fort). However, a breakdown in the Theory of Mind and timing of the effort results in the child's inner rhythm becoming "out of sync" with the other person(s) in the environment.

What is Disorientation to Time?

It's the lack of understanding of the concept of time passing, due to neurological differences in the "hard wiring" of the body clock. Sensory issues and poor episodic memory can also be contributing factors. Children who are disoriented to time often experience difficulties with Causality, narratives, following directions in sequence, answering "why"? questions appropriately and problem solving. They have issues with attention span and Time on Task (TOT), thereby causing attention seeking and avoidance/escape style behaviors when feeling challenged and/or frustrated. Our overall goal with these children is to implement preventive intervention versus crisis intervention. Our starting point for remediation is to teach The If...Then Contingent to mark the passage of time, something neurotypical toddlers learn at 18 months.

Cognitive Symptoms of Disorientation to Time
Poor comprehension of Causality
Expressive Communication Difficulty with Asking/Answering Why? Questions
Reduced or Absent Problem Solving
Inadequate Sequencing Of a Story In Order (Visually and Verbally) and Following Directions In Order
Poor Understanding of Quantity Related Vocabulary ("One/All", "Few/Many" etc.), Counting Accurately, and Telling Time
Poor Comprehension and Use of Verb Tense and Time/Calendar Related Vocabulary (Seasons, Days of the Week, "Before/After", "Now/Later", "Yesterday/Today" etc.)

CASE STUDY

Sam is a seven year old very bright, talkative boy with High Functioning Autism (HFA), and is an avid reader. He attends a regular education class with support services which include speech therapy twice weekly; once individually and once in a group setting, usually during recess. Sam enjoys speech therapy and recess, but not everyone in the group enjoys his company. He can sometimes fixate on a topic near and dear to him, such as the different types of fighter airplanes seen in history. He is now interested and able to observe other children at recess, and know when to approach and join in. He attempts to join a group of peers pretending to dive bomb off the slide, as an act of competitive physical prowess. Nonetheless, Sam excitedly begins to empty his pockets and line up his toy model airplanes on the slide; oblivious that his precious cargo is about to be stepped on. He begins to discuss and expound on his favorite topic, getting more animated, but increasingly technical. He waves around one of his model World War II airplanes, and his dog-eared copy of his illustrated airplane encyclopedia, to show off. The others ask to see and touch, making Sam feel good and part of the group. However, another child starts flying the airplane off the slide, in a feat of imaginary warfare.

Sam becomes confused and agitated. He snatches away the toy and begins talking louder and faster about planes. He does not understand the unscripted play schema unfolding before him. He does not understand the small window he was given to take charge and be center stage in the play. He subsequently snatches back his toys, further alienating himself from the group.

Sam may have initially interested others in his discourse. However, his lack of emotional attunement i.e. difficulty reading facial expressions and body language, and his reduced inner timing i.e. inner stopwatch, caused him social difficulty and "social blindness". He did not modulate his behavior to "live in the moment". His disorientation to time prevents him from realizing at which point his recital went from novel, to boring, to tangential, to insignificant. Sam misunderstood the cues he got and thus becomes agitated and/or withdrawn upon attempts to humorously redirect him and have him join in the current game.

SOLUTION

1. Causality comprehension requires Assistive Technology (AT) and Visual Supports to make sense of time and social cues: Use Visual Schedules with embedded AT Link Clips (like Nuby Click Links or Boomerings™ by Discovery Toys) to teach Causality.

2. Causality execution requires understanding Rules of Engagement and having a sense of humor about outcomes etc. when those rules are broken.

To develop a sense of humor, there needs to be interest in and understanding of how the world "works", causality, and the rules of engagement in various environments e.g. school vs. Grandma's house. Physical humor (ex: laughing at someone else executing a task incorrectly such as putting shoes on the wrong feet) tends to develop before linguistic (ex: laughing at someone's wrong use of a word--grammatically or out of context) humor. I will elaborate on humor development in a different chapter.

I do want to point out that I have engaged in both types of humor deliberately in therapy, to increase awareness of me/we, self-evaluation of performance and to garner a general verbal response that shows me that the child understands Causality. I have pretended on purpose, to misunderstand the student's attempts to correct me (a classic Greenspan technique) to keep the interest, activity and dialogue going, until all avenues are explored and/or rejected. The reader is encouraged to refer to current literature on Floortime™ by Dr. Stanley Greenspan, the seminal works from the 1960s by Dr. Virginia Mae Axline, *Dibs in Search of Self* and *Play Therapy*, and the insightful book from 2003 *Einstein Never Used Flash Cards: How Our Children Really Learn, and Why They Need to Play More and Memorize Less*, by Drs. Kathy Hirsh-Pasek and

Roberta Michnick Golinkoff. These and other excellent resources on play skills acquisition, are available in bookstores and libraries for further information.

3. Mastering Causality fosters the ability to transition from Me to We as needed.

A Developmental Timeline For Causality

There are are several prerequisite skills that children need to have, even lower functioning children, to achieve comprehension of Causality and subsequent problem solving, the pinnacle of social communication proficiency. Over the course of treating a large variety of children, I have discovered several interesting patterns of socialization, in both my regular education and special education students. I have found there to be a timeline of sorts, beginning with the aptly named "Terrible Twos" Stage, continuing with my coined "Police man" Stage, and concluding with my coined "Indian Giver" Stage. I have found correlations between developing empathy, visual attention and imitation skills, and subsequent decreasing of egocentric, "self directed" behavior and language and conversational patterns.

Children who are steadily progressing developmentally, make a cognitive "jump" once they start walking. They then become increasingly oriented to person/place/time, and increasingly curious and eager to explore these parameters. Acquisition of this orientation requires patient, systematic, methodical intervention, using "total body" learning experiences with a clearly defined beginning, middle and end. The rate of progress in orienting to person/place/time is contingent on the degree of sensory overload, length of the adjustment period needed to establish rapport and routine, as well as the quality of the re-calibration of the "inner landscape". This will steadily increase comprehension of a sense of self, allowing for future understanding of the "Big Picture". It will also enhance understanding of the value of self monitoring one's performance and proactively helping children with ASD move from being Me to We.

Acknowledging a child with ASD's different neurology and perceptions, resulting in disorientation to time and inconsistent or delayed performance re: Causality i.e. learning to become a We, is a relatively recent development in special education. Until 2004, when revisions to the IDEA mandated that a Behavior Intervention Plan (BIP) become part of every child's IEP, special education service providers operated within a *Crisis Intervention Paradigm*. For the most part, behavior management and social communication development did not account for the truth....that crisis intervention doesn't teach carryover or consistently decrease the duration and frequency of the tantrum.

Crisis intervention does not help child with Autism and neurological challenges feel that time is passing. It does not provide enough practice re: the need to adapt, to develop episodic memory of what happened last time there was a tantrum and what to do/not do this time. That's why I'm such an advocate of using proactive intervention techniques such as visual supports and Social Stories to foster orientation to person/place/time. Mastering Causality is what self regulation, and this book, are all about!

Disorientation to Time and Problem Solving

I will address behavior management and humor development in different chapters but for now, I want to explain the impact of disorientation to time on social communication development, especially the end result of Causality; problem solving.

I want to repeat that children with Autism have difficulty learning social communication skills i.e. transitioning to becoming We, on their own, due to fluctuating degrees of disorientation to person/place/time. It can be triggered by environmental, biological and neurological, and intellectual factors. My Socially Speaking™ Program is thus designed to methodically, consistently, and proactively address those factors by proactively targeting the disorientation to person/place/time through:

• The careful and creative integration of toys and tech in treatment

• The sequential intervention for social communication challenges specifically related to Body Awareness, Expressing Feelings and Problem Solving; the three components of my social skills curriculum through which all other goals are funneled and targeted.

What is Problem Solving?

Problem solving is definitely a higher level intellectual skill, requiring a certain degree of cognition. Yet it also requires a level of emotional intuition, and protective instinct. Children with special needs all exhibit difficulty mastering this skill. Furthermore, acquiring the ability to problem solve requires a certain degree of psycho-social readiness i.e. the initial mastery of these skills previously discussed.

Readiness Indicators to Learn Problem Solving:
Cause & Effect has emerged and is displayed spontaneously at least 75% time
Orientation to person/place is exhibited without prompting
Communicative Intent has emerged and is displayed spontaneously at least 75% time
Delayed Gratification is being worked on and tracked
Body Awareness has been achieved and mastered in different settings
Transitioning is being worked on and tracked
Inferencing and Causality (understanding how the world works, sequencing events, answering "why"? questions, and predicting outcomes) is being worked on and tracked

A child needs to have somewhat developed both cognitively and psychologically, so he or she can move forward with social development. He or she needs to have an extensive receptive lexicon, an emerging sense of "self", self preservation instincts and an evolving Theory of Mind, to allow for flexibility and empathy with others. He or she will then be ready to work on the final and most important component of a social skills development plan-- learning the sequential five steps to actually solving a problem.

I have developed this hierarchy after much observation, data analysis and treatment of children with pragmatic dysfunction. I have found that they need methodical intervention on HOW to problem solve. This is extremely important, especially if there has been scattered, nonlinear acquisition of the rudimentary social skills and cognitive based language concepts which needed to be mastered first. Furthermore, differences in TOM in children with ASD can account for difficulty recognizing, interpreting and resolving problems that are of a social nature. I consider problem solving to be the corner stone and most advanced skill of good social skills development.

Why is Problem Solving Such a Crucial Social Skill?

Problem solving encompasses all the skills covered earlier in the book and mentioned above. It incorporates the ability to access episodic memory re: feelings, semantic memory re: past events of how things unfolded and how the world works. It results from the ability to "live in the moment", understand time passing and foster emotional connections with others. It is the culmination of acquiring a diverse vocabulary (nouns, verbs, adjectives), a sense of humor and a flexibility to transition from being a Me to We as needed.

What is the Socially Speaking™ "Five Step Problem Solving Hierarchy"?

It's a 5 step process that is usually taught as a **scripted** conversational skill. I frequently use the *Visual Strategies*™ technique to create a Task Organizer and a flow chart, using images/photos, to break down the steps to ensure comprehension and consistency. This also helps the child's entire "inner circle" see what he or she is doing and how he or she is learning to do it. To that end, I am very careful when to start addressing a child's reduced problem solving ability. I want to be sure that the child is really ready, and that his or her team is ready to implement a structured, methodical, collaborative, multi-sensory approach to facilitate this skill.

The Socially Speaking™ 5 Step Problem Solving Hierarchy-A Breakdown:
1. Awareness that a problem exists, why it exists, and how to react (accessing semantic memory and interpreting and expressing feelings evoked by the problem-- in self and in others)
2. Verbalizing the problem to an adult instead of "acting out" (explaining what the problem is and why it is occurring)
3. Exploring solutions/outcomes/options verbally and calmly (making inferences, accessing episodic memory and comprehension of Causality)
4. Verbal Negotiation to come to an agreement or compromise (showing flexibility and empathy, accessing another person's Theory of Mind i.e. "inner landscape" to begin building rapport and trust)
5. Conflict Resolution where both parties agree with outcome politely and graciously (accepting outcomes with serenity, admitting wrong doing and/or mistakes, learning to live with unfairness and repairing communication breakdowns)

Problem Solving and "Social Blindness":

As previously mentioned, a working knowledge of developmental milestones re: language and play development, the child's "inner landscape", and mental age, are all clinical prerequisites for targeting problem solving for remediation. I do not address this skill until the child understands target vocabulary re: body parts, The Five Senses, and Feelings. I do not consider remediating this skill in those children who still have difficulty asking and answering simple, contextual "why"? "when"? and "how"? questions. All of these are indicative of "social blindness" about themselves and others.

In academic terms, I have found that lower functioning children with focusing and interaction-attachment issues, tend to have a hard time reading social cues and also problem solving. Children with below age level language ability and gaps in their pre-reading readiness skills acquisition, namely in the areas of categorizing and sequencing, tend to have noticeable "social blindness" and problem solving difficulty. They have difficulty perceiving a problem, explaining it and providing verbal rationales for their actions and the actions of others.

This leads to the subsequent reduced awareness (i.e. they "shelve it") of the existence of a problem and/or the need to solve it. These children are disorganized thinkers who develop the splintered ability to explain the problem in a situation- specific, concrete manner. They are stumped when it comes to exploring solutions, attempting conflict resolutions and politely accepting consequences and outcomes of their actions. This results in being perceived as "prompt dependent", inflexible, quick to "act out" and "disconnected". These children are also labeled as self- directed, moody, or noncompliant students who either become aggressive or "tune out".

In reality, they are frustrated and working overtime to make sense of the social cues they don't understand, the environment that appears confusing and even hostile, and what is expected of them by the adults in their surroundings. They are the children with organic biological, sensory, cognitive, and/or psycho-social deficits. These deficits mask their potential to overcome their "Social Blindness". They remind me of the biker peddling furiously but going nowhere, because the bike is chained to the telephone poll, unbeknownst to him. They remind me of the old computers that sometimes go haywire in cartoons and spew paper while a voice drones "does not compute".

These children require patient, methodical, structured intervention, involving sensory input, emotional engagement and activities with a clearly defined beginning/middle/ end. We need to remove the obstacles in their way if we can, and provide the building blocks for one day starting to learn this essential skill.

How do we concretely teach these children problem solving? We will cover that a bit later when I provide my cookbook style tips for "social skills kits". In the meantime, it's important to remember that a social skills treatment plan involving the facilitation of problem solving in particular, can only be implemented for those students who are developmentally (cognitively) and behaviorally (psycho-socially) ready! I usually write this on post-it® notes or note Apps and distribute as needed!

How To Foster Readiness to Learn Problem Solving Skills:

1. Address Environmental Modifications and Behavior Management

My "low tech" weapon: "AT Link Clips": Math Clips from Lauri™, BOOMERINGS® Links by Discovery Toys, or Nuby Click Links by Nuby (see Amazon). Attach the clips to the Visual Schedule and other visual supports, to bridge the gap between readiness to learn and actual performance.The use of these clips act as a time duration map, allowing the child to concretely experience the countdown to the completion of a task or activity, and to actually see time passing from starting time to ending time of the "job". Children understand that everyone, including their parents, have jobs to do. This one is theirs.

• Why? To teach The "If...Then" Contingent using tangible reinforcers AND structured activities with a clearly delineated beginning/end.

My "high- tech" weapon: Specific iPad® apps to build rapport, comprehension of Causality, and other pre-requisite skills for social communication proficiency re: problem solving, the culmination of my social skills curriculum. The iPad® teaches Cognitive Causality i.e. the "If...Then" Contingent naturally and methodically. The iPad® naturally gives us a the Causality look of action/reaction, the first step towards comprehending the passage of time. The use of an iPad®, and most apps, intrinsically act as a timer of sorts because activating it signals the start of time passing, of a countdown towards a desired outcome provided by segmenting actions into beginning/middle/end. Using an iPad® gives concrete examples to children with ASD in need of understanding if/then, before/during/after, and what it means to experience Time on Task (TOT) and sustained attention.

2. Address Specific Play, Cognitive Language, and Pre-Literacy Goals

My first line of defense: Teach play in a developmental sequence, using my formula for assessing play skills acquisition in Chapter 8 to see if the "light's on" and there is readiness to learn a specific skill/target vocabulary.

My second line of defense: Address object function and overall categorization (like, unalike objects/photos with a verbal rationale) in treatment.

My third line of defense: Implement the *Pre-Reading Readiness Hierarchy Protocol*.

My fourth line of defense: Implement my *Five Step Problem Solving Hierarchy*.

NOTE

The Socially Speaking™ Rationale

Targeting problem solving in treatment begins when the child starts to develop rapport with you and then learns about Causality and Body Awareness once rapport is cemented. Problem solving is about teaching the child "how the world works" and what the vocabulary of that world is, which is why addressing play and pre-literacy skills are so crucial. Following my 5 step hierarchy leads to mastery of object function, which is needed to develop delayed gratification and resiliency. Both then lead to better problem solving, where the child demonstrates the ability to know *when* to transition from a Me to a We and back, the cornerstone of self regulation and frankly, civilized behavior. It's why a hand shake is the logo of my company, Socially Speaking LLC, since 2010.

3. *Address "Social Blindness" Proactively and Visually, Using Humor and "Social Autopsies"*

What is "Social Blindness?"

Have you seen the Geico insurance commercial where a couple takes Tango lessons? That's a classic example of "social blindness"!

http://bit.ly/1tmWhOI

We previously discussed the role that the five senses play in social skills development by facilitating Body Awareness and proprioception. I would like to move on to "The Sixth Sense" and its effect on verbalization of feelings **of** another, and verbal problem solving **with** another. Let me start by notifying the reader that the #1 challenge of the social skills facilitator is "Social Blindness". It is a term used to explain a group of behaviors seen in higher functioning verbal children who appear to be clueless when it comes to social interactions.

These children have achieved the prelinguistic and early psycho-social prerequisite skills such as Body Awareness, Joint Attention and Cause & Effect. However, they continue to literally be oblivious to body language, facial affect, nonverbal language cues and emotional "vibes" from others. This affects their ability to interpret and express the emotions of another, and then engage in systematic problem solving with another, where conflict resolution forms an emotional connection between that child and someone else.

We now know that many famous people have displayed an impaired "sixth sense" such as Abraham Lincoln and Albert Einstein. Children with ASD often display "Social Blindness". They can exhibit difficulty expressing feelings appropriately, problem solving and conducting conversations in a mature, age appropriate manner due to difficulties with:

- Knowing what to do/say in social situations (starting conversations, staying on topic, asking to play and join in too, as well as sharing)
- Interpreting body language and utilizing eye contact appropriately Timing of questions and answers, which affect maintaining topic appropriately
- Making and keeping friends (special needs students may not transition well, may not handle rejection or losing well, may be quick to anger and may be perseverative in their speech and movements)
- Repairing communication breakdowns when misunderstood and/or things don't go as planned

How Do We Counteract "Social Blindness?"

A child with "Social Blindness" can view the world like a driver passing by covered road signs, preventing him from truly navigating the highway and being oriented to his or her surroundings. I do not want to "reinvent the wheel". I thus refer the reader to Dr. Jed Baker's great book, *Social Skills Training*, for an in depth look at his ideas and insights into the topic at hand. I would like to highlight, interpret and elaborate upon his good advice on how to ameliorate the child's tendency to be oblivious to the social cues and goings-on around him/her:

1. Teach about "The 5 Senses" that help us perceive the world around us, and how it individualizes us as people.
Collaborate with the child's IEP team re: specific techniques and materials to increase tolerance for various input via the five senses.
- Role play different types of activities emphasizing a specific sense (ex: have a sampling tasting party, or an art project for the group using cutting/pasting/drawing)
- Discuss "The Sixth Sense" (*The Social Sense)* and what it means. For children with High Functioning Autism who read, take out books from the library and discuss which famous figures in history displayed it and how "social blindness" can cause difficulties with friendships, conversations and activities such as play dates, gym and recess.

2. Teach the target vocabulary re: feelings, according to cognitive status.
For cognitively intact and bright children such as those with High Functioning Autism, you can use the "all the shades of a rainbow" visual technique using Arts & Crafts and paints to expand the lexicon to include abstract ideas for words such as surprised, furious, hopeful, lethargic disappointed, and confused. I also recommend *The Magic Rainbow Hug*, by Janet Courtney, and *I Feel Silly* by Jamie Curtis.
- Collaborate with the child's speech therapist re: specific techniques and materials to teach labeling, expressing and self recognition of feelings, including interpretation of various facial expressions, through contrived and "free style" play activities.
- Collaborate with others like the school's art therapist for ideas re: materials and technique. Find and order free, online catalogs such as Lakeshore® and Oriental Trading Company® to see what's available in terms of arts & craft items. Do specific searches on Pinterest.
- Collaborate with others like the school's music teacher or music therapist for ideas re: incorporating music into lesson plans. Provide teachable moments to foster the association of various feelings with different music tempos that can be recorded/played/ saved as an MP3 or via a recorder App. Using other musical tools can be an invaluable experience in early intervention, such as the Adventus MusIQ Software and My First MusicIQ Club, which you can learn more about here:
  http://www.myfirstmusiqclub.com/index.html

3. Teach child to problem solve using my 5 step hierarchy, and back track to see if cues were missed.
Children with Autism can learn to better read social cues by having a better understanding of what feelings and problem solving are all about. These are abstract,

conceptually difficult goals that CAN be taught in a more concrete manner by using multi-sensory activities, and a task analysis oriented approach. When a child can predict and accept outcomes, he or she understands the idea of Causality. He or she comprehends that actions have consequences, and that some consequences, especially the undesirable ones, require either accepting or overcoming the obstacle. This is the essence of problem solving. It begins when a child starts to play. I will discuss this in a later point in this book.

Problem Solving Using a "Social Autopsy"

A "Social Autopsy" is an innovative strategy wherein an adult assists a child to improve social skills by jointly analyzing social errors that a child makes and designing alternative strategies.

-- The Montana Autism Education Project , 2013

http://1.usa.gov/1K0AKhe

The Social Autopsy is often done with photos and/or video footage of the child engaged in a problematic behavior, doing something "wrong". It's important to note that there needs to be a level of self awareness, cognition and emotional maturity on the part of the child so that constructive criticism can be taken the right way. There also needs to be understanding of the "rules of the game" i.e. orientation to person/place/time and humor development, so that the child correctly internalizes the constructive criticism and activates episodic memory about it.

Teaching children with Autism to be aware of the "Sixth Sense", the "social sense", is a challenging, multi-sensory, and methodical process that starts with honing orientation to person/place/time and Self Concept. The child must first learn to be a "Me" and all that it entails, both cognitively and emotionally. It continues with having the child develop a sense of humor and master both object function/categorization skills and then sequencing skills, so that he/she can:

• Access Episodic Memory re: how the world "works" when things go awry/routines change.

• Accept constructive criticism and develop resiliency so that tantrums lessen and admitting mistakes and self monitoring/self evaluation of performance increases.

• Improve problem solving and Theory of Mind (TOM); both of which are needed to counteract "Social Blindness".

The overall purpose of a "Social Autopsy" is not to talk a child "off the ledge". That's behavior management using a crisis intervention paradigm which I previously discussed. The "Social Autopsy" is proactive intervention in action where the child is made to understand and string together the "why, what, when, where, and how"? of the episode in question. It's both a preventative measure and a review of what happened, using time, target vocabulary, and visual supports to enhance comprehension and memory.

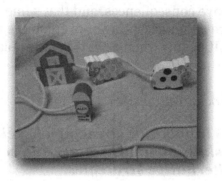

Components of a "Social Autopsy"
What "triggered" the meltdown and/or the ignoring of social cues
What the child's reaction was (good or bad) and how it was perceived
Why it worked/didn't work i.e. what were the consequences (think of the classic behavior management technique, the ABC chart- Functional Behavioral Analysis)
What to do next time i.e. predicting outcomes and strategizing/creating a plan.

Readiness Indicators to Learn About Social Blindness and Benefit From "Social Autopsies"
Self Awareness of The Five Senses
Comprehension of Causality
Ability to Express Feelings
Ability to Problem Solve and Predict/Accept Outcomes

Final Words

I came across a painful, moving blogpost in late July 2013 by Stuart Duncan, a father of a child with Autism, written in July 2010. I don't know him, or what treatment his son was getting for that matter. I don't even know what the IEP team told this father, which resulted in his comment, "my child has no concept of time thanks to Autism".

http://bit.ly/1z8KbYV

I saved the post to my Pocket App and Evernote notebook for future reference. I wish I could have found this post three years earlier and introduced that disheartened father, and the rest of that IEP team to my social skills curriculum. I wish they would see the content of this chapter. I would explain, as I often do in therapy and in my seminars, that Causality, like Theory of Mind, is **underdeveloped**; not absent, and not a lost cause! Children with Autism can and do learn to understand the concept of time passing, despite neurological differences initially affecting the "internal body clock". The resulting disorientation to time can be partially and sometimes completely overcome, like jet lag. It depends on the child's cognition, coping mechanisms re: stress, and ability to access episodic memory. That's why teaching children with Autism to improve their episodic memory and resiliency skills are so integral to a social skills treatment plan.

The whole purpose of following my *Socially Speaking™ Program* is to teach children with Autism to use their episodic memory to recall prior experiences which enable them to be a Me who can then transition to being a We. Even when things don't go as planned. That's why teaching orientation to person/place/time, a sense of humor, and the corresponding social skills trifecta of goals, Body Awareness, Expressing Feelings, and Problem Solving are all targeted in my program. That's why targeting sequencing skills *before* working on problem solving and "Social Blindness" is recommended. That's why implementing behavior management and the use of visual supports in treatment *from the start*, are both recommended as well.

We live in the Digital Age where the use of social media in education and in the workplace is now widespread. It brings a whole new playing field for children with Autism who have social communication challenges. One rife with positive opportunities for new learning experiences and friendships. One also rife with negative opportunities like mismanaging one's digital avatar and subsequent digital reputation, and cyber-bullying.

"Social Blindness" thus needs to be addressed; online and offline, in a methodical, collaborative, and creative fashion. Best practices need to include behavior management protocols, social communication goals involving problem solving when the child is intellectually and socio-emotionally ready, social media etiquette protocols, digital citizenship standards of conduct and the "Social Autopsy". Social communication is part of the skill set needed for a 21st century emerging proficiency-- digital citizenship. It's something I will elaborate on later in Chapter 11. For now, I want to emphasize that we do our children a real disservice if we do not methodically counteract "Social Blindness" and problem solving in treatment. We must prepare them for the realities of 21st century communal life, workplace (if applicable) and culture. It behooves us to carefully and collectively consider where society is headed; in real-time and in cyber-time, and to implement protocols for self regulation and time management for all.

Materials for Your Toolbox

- <u>Key References</u>

Bader, Stephanie et al (2010). *Enhancing Communication in Children With Autism Spectrum Disorders: Practical Strategies Series in Autism Education*. Waco, TX: Prufrock Press Inc.

Baker, Jed (2003). *Social Skills Training for Children and Adolescents with Asperger Syndrome and Social Communication Problems*. Shawnee, KS: Autism Apserger Publishing.

Barbera, Mary Lynch, and Rassmussen, Tracy (2007). *The Verbal Behavior Approach: How to Teach Children with Autism and Related Disorders*. Philadelphia, PA: Jessica Kingsley Publishers.

Baron-Cohen, Simon (1995). *Mindblindness*. Cambridge, MA: MIT Press Baron-Cohen, Simon (2000). Is Asperger Syndrome/High Functioning Autism Necessarily a Disability? *Developmental Psychology* 12, 480-500.

Baron-Cohen, Simon (2002). *Targeting Autism: What We Know, Don't Know, and Can Do to Help Young Children with Autism and Related Disorders*. Berkeley, CA: University of California Press.

Beckerleg, Tracey (2008). *Fun with Messy Play: Ideas and Activities for Children with Special Needs*. Philadelphia, PA: Jessica Kingsley Publishers.

Brady, Lois Jean, et al (2011). *Speak, Move, Play, and Learn with Children on the Autism Spectrum*. Philadelphia, PA: Jessica Kingsley Publishers.

Brady, Lois Jean (2015). *Apps for Autism, 2nd Edition*. Arlington, TX: Future Horizons.

Charman, Tony, and Stone, Wendy (2006). *Social and Communication Development in Autism Spectrum Disorders*. New York, NY: Guilford Press.

Dawson, Peg, and Guare, Richard (2010). *Executive Skills in Children and Adolescents: A Practical Guide to Assessment and Intervention, Second Edition*. New York, NY: Guilford Press.

Grandin, Temple (2005). *The Unwritten Rules of Social Relationships*. Arlington, TX: Future Horizons.

Grandin, Temple (2008). *The Way I See It: A Personal Look at Autism and Asperger's*. Arlington, TX:Future Horizons.

Greenspan, Stanley, and Weider, Serena (2006). *Engaging Autism: Using the Floortime Approach to Help Children Relate, Communicate, and Think*. Cambridge, MA: Da Capo Press/Perseus Books Group.

Prelock, Patricia et al (2012). *Treatment of Autism Spectrum Disorders: Evidence-Based Intervention Strategies for Communication and Social Interactions.* Baltimore, MD: Paul H. Brookes Publishing Company.

Prizant, Barry et al (2003). The SCERTS Model: A Family Centered, Transactional Approach to Enhancing Communication and Socioemotional Abilities of Young Children with ASD. *Infant and Young Children, (16), 4, 296-316.*

Quill, Kathleen Ann (2000). *Do-Watch-Listen-Say: Social and Communication Intervention for Children with Autism.* Baltimore, MD: Paul H. Brookes Publishing Company.

Weiss, Mary Jane and Harris, Sandra (2001). *Reaching Out, Joining In: Teaching Social Skills to Young Children with Autism.* Bethesda, MD: Woodbine House.

Weiss, Mary Jane and Demiri, Valbona (2011). *Jumpstarting Communication Skills in Children with Autism: A Parents' Guide to Applied Verbal Behavior.* Bethesda, MD: Woodbine House.

• Key Links to Peruse

http://bit.ly/1zVSo5C

http://bit.ly/1tmXfug

http://bit.ly/1Df6kWz

http://bit.ly/18rUNtf

http://bit.ly/1JDT7uc

http://bit.ly/1zukvJI

http://bit.ly/1y3Gxgf

http://bit.ly/1D6HnMn

http://bit.ly/15M4KzK

http://bit.ly/1BlJKsN

• Key Concepts to Address:

Play Development, Theory of Mind, The "If...Then" Contingent, Executive Functioning, Pre-Literacy Hierarchy, Problem Solving, Episodic Memory and Social Communication

• <u>Key Toys to Use in Treatment</u>

<u>Toys To Facilitate Comprehension of Causality, Time, and Sequencing</u>
✦ Nuby Click Links: 8 Pack (Similar to Lauri Math Clips)
✦ Fisher-Price™ Brilliant Basics Rock-a-Stack Toy
✦ Fisher-Price™ Brilliant Basics Melody Push Chime
✦ Playskool Explore `N`Grow Busy Ball Popper
✦ Manhattan Toy Push and Spin Carousel
✦ Rainbow Xylophone Piano Pounding Bench for Kids with Balls and Hammer by Musical Toy
✦ Battat Sound Puzzle Box
✦ Melissa and Doug Assorted Puzzles
✦ Melissa and Doug Cutting Food Toy (Half & Half)
✦ Beads and Pattern Card Set by Learning Resources
✦ Playskool Sesame St. Smart Phone
✦ Melissa & Doug Wooden Bear Family Dress-Up Puzzle
✦ Storybooks and Social Stories About the Weather/Seasons
✦ ThinkFun Roll & Play Board Game
✦ ThinkFun Zingo
✦ Before & After Fun Deck Cards by Super Duper
✦ Smethport Pocket Chart Card Set Story Sequencing Game 2-4 Scenes
✦ The Learning Journey Match It! Sequencing 3 Picture Puzzle Game
✦ Learning Resources Sequencing Puzzle Cards
✦ Learning to Sequence 4 Scene Set by Carson Dellosa
✦ Smethport Tabletop Pocket Chart Four Step Sequencing
✦ Lauri Toys Early Learning Center Kit-4-Step Sequencing Card Game
✦ Telly The Teaching Time Clock
✦ Judy Instructo Mini Clocks: Set of 12
✦ Zingo Time-Telling Board Game
✦ Melissa and Doug Wooden Shape Sorting Clock
✦ Eureka Tub of Telling Time Chips
✦ Trend's Telling Time Bingo Game
✦ Learning Resources Write On/Wipe Clocks Classroom Set
✦ Perfection Game
✦ *If You Give a Mouse a Cookie* by Laura Joffe Numeroff and Felicia Bond

<u>Toys To Facilitate Problem Solving</u>
✦ Edushape Educolor Building Blocks: Set of 30
✦ Battat Bristle Blocks Bag
✦ Tinkertoy 100 Piece Essentials Value Set
✦ Playmag or Magna-Tiles® Magnetic Tiles Set
✦ PLAYMOBIL Children's Zoo
✦ Chutes and Ladders Game
✦ Let's Go Fishin' Game by Pressman Toys
✦ Connect Four Game
✦ Hape-Quadrilla Round About: Marble Railway in Wood

✦ Gizmos and Gears
✦ Doctor Set Kits
✦ MindWare Imaginets Magnetic Toy
✦ VTech Go! Go! Smart Wheels - Train Station Playset
✦ Smethport Mind Your Manners Language Cards
✦ Carson Dellosa Key Education What's Wrong? Learning Cards
✦ Webber's "What Are They Thinking?" Cards from Super Duper
✦ *Wacky Wednesday* by Theo LeSieg and George Booth

• <u>Key iPad® Apps to Use in Treatment</u>

☞ **For the Service Provider:** Orientation to time involves both abstract and concrete understanding of both problem solving and reading a clock. It is thus best to use manipulatives during play first, to build a lexicon and improve episodic memory for later recall. This way, we can naturally "set the stage" for the child to learn about verb tense which marks the passage of time, and ensure that the child fully understands the If...Then Contingent, why? questions, and quantity concepts re: part/whole relationships and 1:1 correspondence etc. before introducing these and similar iPad® Apps in treatment:

☞ *Cognitive Problem Solving:* Toca Tea Party, Autism and PDD Reasoning and Problem Solving Lite and Paid, My PlayHome, Super Duper StoryMaker FREE and Paid, StoryBuilder for iPad®, Question Builder for iPad®, LanguageBuilder for iPad®, LanguageBuilderDeluxe, Alex the Handyman Free, Toontastic, Happy Farm Yard, WhQuestions by Smarty Ears, Is That Silly? by Smarty Ears, WH Question Cards Free, What Doesn't Belong? by Tiny Tap, Understanding Inferences Fun Deck, How Would You Feel If...Fun Deck, What Are They Asking? Fun Deck, What's Being Said? Fun Deck, What Would You Do At Home If...Fun Deck ,What Would You Do At School If...Fun Deck, Difficult Situations Fun Deck, Let's Predict Fun Deck, Imagination Questions Fun Deck, A Crazy Farmer Harvest Day Story- Farm Collector Saga, Toca Town, Thinkin' Things 1, and ScratchJr.

☞ *Telling Time- Clocks:* Todo Telling Time, Fun Clock for Kids, Time Match by Apps Rocket, Telling Time the Easy Way, Tell Time- Little Matchups, Interactive Telling Time Lite and Paid, Telling Time Free, Mr. Wolf? Telling Time Game, Kid's Time Telling Tutor, Quick Clocks, Set the Clock- Telling Time, and Amazing Time by Avocado Mobile Inc.

☞ **For the Child:** iPad® apps have intrinsic timing and naturally teach Cause & Effect, verb tense and the visual breakdown of a task into beginning/middle/end. However, a child can only experience this firsthand if he/she is both cognitively and motorically ready to use the iPad®. That's why it's important to monitor the readiness indicators discussed previously, and to monitor the child's ability to reorient to person and place and generalize when using apps, as well as to reorient to time using manipulatives through *play*, before introducing apps that will aid in the achievement and then mastery of orientation to time with carryover. Here's a sampling to try:

☞ *Causality:* Peekaboo Barn, Zoo Sounds Free, Balls by iotic, Touch Follow FREE, Monsters, AnimalPiano, MovePaint, ZoLO Lite, The Animal Sounds, Storybots® Tap & Sing, Stop and Go! HD Free, Injini Lite, Dot Collector, Fingerpaint II, Reactickles Magic, Touch and Born!, Marcus' Discoveries HD, Somantics, Knock Knock Family, Melody Touch Lite, Paint Sparkle Draw, Music Sparkles, Storybots® Tap & Sing, Xylophone from Interactive Alphabet, SpeakColors, Touch the Sound, Touch Baby for iPad®, Video Touch Lite, and SoundWorld+.

☞ *Sequencing:* AnimalMixer, Kid's Patterns, Make a Scene: Farmyard, Babyfirst Match-Up, MugMash, Draw a House by Fjord42, Sago Mini Doodlecast, Drawing Box Free, Let's Create, ZoLO Lite, Kids Beads, Abby- Basic Skills Preschool: Puzzles and Patterns HD Free, Toca Tea Party, Cute Food, Colorforms® Revolution Free, Bamba Burger, Ice Cream Sundae Maker!, Icy Dessert, Puppet Stage, Car Puzzles, Create a Car Lite, Talking Train, Try It On, Cartoon Builder, LiquidSketch Free, Drawing with Carl Free and Paid, Puppet Workshop, Ear Doctor, How? Fun Deck, Making Sequences, Advanced Making Sequences, and Advanced Video Sequences by Zorten, iSequences Lite and Paid, Basic Sequences, Sequences 4 Step, 6 & 8 Step by ColorCards, Speech with Milo: Sequencing, Sequencing Post Office, Video Sequencing by PandaPal, Sequencing Tasks: Life Skills Lite and Paid, Let's Use Language: Basic Language Development by Everyday Speech, Tell a Story with Tommy: Community Sequences, Trixie and Jinx, Car Wash, Plane Wash, Build a Ship, Build a Story, Art Maker, and InnerVoice.

☞ *Verb Tense:* ChatterPix and ChatterKid, MashCAM, Sago Mini Doodlecast, StoryBuilder, My Story, Tellagami, TenseBuilder, Speech Journal by Mobile Education Store, Action Words by Innovative Mobile Apps, iPractice Verbs, Speech with Milo: Verbs, Explain Everything, Stick Around, Baby Hear & Read Verbs Lite, Toy Story Read Along, Scratch Jr., Lil Decorator, Mason's New Friends, The Monster at the End of the Book, Puppet Workshop, Adobe Voice- Show Your Story, Celebrity Ice Cream Maker, Maker- Milkshakes, Cake Bites Maker, Outdoor Fun, StoryBuddy 2, The Expanding Picture Book for iPad®, Syntax City, Verbs NEWS, Fun with Verbs and Sentences HD, Language Labs: ing Verbs + Prepositions, Noodle Words HD-Action Set 1, Verbs Part 1- Fun English Videos, Hay Day, Shutterbugs: Wiggle and Stomp, Animated Verb: First Words (FREE), Intense Home (Lite) by AGFH, Regular Past Tense Verb Fun Deck, Irregular Verbs Fun Deck, and English Irregular Verbs by Abitalk Inc.

Chapter 4
Fostering Compliance:
Socially Speaking™ Social Skills Curriculum: Train Tracks #1
<u>Behavior Management 101:</u> Setting the Stage for Learning Better
Orientation to Person/Place/Time

Anecdote

Neely presents as a friendly, strong willed, easily distracted and moody 5 year old girl with an average IQ, Down Syndrome and "challenging behaviors". She is transitioning from CPSE to CSE status now, making her special education teacher and parents wonder aloud at the IEP Annual Review Meeting if she would benefit from a self contained class placement with children with Autism next year. They are worried about her being mainstreamed to a regular education first grade classroom with support services, which is what has been initially recommended.

Neely has received Early Intervention since birth, which includes individual speech, occupational, and physical therapy twice a week for 30 minutes. She was enrolled in a therapeutic, self contained preschool class for the past two years where she made noticeable yet inconsistent progress in all her goals, especially her social communication goals in speech therapy.

Neely is assigned to my evaluation roster. She has a reputation for being fully verbal, funny, somewhat of a kleptomaniac and having poor transitioning and problem solving skills. When she is challenged to go outside of her comfort zone, initiate/complete higher level language tasks involving reading, or engage in fine motor tasks involving bead patterning and writing, she becomes upset. She then looks you in the eye and announces that she will urinate on the floor. It's not an empty threat....Neely has been doing this for the past year; in class, in therapy, on the bus, at home, in the supermarket, at her neighbor's birthday party-- and especially during evaluations.

When asked what the reaction is to this behavior, everyone provides me with a different answer:

- The teacher puts her in the bathroom to change etc. but Neely plays with the water and faucet instead. She's happy to get out of doing her work etc.
- The OT and/or PT stops the activity and reprimands her publicly, drawing a crowd since OT rooms tend to be like a mini-gym; shared space with other OT's and even PT's. Neely eats up the attention and preens for the crowd.

- The speech therapist reviews a picture chart of "Neely's Rules" in school at the start of each session, and works on IEP goals using various activities and materials. They include sorting photos of children engaged in good vs. "bad" behavior at home/school. Neely loves to practice her oral-motor and articulation exercises, and talk about the "bad behavior" in the photos. They never discusses the "why" of it, and what to do "instead". The If...Then Contingent is never used nor mentioned.

- The parents implement a reward and punishment system where every night, if she didn't urinate at home, Neely gets a star on the big chart hanging on the fridge for all to see. The stars are counted on Friday before grocery shopping, to correspond to how many small bags of potato chips Neely will get. Waiting for Friday is too long, since Neely doesn't have a real sense of time. So she throws a tantrum each time she only gets to have one or two bags, because the chart usually features only one or two stars. Neely's parents have become desperate; putting her in "time out", taking away computer privileges, instituting earlier bed-time and even yelling. She's still urinating on the floor when upset. They're the ones requesting a full team evaluation where I was brought in to assess Neely and troubleshoot. They're the ones very interested in my Socially Speaking™ Program and how it can help their daughter.

Strategy and Technique

Clinical Intervention for Behavior Management:

I usually suggest doing these two things in this kind of situation:

- Indirect intervention without the child's participation-Crisis Intervention though Functional Behavioral Assessment (FBA)
- Direct intervention with the child's participation-Proactive Intervention through these techniques: Visual Strategies™, Social Stories™ and REPLAYS™

Neely exhibits the classic controlling of her environment, due to a disconnect from it. Further assessment reveals that Neely has some sensory issues hindering her orientation to place and the development of the corresponding social communication/ language and literacy skills needed. She also has significant disorientation to time, resulting in her underdeveloped Causality, sequencing and problem solving skills (especially negotiation), just to name a few. Her behavior correlates to gaps in her Episodic Memory (re: vocabulary-what to say, and event-recall of consequence the last time she acted out) and ability to express negative feelings age appropriately. Her act of urinating on the floor is purposeful and fills two needs; attention and avoidance.

Possible "Triggers"-- Connection Attempts to Fill a Need
Attention
Sensory/Biological Needs
Avoidance/Escape from Unwanted Activities/Environments
Lack of Structure i.e. Clarification of Your Expectations of That Child

We previously discussed proactive intervention using direct clinical intervention methods. Now, let's examine indirect clinical intervention method,s which often do not require the child's participation. Let's share some insights about crisis intervention and behavior management.

Behavior Management and the IEP

Federal law, under the 2004 IDEA, requires that both indirect and direct behavior management strategies be documented annually in a child's IEP. Social skills curriculums are thus becoming increasingly scrutinized in the educational community. Social skills building is an ongoing process. It involves the educator's responsibility and ability to use "teachable moments" to the maximum, and the child's own reactions and thought processes about the lesson(s) learned.

A good Behavior Intervention Plan (BIP) will subsequently incorporate both the above stated elements to put the puzzle together, and help develop "The Big Picture" regarding the child's behavioral issues. It is both a privilege and directive for parents and educators to steer a course for children and set an example for them. It is therefore imperative that behavior management have both crisis intervention and preventive intervention measures put in place, to ensure success.

Before we can increase the child's own self awareness of what is expected, and what he/she is doing that is inappropriate, the adults (family, educators) in that child's life need to meet, discuss, agree and document a course of action. We need to decide which proactive measures are needed to facilitate appropriate behavior, as discussed in the previous chapter. We need to document and agree on which crisis and subsequent tantrum to address. This will help bridge the gap between readiness to learn and actual performance.

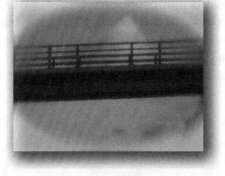

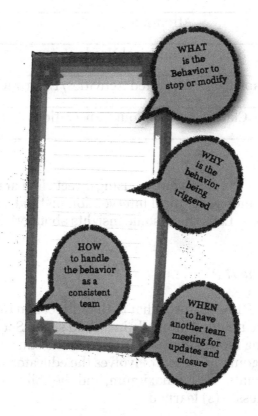

CRISIS INTERVENTION: THE 4 QUESTIONS TO ASK

NOTE

The Four Crisis Intervention Question Infographic can also be found in Chapter 12. We need to use it to specifically target, discuss, and modify the following:

What the child is doing that is inappropriate--target one challenging behavior at a time to ensure success and clarity of purpose by the whole team.
Why he/she continues to engage in the inappropriate behavior- -what's the "trigger"?
How the team will handle the inappropriate behavior in a consistent manner.
When to meet again and as a team, move on to addressing another challenging behavior.

Behavior Management and Crisis Intervention

The first line of defense is the use of a technique called *Functional Behavioral Assessment* (FBA), which utilizes a form called the "ABC Chart" as its backbone. It is usually done when a student is in "crisis mode" and we need to understand why. We will usually have the parent and/or educator or caregiver on duty during the "episode" fill out the ABC Chart and share it with the team. We will then meet and discuss the need to come to a consensus of how to handle the crisis next time, and talk the child "off the ledge" sooner and faster, or decide whether to do so at all.

FAQ: What Do I Need to Remember When the Child is In "Crisis Mode"?

1. Functional Behavioral Assessment (FBA) does not involve student participation. It is therefore the first weapon of choice in the arsenal of behavior management!

2. The "ABC Chart", must be completed by the entire team and include:

- Listing the trigger i.e. antecedent event.
- Defining the problematic behavior which ensued.
- Listing the previously given typical consequences (ex: "time out" etc.).
- Exploring the necessary modifications needed for the next outburst (sensory, structure, level of difficulty).
- Exploring which replacement skills to teach the child for the next time an outburst would be triggered.
- Facilitating skill acquisition using reinforcers and consequences.

FAQ: What's the Difference Between Crisis Intervention and Proactive Intervention?

1. Crisis intervention is all about managing the outburst at the exact moment it happens, and lessening both the duration and frequency of the tantrum. It's meant to ensure that the child is safely handled, the adults understand the "trigger" (not the child), and that steps are taken to help that child calm down and reestablish homeostasis.
2. Proactive Intervention is all about managing both the "trigger" and consequences of the outburst way after it happened, when the child is emotionally removed from the situation and receptive to discussing it. It's meant to teach the child to self-evaluate performance, take "emotional temperature" i.e. understand warning signs and implement strategies to prevent the meltdown from occurring, or occurring with such severity. These strategies involve the use of visual supports and the "Social Autopsy".

★ To enlighten and remind the child of the adult's expectations placed upon him
★ To structure the learning environment for maximum impact, attention and retention.
★ To enable the child to stay anchored to the present i.e. "live in the moment" so he/she can follow and understand the rules and players in the game unfolding.
★ To help the child self regulate when things don't go as planned.

Behavior Management and Proactive Intervention

Now that we shed some light on the <u>why</u> of the tantrums, we can move on to <u>how</u> to deal with them. As science has evolved, the role of preventive medicine has been increasingly discussed. It is felt to be equally if not more important than dealing with the medical emergency as it arises. The same can be said for behavior management. We now know that PREVENTIVE intervention can be more effective than crisis intervention.

Unfortunately, the axiom "the squeaky wheel gets noticed" is still true in many school and home environments. However, the use of proactive methods such as TEACCH™, Visual Strategies™ and a Sensory Diet prescribed by an occupational therapist, can all aid in preventing the wheel from getting "squeaky" in the first place. Proactive measures are now being routinely documented in a child's behavior plan, and incorporated into the annual IEP. The revisions to the IDEA in 2004, make this a federal requirement, as was previously discussed.

I like to compare proactive behavior modification measures to planting seeds in a garden. Certain things need to happen, in a specific order, so that leaves can unfurl and flowers bloom. A child with ASD needs to have the planting done, i.e. the stage "set" to help get him or her ready to learn. Positive Behavioral Supports, visual supports and preventive intervention can go a long way in bridging the gap between readiness to learn and actual performance.

An important proactive measure to consider is structure. It means environmental modifications, setting boundaries and clarifying for yourself and the child what's to be expected and in which parameters. Clarify what you expect of the child using simple, firm verbal instructions, or pictures showing the appropriate response. Explaining your intent at the START of an activity can make all the difference! Structuring your lesson means reconfiguring the learning environment i.e. these parameters:

- The nature of the materials presented (ex: manipulatives such as blocks versus photo cards).
- The physical surroundings (remove all distractors that can potentially "set off" the student).
- The mental framework of the task at hand. Visual Strategies™ (such as "My Rules", "Task Organizers" and Social Stories™ about specific home/therapy/class routines) can clearly communicate what you want from the child. Remember: It is CRUCIAL to

review this with challenging students at the onset of each activity. This really helps bridge the gap between readiness to learn and actual performance. Also, make sure that the *environment* is structured for that particular child! Remove *potential distractors* or possible negative "triggers". Remember to show off the impending reinforcer(s). You can also use verbal reminders with higher functioning children whenever needed, to make sure that they are reoriented to what you want from them. Now the child is ready to stay connected to you and "live in the moment", so that learning can begin. There is now a bridge between readiness to learn and actual performance.

NOTE

A Word About Preventive Intervention: Modify the Structure of Your Activity By Reconfiguring These Parameters

1. *Nature of your demands on the student* - Decide how to present the materials. Does the student need to use tactile manipulatives such as blocks OR visual stimuli such as picture cards, based on sensory concerns?
2. *Physical and mental surroundings* - Remove distractors! Use Visual Strategies™ to negotiate with an "If...Then Contingent" style Visual Schedule. Remind the student of the rules of engagement. Bring in reinforcers that are motivating to that particular student (to use on an ongoing basis or token economy style for delayed gratification).
3. *Timing* of the activity-Modify how many discreet trials to do before stopping. Timing is everything! Time the challenging activity so that it precedes an easier, enjoyable activity, OR trade off between both (ex: "First, play with the dollhouse.....then, go ride the bike.").

A Word On ABA and VBT

Any discussion of behavior modification providing timed, structured intervention and discreet trials is incomplete without mentioning two widely used approaches:

Applied Behavioral Analysis (ABA), and Verbal Behavior Therapy (VBT). An in depth look at these approaches is beyond the scope of this book. Please see the bibliography at the end of this chapter for further information. I would like to emphasize that the use of these two approaches, particularly VBT, can be a beneficial part of any tool box when treating children with ASD. I believe in using these approaches in conjunction with others such Floortime™, TEACCH ™, and Visual Strategies™. Experience proves that all these approaches aid in structuring the environment, configuring the timing of the activity and bridging the gap between readiness to learn and actual performance.

Behavior Management-Implications for Learning

The Socially Speaking™ Train Analogy

I like to compare my approach to social communication development and behavioral intervention to an old fashioned train meandering through the country side. I imagine sitting on the train and observing the terrain outside, created from the student's "inner landscape". I imagine how one sees a scenic view of varying degrees of darkness and light, chaos and order, as the train rolls on by. I think about the train that was made, out of a synthesis of building materials, and brought to that landscape. I think about Verbal Behavioral Therapy (VBT) being the train tracks, laid out in an orderly fashion, and with clear markers.

I compare Visual Strategies™ to the individual cars of the train, running smoothly on the tracks that were laid out in a linear, consecutive design. I then imagine that inside each train car are different people, toys, materials, books and equipment. I also imagine that the terrain outside the train is wondrous and ever changing, and that one needs to pay attention to all the little details. Think of the terrain outside as the environment the child faces daily; in all its structured and unstructured glory. Think of all the teachable moments the child experiences, and the vocabulary learned and paired with those events, forming episodic memories the child can draw from as needed. Think of all the "stuff" the child accumulates in said environment, and the people who populate it and get to meet that child at different "stops" on the train, not to mention the changing surroundings as the train travels onward. Now try to see what the child sees.

I then compare the intervention process to a ride on this train, for varying periods of time, until the next stop. There are stations where people and play things may be added while others get to disembark. A good passenger knows where the train has been, where it is headed and how to ensure it completes its journey. A good observer understands the value in making sure the train's storage bins are fuller upon arrival than they were when it first departed on its trip.

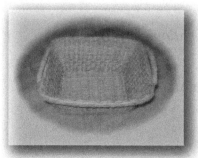

There have been many books written about behavior modification starting points and final results, and individualized methods to help children with ASD get from point A to B. There has been much discussion of laying the groundwork i.e. tracks for learning, using methods such as ABA, and linking moments in time i.e. train cars, using methods such as Floortime™ and Visual Strategies™. These approaches are valuable in helping children with ASD "take off" and depart from the station, so to speak. However, it is also imperative to consider the therapeutic process i.e. the actual train ride. One must keep in mind the gestalt, i.e. the integration of various therapeutic approaches to facilitate the **learning process** for children with ASD.

It is crucial to think about the **journey** of the materials that are loaded and unloaded from the train cars at each station. Parents and educators certainly need to keep sight of the train and make sure it is not derailed. However, they also need to think about **what** materials to pack along for the ride, **when** to stock up, or discard items along the way, and **how** to introduce them to the VIP passenger, our child with ASD. Balance and timing are two crucial components of my goal planning for behavioral and social skills intervention and remediation. It is the essence of my therapeutic process for children in need.

As I mentioned before, this book is about an eclectic approach to learning social skills. I have rarely used just one approach in therapy. An eclectic, integrated approach has proven to be beneficial in deciphering the child's Theory of Mind, in scaffolding my lesson plan, in motivating my students to engage and interact and in generalizing learned skills. It has also proven beneficial in alleviating boredom and "burnout" in educators and students alike. Intervention is all about planting seeds of knowledge, helping those seedlings grow and harvesting the fruit to use outside in the world.

As you have already noticed, this book is different from others you may have read. It is about the journey of a child transitioning from a Me to a We, when to start that journey (what prerequisite skills are needed) and *which specific materials* to bring along on the journey, once the road is defined and the train cars are linked. It is about being able to tell the unique child with ASD, "I see you". It is about better seeing and understanding the child's "inner landscape" and getting that child to join you in the present by really seeing him or her.

NOTE

Compliance Tips for the Service Provider

1. *Visual* redirection to the present is needed on a regular basis to prevent an episode of "acting out". Think of this as letting the child see what's "behind door #1".
2. Structure and consistency are CRUCIAL in all learning environments, and with all caregivers and educators! Think of clear expectations and opportunities for practice.
3. "Crisis intervention" style teaching is not as helpful as "prevention intervention" style teaching when it comes to behavior management for children with ASD.
4. To ensure compliance, especially in the beginning of treatment, tasks need to have a "countdown", to be broken down and have a clearly delineated beginning/middle/end, that is visually depicted-- either using simple toys, visual supports such as a Visual Schedule with embedded AT Link Clips (see Chapter 3), my personal choice, or a picture format worksheet (see Chapter 12).

Final Words

We need to remember that children with Autism exhibit a "different operating system" of sorts due to different neurological hardwiring. This can result in resistance to change, to being challenged, to completing unfamiliar and/or undesirable tasks, and difficulty with transitioning and accepting unwanted outcomes. Children with ASD respond well to structured, clearly delineated routines and expectations which are "spelled out", usually via pictures and props i.e. Visual Supports. It is thus practical and necessary for us to consider these 2 questions:

- How can we proactively counteract all this and try to prevent the behavioral outbursts that can and will pop up?
- How can we explain what's going on to the uninitiated?

I often tell parents and colleagues that there are two unwritten rules of behavior management I never forget. Two rules driving the actions of children with ASD facing today's busy, tech-centric, and sometimes overwhelming surroundings:

1. The environment is *not* our friend!
2. Technology *is* our friend!

<u>Translations</u>
❖ Modifying the environment means physical changes after verbally and visually preparing the child and the uninformed adults around him or her.
❖ We need the child to fully understand what's in store, what's happening now and what will change. We need to therefore prepare the child visually and verbally for the unfamiliar or changing environment. How? By talking to the child *beforehand* about what he/she can expect from seeing____ or doing _____ . We need to emphasize the target vocabulary that can help the child comprehend and internalize that which may be different than expected and different than the usual.
❖ Tablets and smartphones can be loaded with educational and entertaining Apps that can help a child practice and retain learned vocabulary and skills, become "grounded" when overwhelmed by the surroundings and communicate wants/needs more effectively than just "acting out".
❖ "Tech" can be used as both an intrinsic motivator to cooperate i.e. a reinforcer for good behavior, and also as a portable "teacher" to help the child find ways to make requests instead of tantrums, find ways to stay occupied and find ways to review and internalize target vocabulary and/or specific concepts.
❖ We *can* alleviate some of the guesswork and confusion in advance if we do our homework and help the children do theirs. Preventive intervention trumps crisis intervention, particularly when it comes to social skills development! Visual supports, especially digital ones created with the use of mobile Apps, can truly help the child cope with changes in routine. Prepping the setting and those in it, to interact more effectively with our children, is so crucial to future success! Prepping the child's environment and those in it are **as** important as prepping the actual child for noisy, busy and often chaotic surroundings.

"A tantrum usually indicates that the child has misunderstood cues or become disoriented to person/place/time."

I need to point out that a failure to behave properly is actually a failure to communicate properly, and that the tantrum *does* serve a function! It's usually an indication that the child has misunderstood social or environmental cues, or has become disoriented to person/place/time. This is why self regulation is contingent on modifying both our directions/expectations and the child's surroundings. I always quote this immortal quote from Dr. Temple Grandin: *"If I see it, I understand it."* Good luck!

Materials for Your Toolbox

• <u>Key References</u>

Attwood, Tony (2004). *Exploring Feelings: Anxiety-Cognitive Behavior Therapy to manage Anxiety*. Arlington, TX: Future Horizons.

Baker, Jed (2003). *Social Skills Training for Children and Adolescents with Asperger Syndrome and Social Communication Problems*. Shawnee, KS: Autism Apserger Publishing.

Baker, Jed (2008). *No More Meltdowns: Positive Strategies for Managing and Preventing Out of Control Behavior*. Arlington, TX: Future Horizons.

Barbera, Mary Lynch, and Rassmussen, Tracy (2007). *The Verbal Behavior Approach: How to Teach Children with Autism and Related Disorders*. Philadelphia, PA: Jessica Kingsley Publishers.

Barnes, K. et al (2008). Self- regulation strategies of children with emotional disturbance, *Physical & Occupational* Therapy In Pediatrics, 28 (4), 369-387.

Blimes, Jenna (2004). *Beyond Behavior Management: The Six Life Skills Children Need to Thrive in Today's World*. St. Paul, MN: Red Leaf Press.

Chandler, Lynette, and Dahlquist, Carol (2009). *Functional Assessment: Strategies to Prevent and Remediate Challenging Behavior in School Settings, Third Edition*. Upper Saddle River, NJ: Prentice- Hall/Pearson Education.

Dunn Buron, Kari (2003). *Incredible Five Point Scale: Assisting Students with Autism Spectrum Disorder in Understanding Social Interactions and Controlling Their Emotional Responses*. Shawnee, KS: Autism Asperger Publishing.

Durand, V Mark, et al (2001). Functional Communication Training: A Contemporary Behavior Analytic Intervention for Problem Behavior. *Focus on Autism and Other Developmental Disorders 16, 110-119.*

Fouse, Beth and Wheeler, Maria (1997). *A Treasure Chest of Behavioral Strategies for Individuals with Autism*. Arlington, TX: Future Horizons.

Gimpel Peacock, Gretchen, and Holland, Melissa (2003). *Emotional and Behavioral Problems of Young Children: Effective Interventions in the Preschool and Kindergarten Years*. New York, NY: Guilford Press.

Hodgdon, Linda (1999). *Solving Behavior Problems in Autism*. Troy, MI: Quirk Roberts Publishing

Kowalski, Timothy (2002). *The Source for Asperger's Syndrome*. East Moline, IL: Linguisystems.

Levine, Karen, and Chedd, Naomi (2007). *REPLAYS: Using Play to Enhance Emotional and Behavioral Development for Children with Autism Spectrum Disorders*. Philadelphia, PA: Jessica Kingsley Publishers.

Manela, Miriam. (2014). *The Parent-Child Dance: A Guide to Help You Understand and Shape Your Child's Behavior*. Passaic, NJ: OT Thrive Publishing.

Thompson, Thomas (2008). *Freedom From Meltdowns: Dr. Thompson's Solutions for Children with Autism.* Baltimore, MD: Paul H. Brookes Publishing.

Weiss, Mary Jane and Demiri, Valbona (2011). *Jumpstarting Communication Skills in Children with Autism: A Parents' Guide to Applied Verbal Behavior.* Bethesda, MD: Woodbine House.

• <u>Key Links to Peruse</u>

http://bit.ly/1K0KBnl

http://bit.ly/15Hf2Bz

http://bit.ly/1Cf4gkh

http://bit.ly/1D6Mz2Q

http://bit.ly/1Bw2F6w

http://bit.ly/1EOiHtK

http://bit.ly/1Cf4YoH

http://bit.ly/1EOiOp2

http://bit.ly/1z3lrRO

http://bit.ly/1Epmu38

• <u>Key Concepts to Address</u>

Functional Behavioral Assessment, ABC Chart, IEP, Behavior Intervention Plan, Verbal Behavior Therapy, visual supports, AT Link Clips, Theory of Mind, Crisis Intervention, Preventive Strategies

• <u>Key Toys to Use in Treatment</u>

Note: Treatment of self regulation difficulty initially involves:

◉ Giving the child the run of the room to see what he/she gravitates towards, which can be used to build rapport and reinforce compliance

◉ Introducing child to unfamiliar and/or slightly challenging toys to see his/her reaction, update baseline data and generate treatment goals

◉ Toys that readily lend themselves to fostering compliance i.e. toys have an intrinsic, visible, rather short "countdown" to task completion depicting before/during/after:

✎ *For Younger Children:* Winfun Sweet Cake Stacker, Fisher-Price™ Brilliant Basics Snap-Lock Caterpillar, Guidecraft Stack N'Sort Cups, Alex® Early Learning String A Farm, Lauri™ Tall Stacker Pegs & Pegboard Set, TOMY Little Chirpers Sorting Eggs Learning Toy, Melissa and Doug Puzzles, Slinky™ Toy

✎ *For Older Children:* Time Timer's Clock, Toysmith Liquid Motion Bubbler, Tomy™ Gearation Building Toy, Connect Four™, Estone Baby Kid Intelligence Wood Abacus Counting Number Frame Maths Educational Toy

✎ *Toys that Sustain Overall Compliance:* Can double as an instant visual support for a Visual Schedule etc. such as TOMY Megasketcher Magnetic Board, Crayola™ Dry-Erase Fold & Go Pack, Melissa and Doug Deluxe Magnetic Responsibility Chart, Fisher Price™ Travel Doodler Pro

• Key iPad® Apps to Use in Treatment

☞ **For the Service Provider:** Good behavior management involves the use of structured apps which provide visual supports and facilitate self regulation by having a Causality component (token economy) and a clearly delineated beginning/middle/end. Here's a suggested sampling to try:

☞ *Visual Supports:* Choice Works by Bee Visual, Visual Schedule Planner, VTVS HD: First Then Visual Schedule, First & Then by Alisha Forrest, Picture Me Calm, Life Skills: Autism Visual Schedule by iTouchiLearn, Routines by iTouchiLearn, My Visual Schedule HD Lite, PPT: Picture Prompt Timer, iGet...My Schedules at Home Social Skills Stories, Pictello, Stories About Me, My Story, PictureCanPlan, Scene & Heard Lite and Paid Version, Use2Talk, Place My Face™, SonicPics, Chatterpix, ChatterKid, MashCAM, Shuttersong, CanPlan, and PhotoFunia.

☞ *Behavior Management with Causality Component:* Balls by iotic, Monsters, Storybots® Tap & Sing, Stop and Go! HD Free, Token Board by Zorten, Sago Mini Doodlecast, Make a Scene: Farmyard (for token economy), Rewards Chart by Big Red Apps, iReward by Gremble, Chore Pad HD Lite, iTouchiLearn Tasks by Staytooned, Behavior Boost by John Tobia, Cheerful Charts Free, Jo Frost Rewards, iReward Chart for iPad®, Goodie Goodie, ChoreMonster, Behavior Chart by Juan Jose Pons Florit, and My Chores by Eiscuer Apps.

☞ **For the Child:** Learning Style and preferences i.e. Theory of Mind will play a role in determining which app will appeal to the child. It is also important to give apps that act as reinforcers of performance, not the lesson's target vocabulary, especially if the child has real compliance issues. At this stage, the purpose of apps usage is to build/maintain rapport, not generalize learned material. That means providing an app that will allow the child to: a) feel successful and b) feel rewarded for good behavior. That means allowing the child to be in control and choose apps which are either very familiar and perhaps even age inappropriate, such as a musical app or one which has a video clip that is watched passively. That's okay! There will be other opportunities to use apps as springboards for lessons; not here! Here's a sampling to consider, keeping in mind that some of the apps fit into all 3 categories. However, you need to keep the child's dominant learning style in mind:

☞ *Auditory Learning Style:* Storybots® Tap & Sing, PianoBall, TouchAnimals, TappyTunes™, Monsters, Songs for Kids, Zoola Animals Lite, Animal Sound, Vocal Zoo, Sound Touch, Music Sparkles, Melody Touch Lite, Sago Mini Doodlecast, Furry Friend, Talking Tom, Talking Ginger, Singing Fingers, Silly Monsters Music, Knock Knock Family, Little People™ Player, Preschool Toy Phone, Awesome Xylophone Lite, Marcus Discoveries, Sophie's Discoveries, Word Slapps by Zorten, SPOKEnPHOTO Album, Shuttersong, Make a Scene: Farmyard, Bugs and Bubbles, Mega Sounds SFX, Voice Recorder (FREE), Voice Changer Lite, InnerVoice, TalkRocket Go, Call Voice Changer, Toca Band, Toy Story Read Along Book, Talking Train, Educreations, Screen Chomp, Explain Everything, Stick Around, Advanced Making Sequences by Zorten, iPractice Verbs by Smarty Ears Apps, Adobe Voice-Show Your Story, SonicPics, ChatterKid and Smart Baby Free and Pro for iPad®.

☞ *Visual Learning Style:* Balls by iotic, Bitsboard Free and Pro, SonicPics, Chatterpix, MashCAM, I Like Books (37) by Grasshopper Apps, Family Touch Lite, ZoLO Lite and Paid, Sophie's Discoveries, Marcus Discoveries, Paint Sparkles Draw, Paint My Cat, Sago Mini Doodlecast, Kids Rainbow, Try It On, ColorForms® Revolution™ Free, Drawing Box Free, Doodlelicious, Cute Food, Feed Maxi, Let's Create, Who's there? by Leripa AB, Dress Up: Professions, Art Maker, Marvin Fun, Talking Train, Photo Buttons, Popplet Lite and Paid, Comic Life, Strip Designer, ComicBook! Pic Jointer, Photo Collage Free, Juxtaposer, Superzaic, Speech with Milo: Nouns, Categories Learning Center by Smarty Ears Apps, Tense Builder by Mobile Education Store, Toontastic Jr. and Toontastic, StoryLines, Educreations, Haiku Deck, Explain Everything, Stick Around, Use 2 Talk, Photo Slice Pro, The Chalk Box Story by Auryn, InnerVoice, iTube List and Kids Videos HD- YouTube Videos for Kids.

☞ *Tactile Learning Style:* Balls by iotic, Make It Pop, BuzzBack, Somantics, Reactickles Magic, Paint Sparkles Draw, Drawing with Carl, Drawing Pad, Drawing Box Free, BabyTouch!, Kids Rainbow, Car Puzzles for Toddlers, Car Puzzles for Kids, Kids CARS, Injini Lite and Injini, Abby Musical Puzzle, Singing Fingers, Fun Flowers, Kids PlayHome Lite and PlayHome, Put It Away, Animal Games, Toca Tea Party, Toca Tailor, Toca Hair Salon, Toca Train, Toca Builders, Bugs and Bubbles, Puppet Stage, Build a Story, Make a Scene: Farmyard, Felt Board by Software Smoothie, Little House Decorator (Lite version too), Design This Home by App Minis, Home Design: Dream House by Arcade, Dexteria OT Apps, Build and Play 3D Apps by Croco Studio, Question Sleuth by Zorten, Piano Band, SketchASong, Thinkin' Things 1, Animal Puzzle, Writing Wizard, Create a Scene by IcySpark, Jiggle Balls, Toy Balls HD, Monster Physics™, Build a Car with Kate and Harry Buttons and Scissors, Kids Doodle and Kids Doodle Movie, Sleepy Cat Prepositions and Alex the Handyman Free.

☞ *Honorable Mention: Apps to Visually Prepare Child for Doctor Appointments Besides Social Story Apps (to counteract anxiety and behavioral outbursts):* Caillou Check Up-Doctor's Office, Toca Doctor HD (also Lite version), Eye Doctor-Kid's Games, Little Throat Doctor-Kid's Games, Baby Doctor Office, Doctor X-Med School, Pet Vet Doctor-DOGS Rescue, Dentist Office Kids, Dentist Story Kids, Meebie, Puppet Workshop, My Incredible Body by Visible Body, and The Human Body by Tinybop.

Chapter 5
Fostering Development of Humor:
Socially Speaking™ Social Skills Curriculum: Train Tracks #2
<u>The Use of Humor:</u> Demonstrating Orientation to Person/Place/Time

Anecdote

Do you remember watching half hour sitcoms and laughing out loud with the "laugh track?" Do you remember laughing at funny faces as a small child? Making knock-knock jokes in the playground at school with your friends? Abby doesn't remember doing these things because she hasn't done them. In her 9 years of living with older siblings, attending family outings and learning about the world in play group and later in school, she has continued to have difficulty taking constructive criticism, transitioning, "bouncing back" when upset, as well as playing with peers. Abby has real difficulty displaying a sense of humor. Her High Functioning Autism (HFA) has made her miss out on the joke, on that subtle human interaction, on developing emotional attunement and emotional resonance with others.

Abby didn't develop the "Sixth Sense", the social sense on her own when she was learning to talk. This explains why at age 3 her parents realized something was really wrong and took her for countless evaluations. That is how she came to be on my preschool caseload a year later exhibiting "flat affect", "rigid behaviors" and "below age level social communication skills" and tantrums. Following, you will find an explanation of how we filled in the "missing pieces" in Abby's puzzle.

Strategy and Technique

Humor - The Missing Social Skills Piece

Abby and her parents were introduced to my *Socially Speaking™ Program*, which starts with establishing rapport, environmental modifications and implementing behavior management strategies to facilitate readiness to learn. Her parents were told that I designed my program to include the missing piece of the puzzle, for a more comprehensive social skills treatment plan. I explained that the development of humor is often overlooked in traditional treatment but that it is a behavioral side effect of following my program. When done right, humor can be taught as an imitated and later, a spontaneous action/behavior in context-- playfully, methodically and meaningfully. The development of humor is one of the premier signs of developing intelligence, the beginning of emerging resiliency and the ability to take constructive criticism. Development of humor thus hinges on the development of these executive functions: metacognition and flexibility.

Research has shown that resiliency is linked to problem-solving-- one of the cornerstones of good social skills development. Beginning problem solving requires the understanding of how "the world works" and the causality behind events that don't go as planned. A child's self-concept, which encompasses a sense of humor and the ability to transition between desirable and undesirable activities, needs to be somewhat developed in order for that child to develop problem solving skills. A child with Autism who has reduced proprioception, resiliency and Theory of Mind (TOM) will need clinical intervention to develop a sense of humor, which will facilitate his or her later ability to transition, to take constructive criticism and to resolve conflicts.

"Through clinical intervention, children with Autism can develop a sense of humor, which will later facilitate the ability to take constructive criticism and resolve conflicts."

Two Components of Humor: Physical & Linguistic

Humor is made up of two components: physical and linguistic. Developmentally, physical humor emerges together with gross motor development and the child's ability to attend/track and imitate movements of those around him. This includes a social smile and spontaneous laughter as a result of being tickled and/or shown a funny face.

The emergence of physical humor is contingent on the child's development of body awareness and emotional attunement, which is facilitated through early play. Physical humor helps the child make sense of his or her environment and its place in it, leading to increased orientation to person/place/time and overall resiliency; i.e. ability to transition.

Linguistic humor emerges when an intact temporal lobe can process incoming auditory stimuli, process the meanings behind the vocabulary and reference it using past events stored in episodic memory, where sensory impressions and portions of the receptive lexicon are stored. "Getting" the joke often depends on previous knowledge of object function and categorization of the target vocabulary. Children who understand how "the world works" are usually the ones making the joke and/or participating in others' jokes.

Children with Autism, who exhibit difficulty developing the "sixth sense", the social sense, because of "social blindness" and an underdeveloped sense of humor, will frequently miss the point of humorous constructive criticism from adults, and also miss the joke from a peer, resulting in social difficulty with others.

FAQ: What Are the Implications of "Social Blindness"?

These children often exhibit difficulty with knowing what to do and say in social situations, interpreting body language and utilizing eye contact appropriately, making and keeping friends and problem-solving. See the previous chapter for more information.

FAQ: What's Our Game Plan?

We can work on humor within the context of language lessons using play and mobile technology together. We should be working on social skills simultaneously! I prefer manipulatives and iPad® apps for my lessons, but a child's learning style and preference, your time constraints and budget and your location during the "teachable moment" will all determine what to use when!
• Gauge the child's readiness to develop humor, based on behavior and cognition.
• Use real time, play based, concrete activities first before introducing video clips, which are more abstract and therefore take longer to internalize.
• Have a repertoire of video clips to tailor to every child's needs, by building/storing a list of "teachable moment" videos from YouTube etc. on a flash drive/SD Card or cloud based, digital folder somewhere.

I basically plan lessons around my IEP goals keeping in mind the child's inner landscape, mental age and "humor status". To help me determine whether or not to target physical vs. linguistic humor, I suggest using these two formulas I created:

☞ Socially Speaking™ Formula for Physical Humor

PHYSICAL HUMOR= TOM +BODY AWARENESS

For myself and the IEP team that need to collaborate, I practice using flat affect or exaggerated affect when speaking, AKA deadpan humor. Think of Mr. Bean in the movie *Rat Race*, Rachel Dratch as Debbie Downer on Saturday Night Live and this hilarious video clip for adults to see (not to use in therapy) to get an idea of what kinds of videos to search for in the vast universe of YouTube:

http://bit.ly/1CTjieo

For younger children I start by reenacting slapstick humor myself, with my body/ making faces etc. I start by juxtaposing an object in a weird position such as opening the therapy session wearing a shoe on my head and playing dumb (think the Allstate Mayhem insurance guy commercials) and then use actual video clips of other children or people engaged in similar behavior. Here are examples of the kind of video I show the child, and then we reenact it in therapy:

http://bit.ly/1ywtcxt

http://bit.ly/1z78h2R

http://bit.ly/1vpjj8X

For older children, I then move on to vintage, old school "Sesame St". clips where Cookie Monster is being naughty and someone is losing patience with him, or Ernie and Bert are having a funny conversation. Here are 2 more samples:

http://bit.ly/1zyohQK

http://bit.ly/1DpPELK

I also like to peruse Pinterest, Facebook, and even my Zite App's humor category to find funny pictures and funny videos that are good, clean fun and can hit home the points I'm making, such as:
• Specific "prank" videos: Just for Laughs Gags TV on YouTube: http://bit.ly/16niphY

• Specific photos showing animals in funny poses: http://bit.ly/16niClo

• Specific photos "gone wrong": http://bit.ly/1zNB4As

• Creating funny content/positions photos using an App such as Juxtaposer for iPad® or a related one, visit this link: http://bit.ly/1vpjzEZ

Examples of Physical Humor: *Whatever makes you LOOK twice!*
Funny faces
Flat affect
Vocal affect
Deadpan voice
Incongruity
Juxtaposing objects in weird positions
Pictorial humor

☛ Socially Speaking™ Formula for Linguistic Humor

LINGUISTIC HUMOR= COMPREHENSION OF OBJECT FUNCTION + WH? QUESTIONS

Linguistic humor really begins to be internalized and generalized **only when the child understands and explains categorization/exclusion tasks** (which item does not belong with the others or is out of place? Tell me why). This is the gateway to development of higher humor, resiliency and the ability to take constructive criticism. All of these are factors in a child's successful ability to transition and problem solve later on.

For younger children I usually try to start the child off by finding books/games/photos/ videos involving the theme of "What's wrong with this picture/scene? What would you do about it?" Here's a sample hierarchy to check out:

http://amzn.to/1ywvxbv

http://bit.ly/1zNBt5S

http://bit.ly/1uRLcAL

http://bit.ly/1uRLmrJ

For older children I start out reenacting scenarios myself with the student and then move on to showing video clips from YouTube or TV shows. I incorporate these language tasks into my "teachable moment": Knock, Knock jokes, mispronouncing words, using them in the wrong context and sarcasm. One of my favorite YouTube videos showcasing both physical and linguistic humor as well as sarcasm (for adults) is this one from Allstate Insurance about the GPS: http://bit.ly/1D6NyTl

Examples of Linguistic Humor: Whatever makes you THINK twice!
Knock, knock jokes
Puns
Slang
Feigned ignorance
Novelty
Make believe
Shared moments of irony

The ABCs of Humor-Implications for Social Skills Building

FAQ: What's The Difference Between Physical & Linguistic Humor?

- Physical humor relies on exaggerated or absurd facial affect or lack thereof (deadpan voice and/or expressions), causing people to pay extra attention to the words you say.

- Physical humor juxtaposes objects in strange positions, causing us to pay extra attention and "live in the moment" to ponder the visual absurdity.

- Linguistic humor references concepts and nuances behind vocabulary words stored in episodic memory.

- Linguistic humor references the inner workings of one's mind, not the outer workings of one's body.

Suggested Links To Get More Ideas for Treatment

http://bit.ly/16niphY

http://bit.ly/1Klpe0e

http://bit.ly/1HNZkWR

http://some.ly/1BXvM2R

http://bit.ly/1ywQVO2

http://bit.ly/1zvSj6f

http://on.fb.me/1uRVj8H

http://on.fb.me/1zyWCiE

http://bit.ly/1zyX3cR

Final Words

The development of humor (physical and then linguistic) is one of the premier signs of developing intelligence, the beginning of emerging resiliency and the ability to take constructive criticism. We can learn much about a child's state of mind and overall comprehension by the displayed humor or lack thereof. Observations of a child's demonstrated sense of humor can give us real insight into the developmental milestones which have been achieved, and those that are still emerging. Think of the toddler who enjoys bathroom humor while going through the toilet-training phase. Think of the first grader learning to read who enjoys and shares riddles, especially those that are a play-on-words.

Development of humor hinges on the development of these executive functions: metacognition and flexibility. Physical humor in particular helps the child make sense of the environment and his/her place in it, leading to increased orientation to person/place/time and the increased ability to transition. Our overall goal when addressing social-skills building, particularly the development of humor, is to ensure we counteract "splintered," "non-linear" and "situation-specific learning" of the target vocabulary. To do so, we need to understand the impact of play on causality and humor. We also need to understand the difference between physical and linguistic humor. This enables us to better choose our materials, goals and target vocabulary when addressing overall social communication skills.

Many social skills curricula don't incorporate a developmental, methodical and play-based approach to teaching humor. Mine does. I start with behavior management so that the child understands the rules of the game. I continue by teaching object function so that the child understands the role of the players and items being used in the game. I continue with specific play based, interactive techniques such as REPLAYS™ to foster Episodic Memory and retention of learned concepts/vocabulary, resiliency, the ability to take constructive criticism and "get" the joke and even laugh at oneself.

Materials for Your Toolbox

- <u>Key References</u>

Baker, Jed (2003). *Social Skills Training for Children and Adolescents with Asperger Syndrome and Social Communication Problems*. Shawnee, KS: Autism Asperger Publishing.

Brady, Lois Jean, et al (2011). *Speak, Move, Play, and Learn with Children on the Autism Spectrum*. Philadelphia, PA: Jessica Kingsley Publishers.

Chiak, D.F., Wright, R., and Ayres, K.M. (2010). Use of Self-Modeling Static-Picture Prompts Via a Handheld Computer to Facilitate Self-Monitoring in the General Education Classroom. *Education and Training in Autism and Developmental Disabilities*, 45(1), 136-149.

Cohen, L. J. (2001) Follow the Giggles. *Playful Parenting* pp. 76-92. New York, NY: Ballantine Books.

Greenspan, Stanley, and Weider, Serena (2006). *Engaging Autism: Using the Floortime Approach to Help Children Relate, Communicate, and Think*. Cambridge, MA: Da Capo Press/Perseus Books Group.

Gutstein, Steven (2002). *Relationship Development Intervention with Young Children: Social and Emotional Development Activities for Asperger Syndrome, Autism, PDD, and NLD*. Philadelphia, PA: Jessica Kingsley Publishers.

Hirsh-Pasek, Kathy, and Michnik Golinkoff, Roberta (2003). *Einstein Never Used Flash Cards: How Our Children Really Learn, and Why They Need to Play More and Memorize Less*. New York: NY, Rodale Books.

Hirsh-Pasek, Kathy, Michnik Golinkoff, Roberta, and Singer, Dorothy (2006). *Play=Learning: How Play Motivates and Enhances Social- Emotional Growth*. New York: NY, Oxford University Press.

Hodgdon, Linda (2012). *Special Report: Identifying Key Uses and Benefits From Apps for iPad® for Autism Spectrum Disorders*. Troy, MI: Quirk Roberts Publishing.

Kowalski, Timothy (2002). *The Source for Asperger's Syndrome*. East Moline, IL: Linguisystems.

Landreth, Gary (2000). *Innovations in Play Therapy: Issues, Process, and Special Populations*. New York, NY: Brunner-Routledge Books.

Levine, Karen, and Chedd, Naomi (2007). *REPLAYS: Using Play to Enhance Emotional and Behavioral Development for Children with Autism Spectrum Disorders*. Philadelphia, PA: Jessica Kingsley Publishers

Martin, Rod (2007). *A Psychology of Humor: An Integrative Approach*. San Diego, CA: Academic Press.

McGhee, P. (2002). *Understanding and Promoting the Development of Children's Humor*. Dubuque, IA: Kendall Hunt.

Moor, Julia (2002). *Playing, Laughing, and Learning with Children on the AutismSpectrum: A Practical Resource of Play Ideas for Parents and Carers*. Philadelphia, PA: Jessica Kingsley Publishers.

Nwokah, E. (2003). Giggle Time in the Infant-Toddler Classroom. Learning and Connecting Through Shared Humor and Laughter. *ACEI Focus on Infants and Toddlers*, 16, 2, 1-8.

Owens, Robert Jr. (2007). *Language Development; Seventh Edition*. Boston, MA: Allyn & Bacon.

Paley, Vivian Gussin (2004). *A Child's Work: The Importance of Fantasy Play*. Chicago, IL: The University of Chicago Press.

Schmidt, S. R. (2002). The Humor Effect: Differential Processing and Privileged Retrieval. *Memory* 10(2), 127-138.

Wolfberg, Pamela (2009). *Play and Imagination in Children with Autism, Second Edition*. Shawnee, KS: Autism Asperger Publishing.

• Key Concepts to Address

Physical humor, linguistic humor, social smile, resiliency, conflict resolution, emotional attunement, emotional resonance.

- <u>Key Toys to Use in Treatment</u>

Note: The goal is to juxtapose objects in weird positions for younger children and/or have funny conversations and dialogues for older children, with and without perceptual support!

✎ *For Younger Children:* Mr. Potato Head™, Beyond Play's Thread Heads Family, Melissa and Doug™ Family Bear Dress-up Puzzle, Colorforms Silly Faces Stick-Ons Game, Plan Toy Fruit & Vegetable Play Set,, LeapFrog Farm Animal Mash-Up Kit, Fisher Price™ Laugh & Learn Smilin' Smart Phone, *Where Does It Go?* by Margaret Miller, Sesame Street Tickle Me Elmo, Gymnic/Rody Inflatable Hopping Horse, Twister, *Are You My Mother?* by P.D. Eastman, *Moo, Baa, La-La-La* by Sandra Boynton, Do Princesses? Series by Carmela LaVigna Coyle and Mike Gordon, Pinkalicious Books by Victoria Kann, Amelia Bedelia Books by Peggy Parish and Fritz Siebel, The Miss Nelson Collection by Harry G. Allard Jr. and James Marshall, *Sammy the Seal* by Syd Hoff, *Cloudy With a Chance of Meatballs* by Judi Barrett.

✎ *For Older Children:* Melissa and Doug™ Make a Face Crazy Characters Stickers, Carson Dellosa Key Education What's Wrong? Learning Cards, Photo What's Wrong Flashcards? Carson Dellosa Key Education What's Missing? Learning Cards, MasterPieces Highlights Silly Situation Game, Highlights Silly Situations, Bubble Talk by Techno Source, Chalk Book by Bill Thomson, Dr. Seuss Books: *Cat in the Hat, Wacky Wednesday* by Theo LeSieg and George Booth, Mrs. Piggle Wiggle Books by Betty MacDonald, Mary Poppins Books by P.L. Travers, Poetry Books by Shel Silverstein, Sleeping in Class by Tyler Sput, *The Adventures of Captain Underpants* by Dav Spikey, Once I Laughed My Socks Off Poems Volume One by Steve Attewell, *Caps for Sale* by Esphyr Slobodkina, Mad Libs.

- <u>Key iPad® Apps to Use in Treatment</u>

▨ *Physical Humor*

☞ **For the Service Provider**

Apps that juxtapose objects in strange positions are the ones which showcase intrinsic Physical Humor. They will need to be used first, to maintain developmental integrity of the overall management plan. It goes without saying that this kind of humor needs to initially emerge in natural contexts through play with manipulatives and people. These apps will then target specific visuo-spatial, visual memory, gross motor and fine motor skills. It is therefore crucial that baseline data be obtained and an OT and even PT be consulted as needed to determine visual and motoric readiness to use these apps in treatment. It is also important to remember that if a child is not a visual learner, using these apps may be counterproductive and erode some of the rapport we've worked so hard to establish. Proceed with caution!

☞ **For the Child**

Physical Humor: Juxtaposer, Chatterpix, Meebie, Sago Mini Doodlecast, Funny Photo Effects & Stickers, Pics Mix, Toca Hair Salon 1& 2, Furry Friend, Talking Ginger, Pepi Bath, Ear Doctor, American Doctor, Faces Wild+, iFun Face- Talking Photos, Toy Repair Workshop, Cool Finger Face, Funny Movie Maker Lite, What Doesn't Belong? By Tiny Tap, Put It Away, My PlayHome, My PlayHome Stores, Puppet Stage, Puppet Workshop, What Doesn't Belong? Fun Deck, Advanced Making Sequences, iSequences, Sequencing Post Office, Burger Crazy Chef, Funny Cartoon Face Photo Booth, Funny Photo HD, Pix Mix, MugMash, Caillou: What's That Funny Noise?, Funny Voices: Sound of Life FX, and iFunny Faces HD by Mayuir Sidhpara.

Linguistic Humor

☞ **For the Service Provider**

Apps that provide insight into object function and give the opportunity for the child to provide verbal rationales and funny answers to various wh? questions, especially "why"? questions, are the ones which showcase intrinsic Linguistic Humor. They will also target specific cognitive based language goals such as categorization (exclusion--which one doesn't belong) and "why"? questions (what's wrong?). It is important for the child to have mastered object function comprehension in real time in order to actually enjoy and benefit from using these apps in lessons. It is also important for the child to have begun to understand (achieve, not master) "why"? questions and how to problem solve. Linguistic humor, like physical humor, is contingent on a person's ability: to a) understand how the world "works" and b) recall past situations and outcomes by accessing one's episodic memory and lexicon for a frame of reference. It is thus crucial to determine the child's level of orientation to person/place/time and cognitive functioning re: understanding the play on words, before introducing these apps in treatment. Proceed with caution!

☞ **For the Child**

Linguistic Humor: Things That Go Together by Grasshopper Apps, Clean Up: Category Sorting, Is That Silly? by Smarty Ears, StoryBuilder by Mobile Education Store, Sago Mini Doodlecast, Toca Tailor, Toca Cars, Toca Kitchen, This Is My Story (and I'm Sticking to It), You Doodle Plus, Storylines, Mad Libs, Super Duper What Are They Thinking?, What Are They Asking Fun Deck, Meme Factory- Meme Generator Free, CaptionIt, SonicPics, Comic Life, Strip Designer, ComicBook! 2: Creative Superpowers, Text Here, Captions, MashCAM, Distraction Lite and Paid, Bubble by Toto Ventures, Trixie and Jinx, Elephant's Bath HD, Wheels on the Bus HD, and Dr. Seuss Books (misc).

Socially Speaking™ Part II-Implementation

Methodically Determining Starting Points for Remediation: Collaborative Team Evaluations and Goal Planning For Specific Social Skills Goals

Chapter 6:
Assessment Part 1
The Socially Speaking™ Social Skills Assessment Protocol

Anecdote

Joey is a nonverbal, somewhat distractible and passive, adorable boy with a dual diagnosis of Down Syndrome and Autism, who is about to turn 5 years old. That means that he will no longer have "preschool status" and will need new educational placement. This calls for a reevaluation and a parental meeting with the IEP team to transition him to "CSE status" at the end of the school year. Joey has received both home based and center based related services (speech, OT, PT, Ed) since he was born, but progress has been slow. Joey exhibits splintered, inconsistently demonstrated learned skills corresponding to orientation to person (not place or time). He does not spontaneously initiate eye contact or communicate his needs/ wants, play with a toy independently unless he's "stimming" on one of its parts, or using the bathroom independently. His parents want to continue to be active participants in both the evaluation and treatment process. They are worried about the less than anticipated progress and continued episodes of "tuning out" when Joey becomes overwhelmed. They are concerned about the future social implications of his tendency to drop to the floor to rock back and forth, sometimes squealing when upset.

Joey is not really a candidate for standardized testing, but updated baseline data is needed to determine future IEP goals and service delivery. The IEP team holds a pre-meeting to plot a course of action re: the reevaluation. It is decided that formalized assessment using standardized tests such as the Preschool Language Scale 5's Receptive Language Battery and the initial portion of the Expressive Communication Battery will be used in conjunction with informal observations of behavior and play skills by various service providers. They will then work together to generate a written paragraph for documentation purposes. Despite the collaborative nature of this evaluation, the service providers observing Joey's play and behavioral functioning cannot come to a consensus about what to look for exactly, and what to put into the evaluation. They are unaware of the need to observe and document specific skills or lack thereof, which will provide a bread crumb trail and a blueprint for Joey's future academic and simultaneous social skills treatment plan-- NOT just his Behavior Intervention Plan for the IEP. They are also unaware of the benefits of "prepping" Joey to tolerate testing (not the questions he'll be asked but the place and person asking the questions) and the unfamiliar evaluators who are assigned to him and meet him for the first time on testing day.

Needless to say, Joey is uncooperative, underperforms on evaluations across the board, even with those evaluators who are also his therapists and causes turmoil in class and again at home. He has had a really bad day, and didn't realize what was happening, or that it is now assumed that he is lower-functioning than he really is. This sets the tone for the subsequent IEP meeting, IEP goal planning and educational placement. Joey's parents are very unhappy with the outcomes but don't know what could have been done differently. They are seeking advocacy and perhaps legal action to overturn uninformed decisions that were made on Joey's behalf-- something that happens a lot in the United States after annual review IEP meetings!

Many an IEP meeting can be derailed by an unsuccessful evaluation encounter/ process/procedure which prevents the team from "filling in the blanks". This can have a negative cascade i.e domino effect on the IEP team's overall attempts and outcomes re: collaborating on a functional, measurable treatment plan. This also can result in ongoing, across the board misdiagnosis, incorrect current and future educational placement, ineffective generalized goal planning and implementation, as well as fluctuating retention/generalization of previously learned skills. The child is therefore at risk for continued self regulation issues. The child may display boredom and outbursts when faced with re-learning and task repetition, fluctuating rapport and willingness to be challenged to try learning new, harder lessons, splintered skill acquisition and ongoing underdeveloped Theory of Mind (perspective, empathy) plus social communication skills. The parents and service providers (even amongst themselves) may not "be on the same page" re: what the child's areas of strength and weakness really are. This can further impact on overall expectations the adults have of the child's abilities, and the child's consistency of performance in different contexts. The result? The child exhibits situation specific behavior, learning, and carryover, because the test findings and scores don't align with level of functioning and the chosen IEP goals.

Strategy and Technique

Readiness Indicators That Collaborative Assessment Can Begin

I heard Joey's story from his former teacher and therapists when I was asked to reevaluate him, months after his transition meeting and long after he "graduated". We used him as a case study to show what the IEP team had done correctly and incorrectly, and how they underutilized parental input and cooperation, so eagerly offered in this case! They hadn't understood that service providers need to "line ducks in a row" before doing an evaluation, not only before a lesson. They needed to learn readiness indicators for both themselves and the child being evaluated, especially one with Autism and behavioral challenges, who is not an independent communicator!

Precursors Needed Before Child Assessments:
1. Prioritize specific areas to be assessed, based on a previous team meeting about the child's behavior and current level of functioning, and then provide a written memo to parents re: which areas will be targeted during formal/informal observation. Ask for their input by sending home checklists and questionnaires to fill out and return.

2. Have all team members do an ABC Chart together before the evaluation, to understand better which environmental modifications are needed during testing, and how to lessen the child's exposure to potential "triggers" during testing.

3. Motivate the child to start performing by having familiar and unfamiliar tasks done in the testing room, and showing the child who will be there, etc. If the evaluator is unfamiliar with the child (which is often the case in large school districts and charter schools), use an ABA technique knows as "flooding," where desired reinforcers are given up front for a period (to be determined on a case by case basis) before actual testing starts. Remember: start by establishing a good working relationship with the child. It will help facilitate rapport, which itself acts as an intrinsic reinforcer. The child can then try to tolerate being challenged with unfamiliar and/or difficult tasks.

A cohesive team approach goes a long way to maximizing the evaluation process and outcome for children with Autism and special needs who crave structure and routine, which is the antithesis of a testing situation. While standardized testing and the element of surprise is understandably needed, it does not provide enough insight into practical, functional social communication skills needed in today's 21st century classrooms and communities. That's why it is important to synthesize formal, standardized testing results with informal, observation based testing results that showcase areas of strength and challenge re: specific social skills and actions pertaining to self regulation. Both types of assessments are needed to more functionally and specifically document the goals, technique, materials, criteria for mastery, prognosis and desired outcomes.

This way, the child's "inner circle" i.e. the IEP team are all aware of his/her needs. They are all "on the same page" which makes the treatment plan clearer and more consistent to both implement and document. It is time to rethink starting points for assessment and remediation of social communication skills in young children with Autism and/or special needs. It is time to actively seek out parental input which gets documented to "fill in the blanks". It is time to be more collaborative and functional about the way we draft an action plan of which social skill to target, how to target it and how to keep track of progress and future needs.

Think Differently About Assessment and Treatment

The original Apple™ credo "Think Different!" has always resonated with me, especially when I first designed this social skills curriculum. It is why I created my *Socially Speaking™ Social Skills Assessment Protocol* in both paper and digital formats. My Socially Speaking™ social skills checklist and management plan was introduced to the American special education community at large in 2009. My *Socially Speaking™ App* was designed by me and digitally created by Amadeus Consulting in Boulder, CO. It launched in iTunes in May 2012 and introduced my assessment protocol to the world. It is meant to provide readiness indicators for the evaluation team to pinpoint areas of weakness in how well they know the child as well as specific areas to assess and take note of for documentation purposes. It is also meant to provide readiness indicators about the child's level of functioning and potential to be receptive to learning.

How? By providing the team with baseline data that is cross-referenced with everyone's observations, including parents and caregivers who have often felt they are "left out in the cold"! To that end, I purposely created my assessment protocol as a non-standardized, easy to complete and understand checklist that can be filed with other documentation, even in accordance with HIPPA regulations. Please note that further discussion re: IEP meetings, evaluations, and HIPPA regulations are beyond the scope of this book, but readers are invited to peruse the links at the end of this chapter.

The Socially Speaking™ Social Skills Assessment Protocol Template © 2010

The assessment protocol I created (see Chapter 12) is a deceptively simple and easy to document way to aid in determining which skills are crucial to developing better behavior and pragmatic skills. It contains 2 developmental, play-based, non-jargon, segmented checklists re: social skills development and a lesson plan template to help the special education team both evaluate and treat the child in need. It is designed to update baseline data, determine starting points for remediation and succinctly document goals/techniques/materials to be used in the lesson plan both in school/

therapy and at home. Both the layman (parents) and the service provider can use this protocol to customize Behavior Intervention Plans and IEP goals for the child in need of help re: behavior management and social skills development.

I use this checklist as a starting point when evaluating a child and then drafting both IEP goals and a Behavior Plan. The included skills are divided into three areas: introductory, intermediate and advanced. I have categorized them as such from cognitive and psycho-social standpoints. The beauty of a checklist is that it is succinct, easy to score and easy to re-administer at regular intervals. I usually encourage the child's parents, teacher, speech therapist, occupational therapist, physical therapist, and para- professional(s) to fill out the check list before evaluations and certainly before attending the annual review IEP team meeting. I believe that the more organized the baseline data, the more organized the overall IEP and embedded Behavior Plan will be. The team will then have a more organized way of thinking about and collaborating about specific goals and needs for that particular child.

The Socially Speaking™ Social Skills Preschool Checklist, ©2010 Penina Pearl Rybak MA/CCC-SLP
Child's Name_____Teacher/Class_____Speech Therapist_____
Date_____ Completed by_____

(to be filled out before the team meeting, IEP meeting, and /or before a behavior plan is drafted)

Introductory Social Skills	Rarely	Sometimes	Usually
1. Active Listening (attention with eye contact)	☐	☐	☐
2. Making Requests	☐	☐	☐
3. Asking for Help	☐	☐	☐
4. Expressing Feelings Verbally	☐	☐	☐
5. Verbal Rejection (expressing dislikes and displeasure with task etc. using words)	☐	☐	☐
Intermediate Level Social Skills	Rarely	Sometimes	Usually
1. Following Directions Promptly (response time, cooperation)	☐	☐	☐
2. Asking Questions (for clarification and social conversation reasons)	☐	☐	☐
3. Not Getting Discouraged (not giving up, trying when it's hard)	☐	☐	☐
4. Turn Taking in Group Activities	☐	☐	☐
5. Greeting Appropriately (verbal vs. gesture, adult vs. peer)	☐	☐	☐
6. Sharing with Others	☐	☐	☐
7. Transitioning/Bouncing Back	☐	☐	☐
Advanced Level Social Skills	Rarely	Sometimes	Usually
1. Reading Body Language in Others (reading inflection, humor)	☐	☐	☐
2. Offering Assistance to Others (being kind, helpful, empathetic)	☐	☐	☐
3. Understanding Boundaries/Dealing with Feelings (ex:knowing who/when to hug)	☐	☐	☐
4. Problem Solving (The 5 Step Hierarchy © Penina Pearl Rybak MA/CCC-SLP)	☐	☐	☐
5. Stress Management (Self Soothing/Self Regulation re: mood- relaxing)	☐	☐	☐
6. Dealing with Losing During Play with Others	☐	☐	☐
7. Admitting Wrong Doing and Dealing with Mistakes	☐	☐	☐
8. Accepting Unfairness	☐	☐	☐

29

I also like teachers and parents to fill out the checklist before each report card/quarterly report, not just at the start and finish of the school year. The protocol contains social skills I would like a child with Autism/special needs to develop over the course of the school year. It is by no means an exhaustive list! It contains essential skills I believe these children need in order to make the socio-emotional transition from a Me to We. *The Socially Speaking™ Social Skills Assessment Protocol* addresses skills that the child may be missing, which are leading to disorientation to person/place/time and subsequent behavioral "triggers" and outbursts, because of the child's inability to:

☺ Get needs/wants met by making requests and/or expressing feelings.

☺ Make sense of the social rules and the environmental cues before him/her in class.

☺ Have successful play interactions with peers at home and in school.

☺ Engage in productive, meaningful social exchanges with adults and peers.

- Access another person's Theory of Mind, due to reduced empathy and perspective taking, and reduced flexibility when things don't go as planned or desired.

- Independently engage in self soothing behaviors to improve self regulation.

- Demonstrate flexibility and ability to transition from activity to activity.

Changes in YOUR Thinking Can Yield Results By:
Having fun and decreasing passivity by establishing rapport effectively.
Being developmental and sequential about assessment, goal planning, and delivery.
Being multi-sensory, to creatively appeal to child's interests/learning style.
Giving a common language and ground for child's team to collaborate about.

A Word About the Socially Speaking™ Assessment Protocol and iPad® App

It was designed by Amadeus Inc. in Boulder, Colorado and deployed to iTunes in May 2012. It's based on my *Socially Speaking™ Program's* Assessment Protocol (forms in Chapter 12). It is the only digital, developmental, play based, social skills evaluation that I know of, in the world, that:

• Has 2 "user friendly", developmentally *sequenced* checklists, to help parents, pediatricians, teachers, and therapists determine starting points for remediation.

• Has a built in, fully *customizable* lesson plan template for formulating IEP Goals and documenting materials to be used.

• Can be filled out quickly and repeatedly by the entire IEP team to update baseline data for more collaborative and methodical assessment of *functional* social communication.

• Can be easily *shared* i.e. exported as a PDF, to be filed elsewhere, as per HIPPA regulations.

✎ Goals of My App

• To assess social communication development in young children with Autism and special needs.

• To formulate and implement more precise, customized IEP goals, to facilitate self regulation and social communication skills in young children at risk.

• To enhance multidisciplinary collaboration for the child in need of behavior management and social skills strategies.

✎ Solutions My App Provides to the Child's Team

• The *Socially Speaking™ App* provides an easy, succinct and visual way to assess and determine "missing pieces of the puzzle" with regard to the young child's social skills development, play skills development, and self regulation skills.

• The *Socially Speaking™ App* ties the child's current level of behavioral/social skills functioning directly to the future lesson plans aimed at increasing self regulation and social communication skills in young children with Autism and other special needs.

• *The Socially Speaking App™* allows the iPad® user to customize lesson plans with goals and graphics, to give the child's team common ground/language, better perspective and an easier time documenting future IEP goals (which are federally mandated each year for the child with special needs.)

Final Words:

Autism intervention at its core begins with the understanding that proactive intervention trumps crisis intervention. With that in mind, it gives direction to assess the child's readiness to learn, understanding of how the world works, and which coping mechanisms are in place. A functional, developmentally based and collaborative evaluation contains elements that reflect learned academic skills and learned self regulation skills. That's why I advocate for the use of both standardized and non-standardized, play based testing such as the *Socially Speaking™ Social Skills Assessment Protocol*. We need to gain insight into the child's overall outlook and memory banks. We need to determine how well the child performs when given familiar and unfamiliar tasks. We need to see how he/she manages the fluctuating orientation to person/place/time at any given time, without prompting.

We will then be able to pinpoint areas of strength and challenge, and determine practical, measurable, starting points for remediation. As a result, we can foster a more consistent, flexible and sequential performance. Then we can more age appropriately use "whole body learning" to target play, social communication and perspective taking skills. The *Socially Speaking™ Program* uses built in assessment to more organically and contextually shape the child's Theory of Mind, Body Awareness, Problem Solving and journey of transitioning from Me to We. It's difficult to address the child's ability to express feelings and engage in problem solving if we don't have a clear picture of that child's inner landscape.

Remember the Socially Speaking™ Assessment Process!

1. Early detection and intervention based on child observation (play) and a formalized team evaluation, using a variety of protocols, mine included.
2. Collaborative implementation of IEP Goals through methodically updating baseline data (re: behavior management, play skills development, missing developmental milestones, and splintered skills) and documentation, using a variety of protocols, mine included.
3. Integration of toys and tech in treatment to naturally, developmentally and seamlessly teach language, social, executive functioning and motor skills simultaneously.

Why Consider Using the Socially Speaking™ iPad® App for Assessment & Treatment Purposes?
Digital Evaluations Make Sense Environmentally and Financially
Digital Evaluations Can Be Customized and Stored in the Cloud
Digital Evaluations Can Be HIPPA Compliant
Digital Citizenship is a Skill for Both Educators and Students to Hone
Digital Documentation is a Hallmark of the iEra We're In Now

Materials for Your Toolbox

- <u>Key References</u>

Baker, Jed (2003). *Social Skills Training for Children and Adolescents with Asperger Syndrome and Social Communication Problems*. Shawnee, KS: Autism Apserger Publishing.

Barbera, Mary Lynch, and Rassmussen, Tracy (2007). *The Verbal Behavior Approach: How to Teach Children with Autism and Related Disorders*. Philadelphia, PA: Jessica Kingsley Publishers.

Chandler, Lynette, and Dahlquist, Carol (2009). *Functional Assessment: Strategies to Prevent and Remediate Challenging Behavior in School Settings, Third Edition*. Upper Saddle River, NJ: Prentice- Hall/Pearson Education.

Dawson, Peg, and Guare, Richard (2010). *Executive Skills in Children and Adolescents: A Practical Guide to Assessment and Intervention, Second Edition*. New York, NY: Guilford Press.

Goldstein, Sam et al (2009). *Assessment of Autism Spectrum Disorders*. New York, NY: Guilford Publications Inc.

Grandin, Temple (2005). *The Unwritten Rules of Social Relationships*. Arlington, TX: Future Horizons.

Greenspan, Stanley, and Weider, Serena (1998). *The Child with Special Needs: Encouraging Intellectual and Emotional Growth*. Cambridge, MA: Perseus Books Group.

Manela, Miriam. (2014). *The Parent-Child Dance: A Guide to Help You Understand and Shape Your Child's Behavior*. Passaic, NJ: OT Thrive Publishing.

Owens, Robert Jr. (2007). *Language Development; Seventh Edition*. Boston, MA: Allyn & Bacon.

Prelock, Patricia et al (2012). *Treatment of Autism Spectrum Disorders: Evidence-Based Intervention Strategies for Communication and Social Interactions*. Baltimore, MD: Paul H. Brookes Publishing Company.

Westby, Carol (2000). A Scale for Assessing Development of Children's Play. *Play Diagnosis and Assessment, Second Edition, 131-161*. New York, NY: Wiley Press.

Weiss, Mary Jane and Demiri, Valbona (2011). *Jumpstarting Communication Skills in Children with Autism: A Parents' Guide to Applied Verbal Behavior*. Bethesda, MD: Woodbine House.

Whitten, Elizabeth, Esteves, Kelli, and Woodrow, Alice (2009). *RTI Success: Proven Tools and Strategies for Schools and Classrooms*. Minneapolis, MN: Free Spirit Publishing Inc.

• <u>Key Links to Peruse</u>

http://bit.ly/1CFlvK5

http://bit.ly/1zFNmuI

http://bit.ly/18BeYVG

http://bit.ly/1A4VCEd

http://bit.ly/1vcIxYb

http://bit.ly/1LoqqmR

http://bit.ly/162n20R

http://bit.ly/1JRzjDJ

http://bit.ly/15ZAodo

http://bit.ly/1CivaIo

• <u>Key Concepts to Address</u>

Baseline Data, IEP, Goal Planning, Social Communication, Theory of Mind.

• <u>Key Toys to Use in Treatment</u>

Note: At this stage of treatment, the presented toys are either in keeping with the child's preferences (and are thus used to establish rapport and baseline data) or they are meant to correlate to specific test questions and/or visual stimuli (and are thus either familiar or unfamiliar to the child already). The toys may also serve behavioral purposes to promote delayed gratification, maintain attention and enhance compliance/ performance based on the child's Theory of Mind and learning style. Some toys can be introduced into the assessment situation to determine stimulability and help determine prognosis for progress. Each testing situation and context is unique, which is why I decided not to list specific toys here.

• <u>Key iPad® Apps to Use in Treatment (Besides the Socially Speaking™ iPad® App)</u>

☞ **For the Service Provider:** I recommend word processing and productivity apps (see app listing in Chapter 11) which can help with documentation of the evaluation such as Evernote and Notability with its built in mic for audio notes. I recommend Timer Apps (mentioned previously in the listing in Chapter 2) and misc. behavioral/visual support apps (mentioned previously in Chapter 4) to gain compliance and show a countdown to completion of evaluation and/or to a designated "break time". I also recommend entertaining and calming apps (that the child will find fun, not you!) which can be used as rewards (at regular intervals) to reinforce compliance, and which have a "to be continued feature" i.e. can be stopped in the middle to heighten anticipation and maintain participation and cooperation. I suggest using apps from these categories: music, storybook and video apps (ex: Abby Musical Puzzle, Trixie and Jinx Book, Crack the Books Apps and PBS KIDS Video). Remember to use apps which appeal to the child's preferences i.e. inner landscape and learning style. Finally, I recommend using a video-recording App if possible, such as the native Camera app that can provide a behavior sample as needed. Remember to consider collaboration with other members of the IEP team, including parents, by using the *Socially Speaking™ Assessment Protocol iPad® App* as part of the assessment process.

☞ **For the Child:** Limited interaction with the iPad® is recommended during official evaluations using standardized testing. The focus should be on the child's ability to manipulate those relevant and actual items correlating to the test questions, such as those found in the Preschool Language Scale 5, (PLS-5). There is also much to be gained by observing the child play with unfamiliar toys in the environment. Apps should thus only be used to establish rapport, reinforce compliance (give the child a chance to use a preferred App at regular intervals during testing-- see the apps listing in Chapter 4) and determine the need for further testing. Red flags may be raised re: executive functioning and fine motor skills based on cognition and dexterity i.e. how the child handles and navigates the iPad® user-interface. If you want to assess stimulability for specific goals, you may want to consider introducing specific iOS apps (see other listings in Chapters 1-3, 5, 8 and 9) to the child at the *end* of the evaluation, plus taking notes on preference and social communication overall performance for future reference re: goal planning and implementation. In those instances I really like additionally using apps such as Sago Mini Doodlecast and Art Maker, to get a speech/language sample and glean more information on the child.

Chapter 7:
<u>Assessment Part 2</u>-A Closer Look at Executive Functioning: Evaluation and
Treatment Within a Social Communication Framework

Anecdote

Max is an 8 year old gentle, shy, scholarly and serious little boy who loves to read,
tends to "daydream in class, take forever to complete chores at home" and tends
to mumble. He has a history of premature birth, delayed milestones, including
speech and bilateral mild conductive hearing loss due to chronic ear infections
requiring 3 myringotomy surgeries (tubes). He received various Early Intervention
services which really helped. He's back on my "radar" because his teachers want
him to repeat the grade next year. Despite being a rather sweet and eager to learn
youngster, Max is having both academic and social difficulty in school. His parents
requested that he be extensively evaluated by an outside team. I am part of that
evaluation team. The parents want to determine the need for related services,
possible need for medical intervention and try to rule out Autism. Their neighbors
have hinted that Max has Autism, and have given them all sorts of advice about the
need for speech therapy, occupational therapy, "medication to help Max
concentrate better" and how a gluten free diet is a "life saver". I was the first
one to ever mention the words "executive functioning" and "neuropsychological
evaluation" in regard to Max.

I was the first one to combine standardized testing protocols with non-
standardized, informal observation checklists to provide insight into behavior,
social communication skills and executive functioning skills. Here are the tools we
decided to use:
• The Socially Speaking™ Social Skills Assessment Protocol © 2010 by Penina Pearl
Rybak MA/CCC-SLP
• The Executive Functioning Skills Questionnaire Checklist for Parents and The
Parent Interview © 2010 by Peg Dawson EdD, and Richard Guare PhD
• The Executive Functioning Skills Questionnaire Checklist Semi-structured
Interview for Teachers © 2010 by Peg Dawson EdD, and Richard Guare PhD
• The Executive Functioning Skills Questionnaire Checklist for Students © 2010 by
Peg Dawson EdD, and Richard Guare PhD

I asked both parents and teachers to complete the checklists and return them to
me the same day. Max underwent formalized testing by various evaluators. I also
pulled all previous documentation and files to get a clearer picture of Max's prior

history and his level of functioning. My goal is to synthesize everything into a cohesive report. I intend to highlight areas of strength and weakness, particularly relating to social communication and executive functioning-- two areas which standardized educational/speech-language testing in young children don't consistently target. I intend to provide a more detailed "paper trail" for the other evaluators, especially for the neuropsychological evaluation I will recommend at a later date. My priority is to update baseline data and provide concrete recommendations and goals that the entire team can implement, with the full cooperation of both Max and his parents.

Strategy and Technique

What is Executive Functioning?

Executive Functioning essentially describes a set of cognitive abilities that control and regulate other abilities and behaviors. Executive Functioning is necessary for goal-directed behavior. This include the ability to initiate and stop actions, to monitor and change behavior as needed, and to plan future behavior when faced with novel tasks and situations. I wrote about this earlier. Why do we need to know about this?

The Importance of Consideration of Mental Age vs. Chronological Age

All evaluations in special education are meant to determine these puzzle pieces:

◉ Areas of strength and weakness

◉ The need for services and their mandated service delivery

◉ Starting points for remediation based on current level of functioning

That's why it's important to consider the child's mental age vs. chronological age when making decisions about the course of action to take re: behavior management and social skill building. Part of this includes the formulation of suggested IEP goals within the body of the documented evaluation. Part of this includes the recommendations made re: learning, after establishing baseline data based on the child's cognitive performance. IEP goals can then be methodically formulated from the findings, which can be integrated with my *Socially Speaking™ Lesson Plan Template* and my *Social Skills Goals Chart (Chapter 12)*.

It is becoming much more prevalent for service providers to make written recommendations re: treatment goals, as well as recommendations that the child be given additional evaluations. This can include other domains and disciplines; sometimes at a later date, such as neuropsychological evaluations to assess executive functioning skills. The rationale is that besides starting a "paper trail", it is "setting the stage" for the entire team to be simultaneously apprised and encouraged to understand all facets of treatment. This approach will provide increased awareness of the various environmental and neurological factors impacting on said treatment, including both delivery and performance.

Evaluation Endgame - A Bird's Eye View of Executive Functioning Skills

Anyone working on social skills with a child who has Autism should be concerned about current level of Executive Functioning skills at different stages of treatment. As I explained, Executive Functioning, a term coined by neuropsychologists, essentially describes a set of meta-cognitive abilities that control and regulate other abilities and behaviors. It enables us to sustain our focus, switch between tasks flexibly, inhibit (undesirable) responses and carry out actions in a sequential, organized fashion. Executive Functioning is necessary for goal-directed behavior, which is what socialization is all about. This includes the ability to initiate and stop actions, to monitor and change behavior as needed, as well as the ability to plan future behavior when faced with novel tasks and situations. It allows us to anticipate outcomes and adapt to changing situations, i.e. resiliency. It allows us to problem solve and negotiate when things don't go as planned. This is the pinnacle of social communication development, which so many of our children have difficulty achieving, let alone mastering.

We all know that our task as evaluators is to effect change and growth, so that there is a decrease in situation-specific learning, splintered carryover and inconsistent performance; these are three frequently used descriptions in special education evaluations and progress reports.

To do so, we need to adopt a team approach about EF. We need to stop thinking of Executive Functioning as the domain of neuropsychologists and psychologists alone. Speech-language pathologists, special education teachers, occupational therapists, and parents all need to collaboratively address Executive Functioning skills in a more practical and concrete manner, by "thinking outside the box". Start by changing the way we assess both Executive Functioning, and social communication proficiency. How? Through Play. And, through the introduction of two non-standardized assessment protocols that can be used in conjunction with other formalized evaluations:

• *The Socially Speaking™ Social Skills Assessment Protocol* © 2010 by Penina Pearl Rybak MA/CCC-SLP, iPad® App launched in 2012
• *The Executive Functioning Skills Questionnaire Checklists (for Parents, for Teachers, and for Students)* © 2010 by Peg Dawson EdD, and Richard Guare PhD

It is beyond the scope of this book to provide detailed information on what exactly is targeted in a neuropsychological evaluation. Let me provide some insight into implications for social communication proficiency and how to more effectively set the stage for treatment. Understanding what executive functioning skills are in play will help both the child and the educator take the "driver's seat" as needed, at different junctures of the therapy regimen.

Evaluating Social Skills Sheds Light on Executive Functioning Competence

Informal assessment of play skills has proven to be a valuable contribution to the overall evaluation process for social skills, involving parental collaboration and a shift in focus re: Real Time outcomes and performance. Informal observation of play skills can shed light on a young child's developmental, sequential acquisition of specific neuro-cognitive and psycho-social milestones needed to develop Executive Functioning, social skills proficiency, and literacy skills later on. These are some common areas to assess:

• Early Cognitive Based Social Skills (ex: joint attention, communicative intent)

• Early Communication Based Social Skills (ex: initiation of greetings, requesting help)

• Early Play Based Social Skills (ex: social smile, object permanence)

• Introductory Social Skills (ex: active listening, verbal rejection)

• Intermediate Social Skills (ex: asking questions, transitioning)

• Advanced Social Skills (ex: expressing feelings appropriately, problem solving)

Play Development Fosters Both Social Communication and Executive Functioning Competence

Executive Functioning skills can be compared to the train tracks underneath the train of social skills, on which all human beings sit, and use to cross over into each other's "zones". Its activation is the brain's way of making sure that a child's social skills "performance" happens without a hitch. Executive Functioning competence involves taking one's TOM (Theory of Mind) i.e. perspective/empathy, and merging that with episodic memory (the ability to recall one's actions and vocabulary associated with those actions), to formulate intent and a course of action, make good choices, adjust direction/

trajectory in a split second and be resilient (bounce back, adapt, laugh it off, etc.) when things don't go as planned.

Each area of social communication proficiency that we target in special education, especially in Autism intervention, contains categories and skills that correlate to these specific areas of Executive Functioning:

• Response Inhibition
• Emotional Control
• Task Initiation
• Organization
• Flexibility
• Goal-Directed Persistence
• Working Memory
• Sustained Attention
• Planning/Prioritization of Goals
• Time Management
• Metacognition

All of these categories of EF skills have readiness indicators, which can be addressed by facilitating both receptive and expressive language skills in children with Autism. How? Through play! Play bridges gaps between a child's comprehension of the rules, roles, and vocabulary of his/her environment, and imitation and execution of them. Play bridges gaps between a child's readiness to learn and actual performance, with the help of intact Executive Functioning skills. Play thus helps children nurture and hone these skills, preparing them for future "whole body" academic tasks such as reading and writing, and socio-emotional tasks such as tolerating delayed gratification, easily transitioning from a Me to a We by sharing, turn taking, and expressing feelings verbally (instead of acting out), and negotiating and problem solving (instead of fighting).

"Play helps to naturally and cognitively bridge gaps between a child's readiness to learn and actual performance."

Methodical Goal Planning Targets Both Social Communication and Executive Functioning Competence

A child's generalization of learned skills hinges on the team's ability to accurately assess current level of functioning and then pinpoint goals and concrete lesson plans/materials to teach those goals. These goals are important for a child's successful adaptation and performance in real-life situations. Information thus gleaned from both assessment of social skills and play development allows the team to understand the child's level of executive functioning, thereby changing both the nature and the trajectory of treatment.

Methodical goal planning is after all, truly about facilitating the child's ability to initiate and complete tasks, in a timely manner, and to persevere; intra-personally and inter-personally, in the face of life's challenges. So that the child grows and blossoms. So that the child becomes a Me and then a We. Isn't that what Executive Functioning Skills are meant to do?

Life, and one's environment, can be unpredictable at best, and one must react accordingly. Executive Functioning is thus vital to a person's ability to recognize the significance of unexpected situations and to make alternative plans quickly, when unusual events arise and interfere with normal routines. In this way, Executive Functioning contributes to success in work and school and allows people to manage the stresses of daily life. It also enables people to inhibit inappropriate behaviors.

That is why children with poor Executive Functioning, due to cognitive and neurological deficits, such as Autism Spectrum Disorders (ASD), often have difficulty interacting with other people in a socially appropriate manner. They have difficulty with Theory of Mind (TOM) and transitioning, because of underdeveloped neuro-cognitive processes such as:

• Flexibility

• Emotional Control

• Time Management

• Metacognition

Implications for Assessment and Treatment of Social Communication Proficiency

The implications are such that children with ASD, who usually need intervention to develop Executive Functioning Skills on their own, can have difficulty with self regulation and social communication proficiency due to:

❈ Disorientation to person/place/time
❈ Splintered play skills development
❈ Delayed problem solving (especially negotiation) skills, since there is difficulty transitioning from thinking as a Me instead of a We in communal/group situations

"Social communication proficiency is the most important skill we can teach children with Autism."

The practical implications here are that documentation and implementation of goals for these children need to practically and developmentally account for the connection between Executive Functioning and social communication proficiency. It is time for everyone on the team to "think outside the box" about social communication proficiency. It's the most important skill we can teach children with Autism! It is time to be more accountable about facilitating progress and generalization of learned skills by adopting a more methodical, collaborative approach to assessment and treatment.

Sample Executive Functioning Evaluation With Implications for Social Skills Performance

As you read in the anecdote above, Max was evaluated at his parents' request. I used both formal and informal testing protocols to gain a deeper insight into his behavior, social communication and executive functioning skills. It was important for me to document that Max was not a functional verbal communicator, despite having intact receptive language skills and intact cognition. It was not my place as a school based (educational model, not medical model) speech-language pathologist to rule out Autism or provide neuropsychological testing. It was my place to observe Max at play and in conversation, document his answers to my questions and his overall demeanor and pinpoint areas of strength and weakness re: social communication and behavioral performance. All of this would indicate the need for further testing by medical professionals, which is a decision that his parents would need to make.

My approach involved combining both standardized and non-standardized measures to "paint a picture" of Max-- his inner landscape, his current level of functioning and his comprehension of how his world "works". I used the formal *Test of Auditory Comprehension of Language 3* (TACL-3) and *Test of Problem Solving*. I also used the informal *Socially Speaking™ Social Skills Assessment Protocol* (2 checklists) and *Executive Functioning Skills Questionnaire Checklists* (3 checklists) © 2010 by Peg Dawson EdD, and Richard Guare PhD. I needed to scaffold my baseline data and get concrete, practical results. I needed to get an overall picture of areas of strength and weakness and pinpoint starting points for treatment. I needed to synthesize my findings using my formalized/ standardized testing and my informal observations of current behavior and social communication skills.

Here is an excerpt of those findings, from my written evaluation (with changed names):

Test Results:

Both parents completed *The Executive Functioning Skills Questionnaire Checklist for Parents and The Parent Interview* © 2010 by Peg Dawson EdD, and Richard Guare PhD. Results indicated these Executive Functioning Strengths: "Response Inhibition", "Working Memory", "Sustained Attention" (except for writing tasks, possibly due to graphomotor difficulty and tendency to fatigue easily), "Planning" and "Organization". The Brachs reported these Executive Functioning Weaknesses: "Emotional Control", "Flexibility" and "Time Management". They did not indicate that "Task Initiation" is a real issue at home, although they reported that it seems to be an issue in school. They also indicated difficulty with "Metacognition" (i.e. following directions, requesting help and problem solving), "controlling feelings when upset" and "writing things down", as needed. They indicated that "getting started with homework" and "turn taking" have gotten better.

Both parents also completed *The Socially Speaking™ Social Skills Assessment Checklists* © 2010 by Penina Pearl Rybak MA/CCC-SLP. Results indicated that Max rarely expresses his feelings verbally in an age appropriate manner, does not demonstrate verbal rejection skills (expressing displeasure verbally instead of "acting out"), has moderate difficulty transitioning and being resilient when things don't "go his way" (bouncing back), has mild difficulty reading body language and tone of voice in others, has mild difficulty with problem solving in social situations and needs some help with stress management.

Thomas Getty and Shirley Deere, the classroom teachers, completed *The Executive Functioning Skills Questionnaire Checklist Semi-structured Interview for Teachers* © 2010 by Peg Dawson EdD, and Richard Guare PhD. Results indicated moderate Executive Dysfunction in these areas: "Metacognition" (i.e. following directions and problem solving), "Task Initiation", "Follow Through" and "Time Management", (i.e. tardiness, starting and completing work on time), "Goal Directed Persistence" and "Sustained Attention" (i.e. difficulty with writing assignments and asking for help as needed--from teachers and from peers during both learning activities and recess), in addition to "Emotional Control" and "Flexibility" (i.e. expressing feelings, questioning and getting "stuck" during changes in class routine, plus problem solving).

Max and this examiner collaborated and completed *The Executive Functioning Skills Questionnaire Checklist for Students* © 2010 by Peg Dawson EdD, and Richard Guare PhD. Results indicated that Max in now aware of and self motivated to get help through therapy. He knows that he has several Executive Functioning Strengths: "Response Inhibition", "Working Memory", "Sustained Attention" (except for writing tasks, possibly due to graphomotor difficulty and tendency to fatigue easily), "Planning", and "Organization". Results also indicated three areas of moderate Executive Skills Dysfunction: "Emotional Control", and "Flexibility", (which Max is aware of and took responsibility for) and "Time Management", which Max does not seem to be aware of, but the other informants are.

These findings suggest moderate Executive Dysfunction in the areas of "Emotional Control", "Flexibility" and "Time Management". Results also suggest mild Executive Dysfunction in a) "Task Initiation", which may be situation specific (only in school) and have a psycho-social (emotional) component due to noticeable anxiety and b) "Metacognition" due to noticeable auditory processing and graphomotor (sensory processing) difficulties. These areas of weakness appear to be contributing to persistent social skills difficulties. This is especially seen for those social communication skills involving requesting help, expressing displeasure verbally, problem solving and being able to transition/be resilient when there are changes in routine, or unanticipated/ unwanted outcomes to situations Max finds himself in (both at home and in school). Max is increasingly aware of his difficulties and appears to be increasingly self motivated and eager to work on them.

Key Test Indications:

1. Receptive Lexicon is an area of overall strength and appears to be above age level.
2. Auditory Processing Skills seem to be 1½ years delayed.
3. Verbal Reasoning Skills seem to be 2 years delayed and impact upon expressive communication skills.
4. Beginning Problem Solving and Inferencing are areas of real strength and appear to be above age level.
5. Advanced Problem Solving (involving Theory of Mind and Preventive Action Thinking) is an area of weakness and is delayed by 6 months.

Key Findings:

1. The receptive lexicon (understanding vocabulary, concepts, and grammar) is now age appropriate and even extensive!

2. The ability to visually notice small details of things in pictures (not people's faces) and determine potential problems and their causes seem to be above age level, and is a real strength!

3. Max's auditory processing skills are still lagging, as evidenced by the 1½ year delay, and remain an area of real weakness, which may impact upon future academic skills

4. Max's verbal language skills are almost within normal limits. However, the *quality* of overall verbal output, and overall pragmatic skills, is affected by a 2 year delay in verbal reasoning skills involving humor (facial affect, physical and linguistic absurdities) and perspective (Theory of Mind-TOM), a 6 month delay in "preventive action style abstract thinking" involving reading social cues and body language/facial expressions in others, and difficulty with negotiating/verbalizing alternative outcomes when there is a problem. (e.g. Max had difficulty interpreting photos of car accidents and discussing ways to handle a black-out in the neighborhood.)

5. A situation specific, concrete sense of humor, and difficulty with empathizing and viewing another point of view (carryover re: empathy AKA Theory of Mind-TOM). Informal observation (see Appendix), using data recorded from the informal assessment of Max's sense of humor, ability to register and interpret facial affect and "put himself in another person's shoes" (TOM) , suggests significant difficulty sizing up real life situations and people's facial expressions (e.g. Max was given pictures of a boy crying and holding his hand over his eyes due to an empty cup...Max said the boy "was trying to sleep" and did not comment on the facial expression at all).

Notes:

These difficulties affect overall ability and response time when reacting in an emotionally appropriate, more mature manner to social cues around him. This evaluator saw a pattern where Max noticed many details of objects, but did not seem to consistently "tune in" to the person's face and depicted emotions. The exceptions were photos that really interested him, due to previous episodic memory and being able to self reference, such as those of children fighting, (he then really studied the facial affect and frequently commented how much the "boy must hate school and wishes he could stay home") and younger children/little babies getting into mischief and/or getting dirty (he then age appropriately registered facial affect, context and humor for these situations, and enjoyed discussing the mischievous quality of each photo). This all seems to indicate situation specific learning in this regard. However, with time and practice, it is felt that Max can "tune into" a person's body language, store the "visual mapping" details in episodic memory and learn when to access it for future ability to "size up" a social situation/context, and act accordingly.

Max is still exhibiting episodes of "telegraphic speech" i.e. short phrases instead of full sentences, which is especially noticeable when he is being challenged and is upset/confused etc. He is also exhibiting continued difficulty with reading comprehension tasks involving answering questions given in multiple clusters, and retaining multiple oral directions in order and executing them motorically. He still demonstrates a noticeable lag i.e. a Latency Response Time (LRT) as evidenced by difficuty following this multiple step direction: "Cut up all the fruit pictures, paste them onto the paper, put away the scissors, and go get a cup". It appears that possible auditory processing and sensory integration/processing (alertness levels, tendency to fatigue easily) may be contributing factors.

Summary and Impressions:

Max is a terrific 8 year old boy, with a gentle, sweet, serious, cautious, anxious and curious personality. He has a lively mind and visual learning style, and is quick to notice visual details of objects in his environment. Max has a history of premature birth, globally delayed development and academic and social difficulties in school. This is now resulting in increased episodes of "tuning out", "mumbling", "telegraphic speech", anxiety and behavioral outbursts. Self esteem is steadily decreasing, due to episodes of bullying/teasing in class. Max now passively resists attending school. His teachers report fluctuating moods and attention span, and concern about "how to handle" him. His parents report increasing shyness/withdrawal and increasing difficulty with resilience when "things don't go his way" (bouncing back). Max is now reporting that he feels "helpless in school, especially at recess".

This examiner feels that Max is sometimes bored and very unhappy in his current class placement. Max in some ways appears to be more mature, and has a richer vocabulary and understanding of concepts, than his peers. A promotion in grade, with different peers, may be very helpful at this time and really needs to be considered. It should be noted that when asked about his wandering attention in class, Max told this examiner that he "gets it the first time and thinks about something else when the teacher repeats it several more times for others.....hearing things repeated again and again to me makes me very nervous....just like being called on in class for the answer and knowing that those kids are laughing or waiting for me to fail".

This evaluation reveals intact receptive language skills that are not consistently seen, due to moderate Executive Skills Dysfunction in the areas of "Emotional Control", "Flexibility", and "Time Management" and a 1½ year delay in auditory processing skills. Max's visual learning style and strong visuo-spatial skills are currently partially compensating for his delay. He is aware of his difficulty with all the above stated Executive Functioning skills, except for "Time Management", possibly due to his anxiety and moderate auditory processing delay. Max scored above age level in terms of receptive lexicon, understanding "why"? questions/inferencing, and exploring/planning solutions to problems. His overall receptive language skills appear to be an area of relative strength, and appear to be commensurate with his current level of cognitive functioning.

Max's current expressive language skills are less intact and not fully functional, despite adequate speech intelligibility and verbal vocabulary/grammar skills. This evaluator is concerned about the evident 2 year pragmatic language (social functional behavior) disorder, which is the greatest area of challenge at present. It is affecting the *quality* of overall verbal output and socialization with others, especially in his current classroom, where he is now bullied.

This evaluator's current findings reveal moderately delayed pragmatic/social-emotional competency. The recent episodes of "telegraphic speech" and "mumbling", fluctuating detachment re: facial expressions in others, and the situation specific, concrete sense of humor, all appear to partially stem from increasing anxiety and underdeveloped social skills (i.e. transitioning skills, negotiating skills, verbal rejection skills, and verbal inferencing/reasoning skills). These areas all seem to be rooted in possible difficulty with Sensory Integration, Executive Functioning ("Time Management", "Emotional Control", and "Flexibility") and perspective taking (Theory of Mind-TOM).

This results in the inconsistent ability to meet deadlines, interpret body language and emotions/expressions in others ("Social Blindness"), empathize and negotiate with others during a problem solving situation, understand and use both physical and linguistic humor in an age appropriate manner and understand and verbalize ways to avoid problems (as well as change outcomes that are undesirable and/or unexpected). This then impacts upon Max's ability to easily read social cues in context, and quickly "size up" a social situation.

Max therefore does not always behave accordingly, and in a timely manner. He does not verbally resolve conflicts with peers, deal with changes in routine well and engage in stress management on his own. The overall outcome of these growing social difficulties is that Max has become a much more tense, moody and frequently sad child. While he is more self aware, he remains a "slow moving", frequently tardy and often bewildered child, as to why he is bullied and "runs out of time". Max presents with much lower self esteem and resiliency, since the last time he was seen for speech therapy in Early Intervention (see file). This is of tremendous concern and has now been discussed at length with both of his parents (see file). It is felt that the prognosis for improvement is quite favorable, given parental cooperation, Max's cooperative nature and visual learning style and the current overall findings.

Recommendations:

1. Consider both individual and group speech-language therapy to address needs.
2. Consider a neuropsychological evaluation to be completed in time for the next Triennial-Annual IEP Review, to further assess Executive Functioning and Social-Emotional Competency.
3. Consider an OT evaluation as soon as possible, to assess sensory integration and graphomotor skills, which can impact upon overall Time Management and Latency Response Time (LRT).
4. Consider psychological counseling as soon as possible, for both Max and his parents, to address his self esteem, high anxiety, outbursts and tension resulting from being bullied in class.
5. Consider a complete audiological evaluation to update baseline data, and rule out Central Auditory Processing Dysfunction.
6. Consider parent collaboration with school administration re: change in class placement to alleviate bullying (new peers).

7. Consider parental advocacy re: modifying the learning environment in school, and subsequent *management* of the noticeable auditory processing difficulty. Consider parental collaboration and cooperation with the teachers re: these management strategies for improved productivity:

 a) "preferential seating" i.e. change Max's seat closer to the teacher's face for easier "auditory closure".
 b) "enrichment" of the lesson/school curriculum using <u>visual</u> supports.
 c) "post-teaching" i.e. tutoring and reviewing with Max what was taught that day, and continuous consultation between teachers/therapists re: reading comprehension and social communication skills.
 d) "improving the auditory loop" i.e. minimizing background noise, breaking down difficult paragraphs when reading/translating and encouraging Max to ask teacher and peers for help (If the teacher "sets the tone", Max will endure less fighting/ teasing. The teacher will thus demonstrate that he does not tolerate bullying. Furthermore, assigning a rotating "class buddy" can help Max with socialization opportunities that are structured, and afford him a "checks and balances re: time management, without belittling him. This can become a fun team effort, which can be very helpful and reinforcing.)

<u>Therapy Goals:</u>

1. To increase expressive communication skills: *verbal reasoning*/inferencing skills (reading body language/facial expressions and social cues) and sense of humor: explaining physical and linguistic absurdities. (This will address the Executive Function of "Metacognition".)
2. To increase social communication skills: *problem solving* skills: negotiating, accepting changes and outcomes of problematic situations.(This will also help with transitioning/resiliency, and planning how to avoid problems AKA "preventive action style thinking". This will address the Executive Function of "Time Management", "Emotional Control", "Flexibility", and "Metacognition".)
3. To increase verbal conversational skills: *verbal rejection* skills when faced with undesirable/unwanted situations (This will also help with facilitating expressing of feelings instead of outbursts, and the Executive Function of "Emotional Control".)
4. To increase transitioning and self monitoring: ability to use *compensatory strategies* (e.g. external rehearsal/self talk, visual imagery, visual supports, and requesting help) to improve Executive Functioning for: "Emotional Control", "Time Management", and "Flexibility".

Final Words

Starting points for remediation of social communication challenges for children with Executive Skills Dysfunction (which may or may not accompany Autism) needs to be more sequential and holistic. Why? To counteract splintered skills acquisition and situation specific learning. It thus involves so much more than a Behavior Plan to foster compliance and self regulation. The incorporation of developmental, methodical and collaborative assessment to determine goals to facilitate practical Executive Functioning skills is still a missing piece of the puzzle of intervention that more of us need to be aware of. Informal evaluations to update baseline data, through user-friendly checklists such as the *The Socially Speaking™ Social Skills Assessment Protocol* and the *The Dawson-Guare Executive Functioning Skills Questionnaire Checklists* can be beneficial for the whole team! It allows the team members to share common language, common goals and get "on the same page" regarding treatment. This in turn can lead to more consistent generalization of learned skills and more consistent behavior management and social communication proficiency overall.

It is often difficult to rule out Executive Skills Dysfunction in standardized educational and speech-language evaluation protocols. It is also often difficult to therapeutically and developmentally address them if one does not have adequate baseline data re: social communication competency. This baseline data is needed to determine areas of real strength and weakness and to pinpoint starting points for remediation. It is also needed to synthesize concrete goals with creative, more abstract lesson plans for "teachable moments" that really "stick" and get generalized.

That's why I'm a big advocate of parents and educators joining forces to co-evaluate and:
• Lay the groundwork for collaborative intervention that *functionally* addresses both social and executive skills (i.e. targets the *whole* child, not just fragments of skills such as intelligibility, reading skills, or working memory).
• Provide a "paper trail" of concrete observations about *behavior* that can really help medical professionals with their evaluations later on (neurologist, neuropsychologist etc.). It is becoming more widespread for children with learning differences, particularly Autism, to be given neurological and neuropsychological evaluations at some point in life, before considering vocational choices and life after school.
• Implement specific social communication goals which will indirectly, methodically and developmentally target specific areas of executive functioning as well.
• Develop a safety protocol re: wandering, for the child with executive functioning impairment to follow, to counteract frequent poor judgement and problem solving difficulty. Wandering is a real concern, especially for children with Autism. It must be addressed by the *entire* IEP team using both a proactive (environmental modifications, alert protocols etc.) and behavioral (Social Stories, visual supports-My Rules etc.) approach to increase self awareness and self monitoring of surroundings and performance.

Suggested Resources and Links

http://bit.ly/1AXdIrh

http://bit.ly/17iqBjs

http://bit.ly/1F02MI2

http://bit.ly/17xGgeG

http://bit.ly/1CQyEz3

Materials for Your Toolbox

- <u>Key References</u>

Barkley, Russell (2012) *Executive Functions: What They Are, How They Work, and Why They Evolved*. New York, NY: Guilford Press.

Cannon, Lynn et al (2011). *Unstuck and On Target!: An Executive Function Curriculum to Improve Flexibility for Children with Autism Spectrum Disorders, Research Edition*. Baltimore, MD: Paul Brookes Publishing

Cooper-Khan, Joyce, and Dietzel, Laurie (2008). *Late, Lost, and Unprepared: A Parents' Guide to Helping Children with Executive Functioning*. Bethesda, MD: Woodbine House.

Dawson, Peg, and Guare, Richard (2009). *Smart But Scattered: The Revolutionary Executive Skills Approach to Helping Kids Reach Their Potential*. New York, NY: Guilford Press.

Dawson, Peg, and Guare, Richard (2010). *Executive Skills in Children and Adolescents: A Practical Guide to Assessment and Intervention, Second Edition*. New York, NY: Guilford Press.

Densmore, Ann (2007). *Helping Children with Autism Become More Social: 76 Ways to Use Narrative Play*. Westport, CT: Praeger Publishing.

Grandin, Temple (2005). *The Unwritten Rules of Social Relationships*. Arlington, TX: Future Horizons.

Hirsh-Pasek, Kathy, and Michnik Golinkoff, Roberta (2003). *Einstein Never Used Flash Cards: How Our Children Really Learn, and Why They Need to Play More and Memorize Less*. New York: NY, Rodale Books.

Kaufman, Christopher (2010). *Executive Function in the Classroom: Practical Strategies for Improving Performance and Enhancing Skills for All Students*. Baltimore, MD: Paul Brookes Publishing.

Kenworthy, Laura et al (2014). *Solving Executive Function Challenges: Simple Ways to Get Kids with Autism Unstuck and on Target.* Baltimore, MD: Paul Brookes Publishing.

Levine, Mel (2003). *The Myth of Laziness.* New York, NY: Simon & Shuster.

Meltzer, Lynn (2010). *Promoting Executive Function in the Classroom: What Works for Special-Needs Learners.* New York, NY: Guilford Press.

Moraine, Paula (2012). *Helping Students Take Control of Everyday Executive Functions: The Attention Fix.* Philadelphia, PA: Jessica Kingsley Publishers.

Owens, Robert Jr. (2007). *Language Development; Seventh Edition.* Boston, MA: Allyn & Bacon.

Whitten, Elizabeth, Esteves, Kelli, and Woodrow, Alice (2009). *RTI Success: Proven Tools and Strategies for Schools and Classrooms.* Minneapolis, MN: Free Spirit Publishing Inc.

Yeager, Marcie, and Yeager, Daniel (2013). *Executive Function & Child Development.* New York, NY: Norton and Company.

• Key Links to Peruse

http://abt.cm/1BTFHUA

http://bit.ly/1BTFJvV

http://u.org/1uW6FbO

http://bit.ly/1EF3Iou

http://bit.ly/1KaiDaD

http://bit.ly/1z94L86

http://bit.ly/1DciiSU

http://bit.ly/16wenUP

http://bit.ly/1HXReLf

http://bit.ly/1CukvtR

* Honorable Mention:

http://bit.ly/1EF4n9J

http://bit.ly/1zdK7Zr

http://bit.ly/1HXSzBY

http://bit.ly/1Fo81aL

http://bit.ly/1Lj1jAM

• Key Concepts to Address

Executive Functioning, Problem Solving, Transitioning, Play, Theory of Mind, Resiliency, Neuropsychology

• Key Toys to Use in Treatment

Note: Executive Functioning skills cannot be evaluated and/or taught in isolation. They are learned gradually and concretely within the context of language and social communication, starting when the child explores his/her world through play. At this stage of treatment, which is really the assessment phase, the presented toys are either

★ In keeping with the child's preferences (and are thus used to establish rapport and baseline data).

★ Meant to correlate to specific test questions and/or visual stimuli such as those in the Preschool Language Scale -5 (and are thus either familiar or unfamiliar to the child already).

★ Serving a behavioral purposes to promote delayed gratification, maintain attention and enhance compliance/performance, based on the child's inner landscape i.e. Theory of Mind and learning style.

• Key iPad® Apps to Use in Treatment

☞ **For the Service Provider:** The *Socially Speaking™ iPad® App* is of course recommended to dovetail with other assessments and to gain insight from the rest of the IEP team. I also recommend using specific timer, entertainment and language development screener apps, to further update baseline data and pinpoint areas of strength and challenge. Here's a suggested sampling to try:

☞ *Timers* are suggested to countdown to completion of evaluation or to a designated "break time" such as Pie Time, VisTimer Free, Giant Timer, Best Sand Timer, Aida Reminder, and 30/30.

☞ *Planners for High Functioning Children* can help break down tasks, stay on task, remember tasks and more, such as Visual Schedule Planner, Picture Scheduler, Functional Planning System, Beep Me, and Nudge.

☞ *Gaming/Entertainment Apps* such as music, storybook, or video apps to maintain compliance and attention such as these which were previously mentioned: Melody Touch Lite, StoryBots® Tap & Sing, Monsters, Toca Band, Trixie and Jinx, The Monster At the End of This Book, misc. Dr. Seuss Books, iTube List, Mineflix Free, and Kids Videos.

☞ *Language Evaluation/Auditory Processing Screener Apps* to gain insight into Executive Functioning such as: Sago Mini Doodlecast,, Super Duper Data Tracker, Receptive Language Assessment, Common Core Early Language Screener, Basic Concepts Skills Screener, Squirrel Story Narrative Assessment, School of Multi-Step Directions, Processing Pow-Wow, Question Builder for iPad® by Mobile Education Store, and More Fun with Directions HD.

☞ **For the Child:** In truth, limited interaction with the iPad® is recommended during this portion of the standardized evaluation as well. However, that may change as time goes on, advances in tech continue and more and more evaluations are administered via iPad®. The evaluation's focus should of course be on the child's ability to manipulate those actual items correlating to the test questions, as well as unfamiliar toys in the environment. The iPad® should thus only be used initially to update baseline data, to establish rapport and to reinforce compliance (give the child a chance to use a preferred App at regular intervals during testing). When the rest of the formalized testing has been completed, the evaluator can begin to determine the need for further testing of executive functioning , based on how the child handles and navigates the user-interface, both of which will provide insight into current level of performance after all. In that situation, matching an App to a child's learning style, preference and cognitive level will be needed in order to determine stimulability and prognosis. Please see other App listings in previous chapters for further suggestions.

☞ *Executive Functioning Practice:* Sago Mini Doodlecast, Art Maker, Draw in 3D, Scribble Press, My Story, Show and Tell, Can Plan, Faces iMake- Right Brain Creativity, Create a Car Lite, ZoLO Lite, PlayWorld- House LITE, Recycling Workshop Free, Easy Studio, Draw and Tell HD, Trucks and Things That Go Jigsaw Puzzle Free, Nick Jr. Draw & Play HD, Toontastic, StoryMaker Free, Stick Around, Scratch Jr., Build a Ship, Car Wash, Cut the Rope, iMazing, Minecraft, and Superzaic- Kids' Mosaic Activities.

☞ *Executive Functioning/Productivity Apps for Older, Higher Functioning Students Who Read:* Evernote, Notability, Plan It/Do It/Check It Off, Grafio, 30/30, Forgetful, HabitRPG, Dragon Dictation, YouNote!, Minecraft, Working Memory App-Quizlet, Junganew Herd of Sounds "S" and Crack the Books Apps.

Chapter 8:
<u>Treatment Part 1</u>-The Importance of Play: The Precursor to Social Communication and Pre-Literacy Development

Anecdote

Emily is a cute, mischievous, highly distractible, fully verbal 4 year old girl with a diagnosis of Autism, Sensory Processing Dysfunction, and a seizure disorder for which she takes medication. She was hospitalized for an extended period at birth and spent much time there during the first year of life due to illness and complications from emergency brain surgery. Emily thus craves structure and routine, dislikes loud noise and bright lights and only tolerates smooth textures and bland, soft, pureed foods like yogurt or mashed potatoes. She doesn't like to try new things or to be challenged, and doesn't like to play with new toys, let alone with other children. When upset, she can be rude, and when really upset, she can hit and/or drop to the floor. She has responded well to early intervention, which she has received in the past. She received a home based therapy regimen which includes 2 hours a week of Verbal Behavior Therapy, speech therapy twice a week individually for a half hour and one feeding consult with parent, plus occupational therapy three times a week for a half hour, all with certified service providers from the nearby school district.

Emily appears to be a visual learner who gravitates towards visual stimuli,such as photos, picture games, videos, and of course, the iPad®. She will work for these items which double as teaching materials and reinforcers for good behavior. Her first introduction to special education was an evaluator who told her parents to consider ABA and discrete trials for behavior management, and think about social skills groups when she's older.

Emily is assigned to my caseload when she moves to the district, and is now eligible for enrollment in a center-based therapeutic preschool class with related services. Her parents tell me they want me to only use ABA and "group play time" to help her self regulate and become more social. After careful observation and assessment, I see that Emily may be functionally verbal and may have mastered some early pre-literacy skills such as matching and sorting by shape/color/size but her overall generalization, especially re: comprehension and social skills is significantly below age level. So are her play skills and her overall fine motor skills. A team meeting is held with parents/providers to discuss combining ABA/VBT techniques with Floortime™ to fill in gaps and foster carryover of all IEP goals.

Strategy and Technique

The Importance of Play

"Play is the vehicle through which children reveal and reenact the rules of their world."

Play is the vehicle through which children reveal and reenact the rules of their world. Play is the medium through which practice, role play, and self-directed actions enable them to make sense and work through the rules and roles they see around them, some of which may be hard to live with-- especially if they have Autism. Play allows children to naturally and methodically develop social communication skills by learning about Body Awareness, Causality, Emotional Attunement and resiliency. Play fosters Self Concept, emotional engagement with others and the ability to self regulate. It facilitates the child's sequential understanding of the environment (i.e. the structure and routine, rules and expectations of said environment). It provides social referencing through empathy (i.e. it integrates emotional and cognitive development through perspective, AKA Theory of Mind). That is why I advocate for the use of both Applied Behavioral Analysis (ABA) and Verbal Behavior Therapy (VBT) principals along with the Floortime™ Technique in treatment. The use of both foster Theory of Mind and social communication, which can be learned more methodically and naturally, while taking the child's inner landscape and lead into consideration.

It is beyond the scope of this book to delve into the benefits and implementation of ABA/VBT and Floortime™, and overall play development milestones in neurotypical children vs. those with Autism. The reader is invited to peruse this chapter's suggested reading list for more information. I do want to share some salient points re: play and social communication development, and their interrelationship. The reader is invited to learn more from the recommended bibliography in this chapter and from a careful Google Search. Play development, unlike other areas of cognitive development, shares six unique traits, which are listed in Janet Moyle's *The Excellence of Play:*

Six Aspects To Play:
1. It is enjoyable
2. It lacks extrinsic goals
3. It is spontaneous and voluntary
4. It has an element of pretend ("make believe")
5. It requires active participation
6. It facilitates development of self regulation

In the excellently written and easily understood *Einstein Never Used Flashcards: Why Children Need to Play More and Memorize Less*, I found an interesting hierarchy of intelligence re: stages of play. It correlates to the hierarchy of my Socially Speaking™ Program: Body Awareness, Expressing Feelings and Problem Solving. Here it is:

<u>Developing Intelligence-The Hierarchy:</u>
1. Cause& Effect
2. Conservation (quantity)
3. Inferencing
    ❖Creativity
    ❖Independent thinking
4. Self Concept
    ❖ Delayed gratification
    ❖ Social skills (pragmatics)
    ❖ Imitation
    ❖ Empathy
    ❖ Self regulation (self monitoring)

The Truth About Play and Childhood

"Play is often talked about as if it were a relief from serious learning. But for children play is serious learning. Play is really the work of childhood."
– Mr. (Fred) Rogers, PBS

This specialized work of childhood can be particularly difficult for children with Autism. These children need to make sense of their experiences, formulate episodic memory and build social skills. They are enduring more transitions i.e. a busier day and more structured tasks to complete, than previous years, affecting their overall orientation to person/place/time, which we need to monitor.

We thus need to be vigilant about putting play back into daily routines in special education schools and homes of children with Autism and special needs. Why? Why target play skills in a population that may not "take to it" naturally, may start to "stim" on parts of a toy, or may gravitate to select toys over and over, ignoring and possibly rejecting others?

Why Target Play Skills Development in Treatment?

Play contributes to, and prepares for, being receptive to learning social skills. Play helps generalize those skills to other settings/environments. Play helps children learn to be resilient and manage stress, by teaching important skills that foster a sense of self, a sense of belonging, and a sense of right and wrong. Here are my top 3 reasons why I advocate for play, and actually integrate elements of both VBT/ABA and Floortime™ in my intervention. Why I target play skills development in treatment, to foster social communication proficiency:

1. **<u>Play Improves Body Awareness:</u>**
Over the years "in the trenches" I have worked together with so many parents, teachers, therapists from all domains and paraprofessionals. We have all noticed a pattern. If a child came to us with very few lines on their hands, it seemed to indicate that they did not play with toys easily. They either rejected them outright, couldn't hold/manipulate them with fingers/both hands, or mouthed them indiscriminately. We need to address that situation during the first two stages of play development, the Sensory Play Phase and the Exploratory Play Phase, so that children can learn to:

- Use toys to develop cognition (Joint Attention, Object Permanence etc.) and Self Concept i.e. the ability to be aware, have preferences and make choices etc.
- Use toys to enhance motoric dexterity for better execution of Activities of Daily Living (ADL): walking/running, feeding, dressing, toileting, vocational skills and hand-eye coordination. Play, especially when using both hands, prepares the child for engaging with his/her environment more independently and functionally.
- Use toys to enhance comprehension of how the world "works" re: sights, sounds, textures and location, etc. Play fosters "whole body learning" by building a lexicon of both vocabulary and routines comprised of "muscle memory", "episodic memory" and repetition/practice

✎ Suggested Resources and Links:

http://www.melissaanddoug.com

http://www.beyondplay.com

http://touringteddies.com

2. **<u>Play Improves Understanding/Expressing Feelings:</u>**
Over my years of doing both individual and group speech therapy sessions, I have seen the power of play, and how it provides unique opportunities for children to practice and internalize both the roles and rules they see in their environment. We need to address

this through the third phase of play development, the Replica Play Phase, so that children learn to:

- Use toys to emotionally engage with themselves and with others. Children use play to access memories of events they remember fondly, (or not so much), and need to come to terms with. That's why some play schemas are reenacted again and again, until the child has memorized a favorite activity or resolves feelings about an unpleasant one.

- Use toys to facilitate social referencing through empathy. That means that play integrates emotional and cognitive development through perspective, AKA Theory of Mind (TOM). Children use play to learn how to imitate, empathize and emote with/ for others, especially when engaged with anthropomorphic toys such as dolls etc.

- Use toys to facilitate resiliency i.e. multi-sensory self-soothing and ability to "decompress" and manage stress. We need to teach children to use toys to learn from, and also to act on, to deal with challenging life cycle and unexpected events. That's why I believe in combining Cognitive Behavioral Therapy and Play Therapy techniques in treatment. We all give ourselves a "time out" to play with toys; adult toys are just more sophisticated and expensive! (Mobile apps, cars, Kitchen Aid™ mixers, electronic gadgets etc.)

✎ Suggested Resources and Links:

http://meebie.com

http://bit.ly/1Lj4ngj

http://www.adventus.com/musiq-lab/

3. Play Improves Problem Solving:
In my time spent as both a speech therapist and an entrepreneur, I have seen the importance of learning problem solving skills as both a child and an adult. Consider the importance of learning to become a Me, and then a We. A person needs to understand the structure and routine, rules, time-frame and expectations of his/her environment so that if/when one veers "off course" one can adjust accordingly. Play accomplishes all that, if used correctly, during the fourth phase, the Symbolic Play Phase. That's where children learn to:

- Use toys to sequence events of a process, or steps in multiple directions. We need to use play to help children learn to physically and mentally pattern what they see/hear in front of them, then duplicate that and generalize that learning to other activities.
- Use toys to learn time management, the Causality Loop i.e. "The If-Then Contingent", on which all of life hinges! This leads to a better understanding of time passing and the need to wait for delayed gratification, which is the start of negotiation, a key component of problem solving. How many of us bargain with children? With ourselves?
- Use toys to collaborate and creatively explore solutions to challenging situations/outcomes. We need to teach/let children play, in order to learn via trial and error how to resolve conflict--both inner and outer (when toys don't "work" or things don't go their way). Conflict resolution is the highest form of problem solving and social proficiency. It is a life long struggle that all human beings work on.

✎ Suggested Resources and Links:

http://www.lekotek.org

https://www.fatbraintoys.com

http://bit.ly/17iAjCC

The Impact of Delayed Onset of Play on Social Skills

Children with delayed onset of play skills development usually don't display age appropriate self regulation skills. They are the ones who seemingly have real difficulty with self-soothing and resiliency, understanding Causality, especially the If...Then Contingent (so it's hard to reason with them, especially mid-tantrum), and with expressing their Theory of Mind. These children also usually don't exhibit the necessary readiness indicators to learn specific social communication skills at developmentally relevant junctures in time such as Body Awareness, Rejection and even making inferences.

Lev Vygotsky said that the best learning is within reach during "real life" situations, not during rote learning, and emphasizes process over product, to instill a love of learning.

This is what play is all about! In my *Socially Speaking™ Seminars* I have often said that play skills, which are the culmination of receptive and expressive language development, are not functionally demonstrated without using social skills i.e. self regulation and negotiation skills in context. How does that occur? Children show their understanding of contextual cues and target vocabulary through following directions, self regulating, and playing; all of which provide insight into their state of mind, Theory of Mind, and memory banks i.e. episodic memory.

Play = learning in context, and the manifestation of one's "inner landscape" and perspective, i.e. Theory of Mind (TOM).
-- Penina Rybak, Socially Speaking™ Seminars

<u>Clinical Implications of Failure to Develop Play Skills:</u>

1. Reduced ability to "live in the moment" and develop episodic memory of past experiences and events, through perceptions gleaned from The Five Senses, based upon having Body Awareness and good proprioception and sensory processing/integration skills.
2. Reduced comprehension of time passing and later comprehension of time concepts (seasons, sequencing, correct use of past tense syntax).
3. Disorganized Theory Of Mind (TOM) leading to difficulty with:
   ❖Comprehension and use of quantity concepts (accessing math concepts/numbers readily
   ❖Use of appropriate sentence length (MLU) due to distractibility/anxiety (i.e. child relies on "telegraphic speech").
   ❖Problem solving (low threshold leads to tantrums instead of verbalization and exploring solutions etc).
   ❖Executive Functioning.

Take These Factors into Account When Assessing Play (they are all connected and will affect the rate of development re: social communication & sense of humor)
Cognitive skills
Language skills
Sensory Processing Skills
Facial Affect & Facial Recognition Skills
Motor skills

Incorporating Play Development and Social Communication Development Together:

We now understand how important play is for children with special needs, particularly those with ASD. We now see that the level of play they demonstrate, or lack thereof, gives us deep insights into their Theory of Mind, Executive Functioning and Episodic Memory Skills. We can commence with methodically and developmentally integrating play into lessons aimed at targeting social communication skills. Before we begin, we need to understand which cognitive and psycho-social level the child is on, based on the displayed level of play, and how to choose toys that "speak" to the child. We need to keep in mind preferences/learning style and degree of behavior management needed during intervention to reorient the child to person/place/time if called for. We need to plan accordingly how to maximize our staged "teachable moment" during play with specific toys, using specific activities which will foster:

1. **Cognitive causality** to foster self regulation and comprehension of time, including specific related language concepts such as sequencing, verb tense, and inferences

2. **Psychological Theory of Mind** (perspective/empathy) to promote awareness of the need to transition from Me to We depending on the situation

3. **Fine motor/graphomotor practice** to enhance muscle memory and episodic memory re: experienced events and associated vocabulary which get paired in the brain's "cloud storage"

These are focal points for children with Autism in particular, who often exhibit challenging behaviors and pragmatic difficulties hampering their self regulation and social skills development. This is especially true if they have experienced delayed onset of play skills development, display immature or repetitive play, or a decreased interest in play to begin with.

To counteract this, parents and professionals need to provide these 3 modifications for a successful "teachable moment" involving play:

● Environmental Modifications:
Positioning, Visual Supports, Sanitizing the Environment (to remove distractions) and physically and concretely demonstrating the If...Then Contingent. This can include: Visual Schedules and Reinforcer Rosters, Activity Centers, open cubbies, low hanging shelves, open bins, shoe-box tasks (TEAACH style), and a Sensory Break Area.

● Toy Modifications:
Hand-Over Hand Assistance, Specific Toy Selection, and Repurposing parts of toys (or broken toys) for later Verbal Description, Wh? Question, and Problem Solving Tasks

● Adaptive Play Modifications:
Here are my suggestions for 11 toys and activities perfect for adaptive play settings:
1. **Therapy balls** to sit on while engaged in play for increased attention span
2. **Swings, rocking chairs, or Dycem™ squares** to sit on while engaged in play
3. **Toys with non-slip surfaces and/or textured handles** to facilitate a more secure grip (I sometimes laminate or modge podge relevant toys, use raised buttons, and punch smalls if possible and use fuzzy pipe cleaner handles for grip.)
4. **Toys with embedded audio or visual component** (books and puzzles that make noise, have flashing lights within etc.)
5. **Puzzles with knobs** of varying height/width for an easier grasp (I like Melissa and Doug™ puzzles.)
6. **Structured "touch & feel" activities** and/or arts&crafts for increased sensory/tactile input which builds muscle memory and subsequently episodic memory
7. **Adaptive bikes and adaptive outdoor playground equipment**
8. **Adaptive books and board games** with velcro pictures & PECS, raised surfaces, and modified game pieces and page corners. (For example, I put styrofoam packing noodles at the bottom corner of every page of a book to facilitate turning the pages. I also put dice in a tiny Rubbermaid™ container so that they can be seen and used more easily. I sometimes use Fisher Price™ Little People as game pieces for better handling and understanding re: representation).
9. **Adaptive Switches** and levers using one's head or hand etc.
10. **Adaptive Visual Supports** using mini magnets, velcro dots, brass fasteners, jumbo paper clips, 3M mounting squares, play dough, keychains, pieces of cardboard boxes, container lids, and actual objects as needed. (For example, I use old, worn out cookie sheets that are still magnetized for PECS and picture vocabulary sorting for categorization. I use cardboard squares with actual objects glued on such as a plastic car or a light colored or beige wooden block with a black square drawn on it to represent computer/video etc. for AAC beginners.)
11. **Assistive technology** or mobile technology devices such as the iPad®

Assessing Play Skills and Determining Starting Points for Treatment

Play is a crucial stepping stone in child development, especially for children with Autism. It is important to collaborate and implement a team approach for increased performance and carryover, so that social communication skills can develop more naturally and sequentially. It's a good idea to methodically and developmentally assess and then incorporate play skills into IEP goal planning and implementation in special education, especially during the preschool years. That's why I created *The Socially Speaking™ Play Stages Formula* which I use in conjunction with my *Socially Speaking™ Assessment Protocol*. Both are parent-friendly and informal.

The Socially Speaking™ Play Stages Formula
Solitary Play + Simple Play= Awareness/Sensory Play  (musical mobiles, rattles, Little Tikes™ piano, toy mirrors)
Parallel Play+ Awareness of Others=Discovery/Exploratory Play (Cause & Effect "button" toys, balls and simple chunky knob puzzles)
Associative Play+ Concrete Representations=Imagination/Replica Play (everyday themes are recreated; dolls, toy bus/kitchen and accessories)

Cooperative Play+ Abstract Representations= Critical Thinking/Symbolic Play

(coordinated and goal oriented imaginary schemas, ex: making bridges out of tissue boxes, building Lego™ constructs and playing Chutes & Ladders

Incorporating Play and Social Communication Development Into "Input" Goals

Play development involves a learning process that is multi-sensory, holistic, developmental, personalized and contextualized. What is becoming clear to special education service providers and parents in the Autism and special needs communities, is that the same holds true for literacy. My *Socially Speaking™ Program* is based on two areas that have fallen by the wayside in many therapeutic regimens today, play, and pre-literacy. Both facilitate the orientation of person/place/time, which is why I am a such a vocal, passionate advocate for increased "free play times" and "Circle Time" in self-contained classrooms, particularly in preschools.

In a child's early years, especially in a preschool special education setting, there is usually much overlap between play and pre-literacy goals. It is helpful to organize these goals into communication based i.e. social behavior (pragmatic) goals and cognitive based language (conceptual) goals. This helps document what the child must do to prepare for being a student long term, to learn to get along with others and eventually to learn to read. I suggest that we rethink our social communication paradigm and divide the IEP goals into "input" (receptive language) and "output" (expressive language) categories. Here is a sampling of what I mean when I use the term "input" goals:

Suggested "Input" Goals for the IEP:
☑To improve attention i.e. orientation to person/place/time.
☑To improve play skills and the understanding of Causality (cause and effect) and ability to make inferences and predictions about events, both seen and unseen.
☑To improve pre-reading readiness skills (the beginning of a conceptual framework of ideas and vocabulary regarding how the world works).

We can facilitate the child's own understanding and the team's understanding of the importance of Circle Time in class, to proactively counteract behavioral "triggers". A Circle Time routine at the start of each school day, and even again every afternoon before dismissal, fosters orientation and understanding of the language concepts of space and time. If the child is oriented to person, place, and time, he/she can "live in the moment", access Episodic Memory, process incoming information and stimuli, as well as engage in social exchanges more age appropriately. A good Circle Time routine encompasses learning about orientation and pre-reading readiness language concepts in a structured, repetitive and fun manner.

Orientation to person/place/time facilitates the ability to answer "who"? "what"? "where"? and "how"? questions. Therefore, remember to use picture identification and matching activities, along with various games and manipulatives to increase vocabulary and categorization skills. This will help foster comprehension of how the world works. We can then enable the child with ASD to understand and more accurately answer wh? questions. A story book read during Circle Time and reenacted visually with props can facilitate the child's understanding of time (sequencing) and Causality (cause & effect). This can later facilitate problem solving development (inferencing, predicting outcomes, exploring solutions, negotiation and conflict resolution).

These are important cognitive concepts one needs in order to develop appropriate social skills. They should be routinely addressed in a comprehensive Circle Time routine in all preschool special education settings. In essence, a good Circle Time routine builds a receptive lexicon and conceptual framework about the child's world, using language. Lessons learned in Circle Time then result in developing Self Concept and self regulation. Circle Time thus becomes a profound, insightful ritual that gives us a daily glimpse into the child's "inner landscape" i.e. Theory of Mind.

A service provider who collaborates with others, including parents, on Circle Time routines, has a better chance of entering the child's inner landscape. This makes it easier connecting emotionally with the child to build trust/rapport and easier to then gently lead him/her into our landscape to view and to learn. Circle Time is usually the first experience children with ASD have in Joint Attention, Emotional Attunement, social referencing through TOM, including sitting with a group. It is the beginning of the awareness of the need to transition from a Me to a We. Finally, it is the start of that child interacting with the environment,and impacting upon his/her surroundings and those in it. Why does this work?

Circle Time provides structured learning, disguised as a play activity, which is inherently reinforcing/motivating. It thereby enables the child with ASD to become a more active participant in the activity, which fosters episodic memory. I actually recommend two Circle Times a day in special education settings to teach before/after and review the schedule of the day, i.e. all those things that happened in between.

This allows the child to actively experience time passing, verb tense, teachable moments re: target vocabulary and a group learning activity that is made interactive with visual supports, tangible props, songs and turn taking.

Incorporating Play and Social Communication Development Into "Output" Goals

Part of becoming a more active participant in life and life's activities, whether they be related to literacy or Activities of Daily Living (ADL) means becoming more active in play. Play is actually the first social skill set that we want to put in a bin and take with us on our proverbial "train ride" with that child in need. A child's play skills feature both receptive and expressive language components, both of which are usually targeted in intervention. Verbal children with ASD in particular have real difficulty with the quality of their verbal performance, especially during verbal play and socializing. Pragmatic skills are thus the quality of "output" of language, which is targeted extensively in treatment for these children. Play is the vehicle for implementing changes in how the child views the world around him/her, and how he/she communicates with those in it. A team approach thus calls for synthesizing play and pre-literacy goals with overall output goals, to facilitate and magnify overall performance. Here is a sampling of what I mean when I use the term "output" goals:

Suggested "Output" Goals for the IEP:
☑To improve expressive communication skills: verbal lexicon, syntax and phrase length.
☑To improve self monitoring and problem solving (social functional communication) skills for increased self regulation.
☑To improve articulation (speech clarity) skills of these sounds.

A good team facilitates a child's overall social communication skills, input and output skills, which grow through the acquisition of play and pre-literacy skills. Play skills are where cognitive and emotional development intersect, to foster Self Concept, Communicative Intent and Causality. Targeting pre-literacy skills in treatment further cements the child's psycho-social and intellectual development. How? It addresses both receptive and expressive language development in a sequential manner (ex: matching pairs of pictures, categorizing like/unalike items, sequencing a 3 picture story, counting accurately, and following directions containing spatial relationships AKA prepositions).

When I first started my career in speech therapy, teaching pre-literacy in this order was often the domain of the speech-language pathologist. He or she was the one who actually ran group sessions together with the special education teacher, which sometimes doubled as a Circle Time routine where the target vocabulary was "plugged in" to different levels of the hierarchy shown below. Since I always advocated for Circle Time, I took to this practice naturally, in keeping with my now dubbed Socially Speaking™ philosophy where orientation to person/place/time is taught initially through play and structured "teachable moments" such as those found in these show and tell routines.

Suggested Components of a Classic Circle Time Routine
Orientation to Person/Place/Time
"Good Morning to You" song with mirror and body part photos (review The 5 Senses and child's personal information ex: name, age, gender, address, phone number).
"Who Came to School Today" song with props e.g. toy bus and little people (review prepositions and allow for requesting and turn taking during play task).
"I'm a Boy/Girl" song with articles of clothing to identify and categorize.
"Days of the Week" song with relevant props (review calendar skills and night vs. day target vocabulary).
"What's new with my family?" with relevant props (such as photos, new baby doll, van, doctor's kit).
Environmental Awareness
"What's the Weather/Season" song with real photos and props.
"What Do I Do/See in School" song with props-including discussing Class Rules and Safety Issues ex: Fire Drill Prep, Community Helpers, School Furniture vs. Home.
"What Belongs" in My Classroom? i.e. singing the classic Sesame St. "Same and Different" song while sorting familiar class objects, categorization-inclusion and exclusion tasks using props.
Temporal Awareness: Reviewing Schedule of the Day
Verbal review of today's activities....use visual props to review sequencing of Visual Schedule and time related vocabulary.
Discussion of today's special activity and target vocabulary (ex: trip, baking cookies).
Show n' tell activity by students who are capable (connecting home to school).....allow each student to talk, feel important, build self esteem, and have a turn in the "limelight".

FAQ: What is the purpose of a Circle Time regimen in treatment?

- Teach idea of time passing and everyone has a role to play at different times.
- Facilitate internal organization; i.e. teach child about the world.
- Develop Self Concept, self esteem and self regulation skills.

I recommend having 2 Circle Time activities a day , with 2 opportunities for reviewing the schedule of the day. Why? Because it gives the child the chance to understand the passage of time, Causality, and the vocabulary of verb tense; all areas of challenge for many children with ASD. Discussing what *will* happen and visually preparing the child is so important. Discussing what *did* happen, using those same visual supports, is even more crucial. It can go a long way in facilitating episodic memory, carryover of learned skills, and overall self regulation, for future events and possible transitioning difficulty. The result? It's easier for the child to learn to reorient to person/place/time more quickly and more independently. It's also easier for the child to learn the specific pre-literacy language skills needed for future social communication proficiency, because the journey towards understanding how "the world works" has begun.

What Are Pre-Literacy Skills?

Pre-literacy skills, also called *The Pre-reading Readiness Hierarchy* by many speech-language pathologists, including myself, refers the understanding and use of specific vocabulary which demonstrates the child's ability to do these four things:
1. Identify and label common objects/pictures and their function
2. Group like and unalike items/pictures and explain why using a verbal rationale
3. Follow directions and tell a simple story in the order it happened, using correct grammar (verb tense etc.)
4. Compare and contrast familiar objects/pictures or events using quality (adjectives) and quantity (amounts) concepts

Pre-Reading Readiness Skills Hierarchy
Categorization (object use and object association)
Same
Same vs. different
Inclusion (what goes together)
Exclusion (which one does not belong)
Sequencing (order of events)
Cause and effect (18 mo. old learns "If...Then" Contingent)
Directions (one step vs. multiple)
Procedure (ex: how to make scrambled eggs)
Story/narrative (from pictures to paragraphs)
Spatial Relationships
Part/whole relationships
Prepositions
Quantity (Vocabulary Such as Empty/Full, More/Less)
1:1 correspondence (counting numbers)
Time (week days, seasons, holidays, telling time)

"Output" goals must also increase the child's ability to self monitor, self correct and self evaluate the "melody" of talking, called prosody (i.e. intonation, rate, fluency and vocal quality). Early social skills development involves a child's ability to interpret the meaning and feelings behind the various ways a person uses the voice and speech to communicate. Communication and social skills development thus go hand in hand, resulting in the need for a team approach when implementing IEP goals to improve social skills.

Targeting Orientation and Social Communication Skills Through Play

It takes team collaboration as well as the integration of toys and tech in treatment to successfully plan and execute an effective and enjoyable "teachable moment". I suggest following this roadmap of sorts re: play. I have experienced the power of synthesizing both toys and tech, namely iPad® apps (see Chapter 11), for more productive intervention that facilitates both cognition and self regulation. I have also experienced firsthand the power of play to teach orientation to person/place/time and the Socially Speaking™ Trifecta: Body Awareness, Expressing Feelings, and Problem Solving.

I suggest using play schemas to teach these concepts in this order, following these guidelines, and my suggestions at the end of this chapter.

1. Object Function Comprehension

Children *first* need to understand the vocabulary of their environment i.e. how their world "works". That involves learning to identify basic objects by their appearance, texture, sound, and function. This can be done with various toys including chunky puzzles, picture books, dolls and accessories, matching objects, matching photos and related materials.

2. Categorization: What Goes Together or Not (Inclusion & Exclusion) with Rationale

Children begin to master orientation to person/place/time when they can group alike/unalike objects/photos into categories and explain why. This skills helps develop higher level social skills and Executive Functioning skills needed for later self regulation and literacy skills. This skill is the precursor to developing the ability to ask and answer "why"? questions, to have resiliency and to learn problem solving skills when things don't go as planned and improvisation/adjustment is needed. This is the point in time that I introduce humor into the interaction by purposely grouping items that "don't fit" and help the child see why that's funny. This is also the juncture in time when I introduce more picture board style games into the repertoire.

3. Sequencing

Children learn to sequence a pattern, oral directions, or events in a story *after* they learn about object function and how to categorize the vocabulary and images in their memory banks. This skill is a later one to emerge, and is essentially the bridge between language and social skills. It can thus take the longest to develop. It also requires mastery of the first two skills I mentioned. Sequencing is the gateway to mastering literacy and problem solving, as well as math concepts and self regulation (following a schedule, tolerating changes in routine/transitions, accepting delayed gratification). Sequencing is where "whole body" learning really counts; where the child reenacts and explains the order of what he/she is doing while doing it, building "muscle" memory and episodic memory for later scaffolded learning.

Targeting Stress Management and Resiliency Through Play

A collaborative team understands the importance of working social communication "teachable moments" into all aspects of treatment across all domains. A good treatment plan involves methodical, developmental and creative joint efforts to facilitate self regulation through play, so that the child can learn important concepts needed for literacy acquisition and later social skills. This will also help the child learn to self monitor behavior, make sense of the surrounding world and his/her role in it. A child with Autism in particular also needs to learn to play to self-entertain and self soothe, maximizing "down time". Learning to play means learning resiliency, causality and even the foundation of humor. All of these help with orientation to person/place/time, which epitomizes self regulation and the foundations for literacy. Both are targeted in deliberate activities such as play schemas and Circle Time, both of which are a lost art in many special education settings today. The introduction of play and Circle Time into the therapeutic regimen can help a child with ASD know what to expect and to manage stress and anxiety, especially when schedules are changed and unanticipated events occur.

Stress management is in itself a large part of social skills building and self regulation. As we now know, the root of the problematic behaviors seen in many youngsters with ASD is their neuro-biological disorientation to person/place/time. Another root cause is poor transitioning, especially when the routine and/or expectations change. This can lead to delayed onset of play and pre-literacy development, not to mention gaps in social communication proficiency. We therefore see how all this plays a crucial role in bridging the gap between readiness to learn and actual performance re: social skills development. A comprehensive team approach which targets play skills and pre-reading readiness skills for remediation will help to facilitate the child's orientation, Self Concept and acquisition of neuro-cognitive processes such as Theory of Mind and Executive Functioning. This will then facilitate later social skills involving humor, resiliency, accepting unfairness and change, along with problem solving; all of which are needed to help children and later, as adults, navigate their environment and take steps to turn Me into We. For more information visit: http://bit.ly/1AXkYDf

Final Words

Play is truly the "work" of children, and its "workflow' and schemas help children make sense of their environment and those in it. How? By providing structured and unstructured, novel and familiar and educational and entertaining opportunities. Opportunities to grow. To learn. To remember. To relate to others. Opportunities for replicating and reframing, and practicing and internalizing both the rules and roles of said environment. It is thus self evident that play needs to be the ultimate vehicle through which service providers/clinicians/parents/educators introduce children to their world; its realities, regulations and rewards.

What is so important about play? Play fosters Self Concept, emotional engagement with others, and the ability to self regulate. It facilitates the child's understanding of the environment (i.e. the structure and routine, rules and expectations of said environment). It provides social referencing through empathy (i.e. it integrates emotional and cognitive development through perspective, AKA *Theory of Mind.*)

For many children with Autism, readiness to play indicates a cognitive and socio-emotional readiness to learn social skills; this is something to keep in mind when determining starting points for remediation and goal planning. Another thing to keep in mind are the pitfalls and outcomes of delayed onset of play skills development due to a variety of contributing factors. They can include sensory processing issues, behavioral issues, cognitive issues, gross/fine motor issues and unfamiliarity with toys due to environmental deprivation/poverty. This can all result in the situation specific, splintered learning and performance which contributes to the gap between readiness to learn and actual social communication proficiency. This is exactly what properly planned and executed Autism intervention tries to counteract.

Materials for Your Toolbox

- <u>Key References</u>

Axline, Virginia (1964). *Dibs in Search of Self.* New York, NY: Ballantine Books.

Axline, Virginia (1964). *Play Therapy: Second Edition.* New York, NY: Ballantine Books

Baron-Cohen, Simon (1987). Autism and Symbolic Play. *British Journal of Developmental Psychology,* (5), 2, 139-148

Beckerleg, Tracey (2008). *Fun with Messy Play: Ideas and Activities for Children with Special Needs.* Philadelphia, PA: Jessica Kingsley Publishers.

Brady, Lois Jean, et al (2011). *Speak, Move, Play, and Learn with Children on the Autism Spectrum.* Philadelphia, PA: Jessica Kingsley Publishers.

Bundy, Anita, Shia, Sue, et al (2007). How Does Sensory Processing Dysfunction Affect Play? Conceptualizing and Identifying Sensory Processing Issues. Sensory Integration Treatment: Special Issue. *The American Journal of Occupational Therapy, March/April,* 61, 2

Burdette, H. L. & Whitaker, R. C. (2005). Resurrecting Free Play in Young Children: Looking Beyond Fitness and Fatness to Attention, Affiliation, and Affect. *Archives of Pediatric and Adolescent Medicine,* 159, 46-50

Charman, Tony, Baron-Cohen, Simon, et al (1997). Infants with Autism: An Investigation of Empathy, Pretend Play, Joint Attention, and Imitation. *Developmental Psychology* 33, 781-789

Charman, Tony, and Stone, Wendy (2006). *Social and Communication Development in Autism Spectrum Disorders.* New York, NY: Guilford Press.

Christie, Phil et al (2009). *First Steps in Intervention with Your Child with Autism: Frameworks for Communication.* Philadelphia, PA: Jessica Kingsley Publishers.

Courtney, J.A. (2012). *Touching Autism Through Developmental Play Therapy.* In L. Gallo-Lopez & L.C. Rubin (Eds.), *Play-Based Interventions for Children and Adolescents with Autism Spectrum Disorders* (pp. 137-157). New York, NY: Routledge.

Densmore, Ann (2007). *Helping Children with Autism Become More Social: 76 Ways to Use Narrative Play.* Westport, CT: Praeger Publishing

Delaney, Tara (2009). *101 Games and Activities for Children with Autism, Asperger's, and Sensory Processing Disorders.* Europe: McGraw Hill.

Gallo-Lopez, Loretta, and Rubin, Lawrence (2012). *Play-Based Interventions for Children and Adolescents with Autism Spectrum Disorders.* New York, NY: Taylor and Francis Group.

Greenspan, Stanley, and Thorndike-Greenspan, Nancy (1995). *First Feelings.* New York, NY: Penguin Books.

Greenspan, Stanley, and Weider, Serena (1998). *The Child with Special Needs: Encouraging Intellectual and Emotional Growth.* Cambridge, MA: Perseus Books Group.

Greenspan, Stanley (2002). *The Secure Child: Helping Our Children Feel Safe and Confident in an Insecure World.* Cambridge, MA: Perseus Books Group.

Greenspan, Stanley, and Weider, Serena (2006). *Engaging Autism: Using the Floortime Approach to Help Children Relate, Communicate, and Think.* Cambridge, MA: Da Capo Press/Perseus Books Group.

Griffin, Simone, and Sandler, Diane (2009). *Motivate to Communicate: 300 Games and Activities for Your Child with Autism.* Philadelphia, PA: Jessica Kingsley Publishers.

Hirsh-Pasek, Kathy, and Michnik Golinkoff, Roberta (2003). *Einstein Never Used Flash Cards: How Our Children Really Learn, and Why They Need to Play More and Memorize Less.* New York: NY, Rodale Books.

Hirsh-Pasek, Kathy, Michnik Golinkoff, Roberta, and Singer, Dorothy (2006). *Play=Learning: How Play Motivates and Enhances Social-Emotional Growth.* New York: NY, Oxford University Press.

Landreth, Gary (2000). *Innovations in Play Therapy: Issues, Process, and Special Populations.* New York, NY: Brunner-Routledge Books.

Leber, Nancy Jolson (2002). *Easy Activities for Building Social Skills: Dozens of Effective Classroom Strategies and Activities to Teach Cooperation and*

Communication, Manners and Respect, Positive Behavior and More! New York, NY: Scholastic.

Levine, Karen, and Chedd, Naomi (2007). *REPLAYS: Using Play to Enhance Emotional and Behavioral Development for Children with Autism Spectrum Disorders.* Philadelphia, PA: Jessica Kingsley Publishers.

Manela, Miriam. (2014). *The Parent-Child Dance: A Guide to Help You Understand and Shape Your Child's Behavior.* Passaic, NJ: OT Thrive Publishing.

Mannix, Darlene (2009). *Social Skills Activities for Special Children, Second Edition. San Francisco, CA:* Jossey-Bass/Wiley & Sons Inc.

Mannix, Darlene (2009). *Life Skills Activities for Special Children, Second Edition.* San Francisco, CA: Jossey-Bass/Wiley & Sons Inc.

Martin, Nicole (2009). *Art As an Early Intervention Tool for Children with Autism.* Philadelphia, PA: Jessica Kingsley Publishers.

Moor, Julia (2002). *Playing, Laughing, and Learning with Children on the AutismSpectrum: A Practical Resource of Play Ideas for Parents and Carers.* Philadelphia, PA: Jessica Kingsley Publishers.

Paley, Vivian Gussin (2004). *A Child's Work: The Importance of Fantasy Play.* Chicago, IL: The University of Chicago Press.

Rybak, Penina. *Friendship Circle of MI Blog,* 2013-present

Schwartz, Sue and Heller Miller, Joan (1996). *The New Language of Toys: Teaching Communication Skills to Children with Special Needs.* Bethesda, MD: Woodbine House.

Seach, Diana (2007). *Interactive Play for Children with Autism.* New York, NY: Routledge.

Smith, Melinda, and Julian, Linda (2001). *Teaching Play Skills to Children with Autistic Spectrum Disorder: A Practical Guide.* New York, NY: DRL Books.

Stegelin, D.A. (2005). Making the Case for Play Policy: Research Based Reasons to Support Play-Based Environments. *Young Children,* 60, 76-85

Westby, Carol (2000). A Scale for Assessing Development of Children's Play. *Play Diagnosis and Assessment, Second Edition, 131-161.* New York, NY: Wiley Press.

Wolfberg, Pamela (2003). *Peer Play and the Autism Spectrum: The Art of Guiding Children's Socialization and Imagination.* Shawnee, KS: Autism Apserger Publishing

Wolfberg, Pamela (2009). *Play and Imagination in Children with Autism, Second Edition.* Shawnee, KS: Autism Asperger Publishing

• <u>Key Links to Peruse</u>

<u>http://bit.ly/16fQz6l</u>

<u>http://bit.ly/1zHgLTH</u>

<u>http://bit.ly/1EF5K0R</u>

<u>http://bit.ly/1zHhapa</u>

<u>http://bit.ly/1LKpHwh</u>

<u>http://bit.ly/1zdN0cB</u>

<u>http://1.usa.gov/1Dw865s</u>

<u>http://bit.ly/1z96fzj</u>

<u>http://bit.ly/1zHipEN</u>

<u>http://bit.ly/1Dw8As0</u>

Honorable Mention:

<u>http://www.friendshipcircle.org/blog/</u>

<u>http://www.fisher-price.com</u>

<u>http://bit.ly/1DFKmxX</u>

Suggested YouTube Videos:

<u>http://bit.ly/1LKq0WC</u>

<u>http://bit.ly/1LKqyx4</u>

<u>http://bit.ly/1u5O0iv</u>

<u>http://bit.ly/1F4iwKJ</u>

• <u>Key Concepts to Address</u>

Play, Theory of Mind, Orientation, Body Awareness, Self Regulation, Causality, Episodic Memory, Pre-Literacy, Resiliency, Circle Time and "Teachable Moment."

• <u>Key Toys to Use in Treatment</u>

1. ***Object Function- ID and Matching Same/Different:*** Fisher Price Peek-a-Blocks (Vehicles), What's Inside? Soft Feely Box by Lakeshore, Melissa and Doug™ Puzzles, Alex™ Early Learning Wash & String-Little Hands, Mr. Potato Head™, Language Builder Photo Cards- Nouns, Lauri-Smethport™ Foam Magnets-Objects, Kidoozie Fun Time Tractor (paired with assorted farm picture books), ThinkFun S'match Game, Little Tikes Farm 3-D Memory Match-Up, Make a Match Language Lotto by Lakeshore, The Learning Journey Match It-Who Am I? Game, dot paint and blank paper to make pairs and/or same/different, and decorate the "balls" with other arts and crafts items.

2. ***Categorization (Inclusion & Exclusion):*** Ravensberger™ What Goes Together? Carson-Dellosa™ Publishing Opposites Attract, Webber™ "What Doesn't Belong?" Photo Card Deck from Super Duper, Create-a-Scene Magnetic Playset, Spot It! On the Road, Miss Weather Girl Colorforms, Farm Sorting Center by Lakeshore, Discovering Language Sorting Boxes by Lakeshore, Learning Resources Goodie Games Cookie Shapes, dollhouse and furniture, arts and crafts items, such as OTC Barnyard Foam Self-Adhesive Farm Shapes for sorting and pasting etc.

3. ***Sequencing:*** Childcraft™ Attribute Beads and Activity Cards, Learning Journey™ Sequencing Cards, Battat Bristle Blocks Basic Set, Melissa & Doug™ Wooden Bear Family Dress-Up Puzzle, Play-Dough Doctor Drill & Fill, Querrcetti Georello Kaleido Gears, Magna Tiles, Little Tikes Clearly Sports Bowling Set, Fisher-Price Servin' Surprises Ice Cream Party Set, Learning Resources Pretend and Play Kitchen Set, Zingo by Think Fun, Connect Four, Smethport Tabletop Pocket Chart Four Step Sequencing (can be used as 2, 3, and 4 step sequencing tasks), Crayola Wide Screen Light Designer.

4. ***Ten Adaptive Play Suggestions:***

   ✦ **Swings, rocking chairs, Therapy Balls, or Dycem™ squares** to sit on while engaged in play.
   ✦ **Toys with non-slip surfaces and/or textured handles** to facilitate a more secure grip (I sometimes laminate or modge podge relevant toys, use raised buttons, and punch smalls if possible and use fuzzy pipe cleaner handles for grip.)
   ✦ **Toys with embedded audio or visual component** (books and puzzles that make noise, have flashing lights within etc.) See: www.smartkidzmedia.com
   ✦ **Puzzles with knobs** of varying height/width for an easier grasp (I like Melissa and Doug™ puzzles.)
   ✦ **Structured "touch & feel" activities** and/or art s &crafts for increased sensory/tactile input which builds muscle memory and subsequently episodic memory.
   ✦ **Adaptive bikes and adaptive outdoor playground equipment**
   ✦ **Adaptive books and board games** with velcro pictures & PECS, raised surfaces, and modified game pieces and page corners. (For example, I put styrofoam packing noodles at the bottom corner of every page of a book to

facilitate turning the pages. I also put dice in a tiny Rubbermaid™ container so that they can be seen and used more easily. I sometimes use Fisher Price™ Little People as game pieces for better handling and understanding re: representation).

✦ **Adaptive Switches** and levers using one's head or hand etc.
✦ **Adaptive Visual Supports** using mini magnets, velcro dots, brass fasteners, jumbo paper clips, 3M mounting squares, play dough, keychains, pieces of cardboard boxes, container lids and actual objects as needed. (For example, I use old, worn out cookie sheets that are still magnetized for PECS and picture vocabulary sorting for categorization. I use cardboard squares with actual objects glued on, such as a plastic car or a light colored or beige wooden block with a black square drawn on it to represent computer/video etc. for AAC beginners.)
✦ **Packing Noodles or "Puffy" Stickers** to stick on page corners to help little fingers turn book pages.

• Key iPad® Apps to Use in Treatment

☞ *For the Service Provider:* Play and pre-literacy apps must be chosen with care and correlate to both the child's cognitive level and Theory of Mind. That means that the child's learning style, understanding, preferences and familiarity with a specific concept and/or user interface of a particular app must be carefully addressed. Please see app listings in other chapters, especially Chapter 4, for further considerations.

☞ *For the Child:* Play and language development usually follow this pattern:

1. *Object Function re: ID and Matching Same/Different:* Bitsboard, Talking Picture Board, Shuttersong, Marcus' Discoveries HD, Touch the Sound, Sounds by Different Roads to Learning, Touch, Look, Listen-My First Words, Injini Lite and Paid, My First Words- Flashcards by Alligator Apps, Baby Flashcards- Free: Staple Goods, Photo Buttons, Meebie, Autism iHelp- WH Questions, Describe It To Me by Smarty Ears, My PlayHome Lite and Paid, My PlayHome Stores, Word Slapps, Question Sleuth, Baby Flash Cards FREE, Knock Knock Family Expanding Language, Pair Animals, Farm Flip, Memory King, Montessori Matching Game, SoundTouch Lite, AnimalMixer, Babyfirst Match-up, Same/Different by I Can Do Apps, Autism iHelp- Same and Different, Make a Scene: Farmyard, Abby- Basic Skills Preschool, Preschool EduPlay Complete and Lite, What's Different? Free by Remarkable Games LTD, My Little Suitcase, and What Is Different (visual discrimination only, not object function!) by James Rouse.

2. *Categorization- Inclusion- What Belongs Together?* Things That Go Together, Montessori- Things That Go Together Matching Game, Clean Up: Category Sorting, What Goes Together by Different Roads to Learning, Autism iHelp- Sorting, Sort It Out 1 & 2 and Families 1 & 2 by MyFirstApp, WhereDoIGo? by Camigo Kids, Let's Build a Bedroom, Put It Away, Sort It Out by School Zone, Question Sleuth by Zorten, Describe It To Me by Smarty Ears, House of Learning by Smarty Ears, Categories Learning Center by Smarty Ears, Abby- Basic Skills Preschool, Let's Name Things Fun

Deck, Language Builder® from Stages, LanguageBuilder for iPad®, and Popplet Lite and Paid.

3. *Categorization- Exclusion- What Doesn't Belong Here?* Disclaimer: Exclusion skills are the main prerequisite skills needed to learn sequencing/problem solving/ orientation to time. I have seen that not enough time is spent on this goal in therapy/ class, using manipulatives during play and then picture worksheets/art projects. I strongly urge that those activities must be provided first before introducing apps to teach exclusion. There is much misunderstanding surrounding this concept, which is being dubbed "problem solving" and targets same/different comprehension, not exclusion comprehension. Exclusion is often unfortunately being taught incorrectly with/without apps from a *visual discrimination* perspective, not the necessary *object function* perspective. This defeats the whole purpose of the exercise! I'm referring to apps with such a confusing misnomer in the iTunes Store like the ABA Problem Solving: "What Does Not Belong?" I am thus uncomfortable with most of the apps reportedly addressing exclusion skills. Here's a finite list of which apps I recommend to teach exclusion, requiring you to be creative and think "outside the box" when preparing lessons and teachable moments using ready made photos/stamps or importing your own from your Camera and/or Photos App: Question Sleuth, Photo Buttons, Doodlelicious, SonicPics, Glow Draw®, Drawing Box Free, Drawing Desk, You Doodle and You Doodle Plus, Bingo Card Generator, Bitsboard, Odd One Out by Dana Israel, What Doesn't Belong? by Tiny Tap, and Dress for Winter by Tiny Tap.

4. *Sequencing:* AnimalMixer, Kid's Patterns, Make a Scene: Farmyard, Abby- Basic Skills Preschool: Puzzles and Patterns HD Free, Glow Draw®, Draw a House by Fjord42, Sago Mini Doodlecast, Let's Create, Kids Beads, Toca Tea Party, Making Pizza by Tiny Tap, Cute Food, Colorforms® Revolution Free, Bamba Burger, Ice Cream Sundae! Icy Dessert, Car Puzzles, Create a Car Lite, Drawing with Carl Free and Paid, Puppet Workshop, Ear Doctor, American Doctor, How? Fun Deck, Making Sequences, Advanced Making Sequences, and Advanced Video Sequences by Zorten, iSequences Lite and Paid, Speech with Milo: Sequencing, Sequencing Post Office, Video Sequencing by PandaPal, Sequencing Tasks: Life Skills Lite and Paid, Let's Use Language: Basic Language Development by Everyday Speech, Tell a Story with Tommy: Community Sequences, Abigail and the Balance Beam, Car Wash, Plane Wash, Build a Ship, Build a Story, StoryBuddy 2, Art Maker, and My Story.

5. *Honorable Mention:*

☞ *Adjective/Descriptive/Quality Concepts:* Comparative Adjectives by Grasshopper Apps, Speech with Milo: Adjectives, SpeakColors, Adjectives Part 1- Fun English Videos, Adjectives Fun Deck, Adj & Opposites: First Words (FREE) and (LITE), Drawing With Carl Free, Canvastic, SpeakColors, Music Color Lite- Baby flash cards, Draw in 3D, Drawing Pad, Kids Doodle, Drawing with Carl, Toca Hair Salon 2, Toca Tailor, and Autism & PDD Comparatives/Superlatives Lite.

☞ *Opposites*: Preschool Game: Photo Touch Opposites and Little Matchup Opposites by Grasshopper Apps, Opposites- A Montessori Pre-Language Exercise, Opposites 1& 2,

Zoola Opposites Free and Paid, Opposite Day, Autism iHelp- Opposites and Opposites SLP Edition, Autism & PDD Opposites Lite, Opposites Adventure: Puppy Playtime, Find the Opposites, The Opposites, Opposites Fun Deck, Kids Opposites Free by suavesolutions, Kitty Likes Learning, EduPlay, What's Up Duck? The FOOT Book- Dr. Seuss, Let's Use Language: Basic Language Development by Everyday Speech, Popplet Lite and Paid, and Photo Buttons.

☞ Find More Apps for Children with Special Needs here:

http://bit.ly/1FouyUW

https://momswithapps.com/discover

Chapter 9:
<u>Treatment Part 2</u>-Social Skills Kits for Staged Teachable Moments

Anecdote

Caleb is a 10 year old cute, belligerent, prickly and temperamental little boy who speaks in single words or two word phrases, and has fluctuating eye contact and a tendency to "flap his hands". He has been placed in a mainstreamed (inclusive) public school class and a foster home two years ago. He hasn't seen his real family or twin brother in over 2 years. He has been labeled "selectively mute", a "problem child" in school and at home. He was assigned to my caseload mid-year after being medically misdiagnosed with "oppositional defiance disorder and Attention Deficit Hyperactivity Disorder (ADHD) for which neurological medication was prescribed but wasn't taken. It was unclear if Caleb refused it or it wasn't administered. Caleb has been given "pull-out" speech therapy twice a week; once in a small group with one therapist, and once individually with another, both sessions for 30 minutes per week since he was 3. Progress has been slow and splintered, and he is often reassigned to new providers mid-year at his biological parents' insistence. That's how I came to know him.

There isn't much stability in Caleb's life. His foster parents have 3 other children, all younger than him. Both work full time and life's been a revolving door of babysitters for the four children after school. His teacher went out on maternity leave and the new substitute teacher was just transferred to a different class. His bus driver, whom he really liked, was just assigned a different route after transporting Caleb for 5 months. His favorite classmate's dad works for a company which just transferred him to another state so his pal (for two years) is moving at the end of the week. Caleb has a rotating 1:1 aide in class and two different speech therapists, one of them now being me. When I meet him, I remark that this poor kid seems all alone and seems to be having a bad week, I'm told that it's been a bad year and an even worse life. Caleb looks big for his age and is starting to get bullied and/or do the bullying. There is absolutely no documentation about possible Autism and the need for social communication intervention.

When I first meet Caleb he displays a neutral, flat affect i.e. an expressionless face, and is very quiet, studiously looking at the floor, at the walls, anywhere but in my direction. When I allow him and encourage him to have "the run of the room" and play with whatever he wants, "no strings attached", he freezes, then starts flapping his hands. He then hesitantly chooses a remote control car, becoming more animated as time goes on. He chooses a book about cars, a lego car set, twin "drivers" and adds to his pile. This becomes a ritual for the next 4 weeks. I let Caleb choose these exact items and put them in a clear plastic container marked as his because a) he gravitated towards them and b) it's the first time there's been a sense of permanence in his life recently. He knows where they are and he knows what to do with them. He isn't interested in further communication with me beyond basic requests or labeling, or in trying to play with other toys, or with me for that matter. But he does eagerly come to my room, starts to look at me when I speak to him, starts to smile more often and seems sad when our session is over. At the end of the four weeks he starts to spontaneously speak to me in single words, but I still don't place demands on him or change the therapy regimen--yet. He's actually only seen me four times.

The group speech therapist questions me about this, and is surprised when I tell him that it's part of the plan. I explain that building a rapport is my priority right now, and that these toys will become part of Caleb's Social Skills Kit (and will still be marked his with name and photo). They will be used repeatedly and creatively, first by themselves, and eventually in conjunction with other materials and toys I'll add to the mix. The goal is to work up to addressing his IEP goals and social communication skills simultaneously. The therapist's even more surprised when I ask if he wouldn't mind spending a few minutes of his group session playing Show & Tell.

I suggest having everyone discuss their favorite toys and display them. Caleb will of course be invited to show off the toys in this kit, and he will be responsible for caring for them and transporting them to/from my room. The therapist tells me that he's worried about the students experiencing boredom and because he always wants to foster carryover, he usually brings new materials to the group session each week. I discuss the value in pairing like items and collecting them in one place. I advocate for them to be used again and again, especially for a psychologically traumatized boy like Caleb, whom I believe has Autism. The therapist finally agrees to try my suggestions after a very long conversation, with very positive results. A few months later, he asks me to help him assemble a Group Therapy Social Skills Kit. Soon after, other therapists are asking me to help them assemble specific kits for specific IEP goals and/or students.

Strategy and Technique

Setting the Stage for Team Success: Is the Team Ready to Build So "They Will Come"?

The philosophy behind the Socially Speaking™ Social Skills Kits is based on the premise that we are all visual creatures who respond well to the familiar, to that which is routine. I thus create Social Skills Kits that can be used across all domains and settings and that are shown to all service providers <u>after</u> I establish both rapport and baseline data. I need to know the "lay of the land" i.e. the child's inner landscape <u>before</u> I proceed, which is why I use this checklist with the team beforehand. Remember the imaginative movie *Field of Dreams* and the famous line about building the baseball field etc. so that "they will come"? Social skills intervention requires the same finesse, creativity and planning!

<u>Readiness Indicators for the Team To Build a Social Skills Kit:</u>

1. The team is able to prioritize goals based on documentation about the student's behavior and then provide a written memo re: which goals will be targeted, and why and how (AKA *The Socially Speaking™ Management Plan,* Chapter 12)

2. There is an ABC chart on file because the team knows to:
   - Draft a Management Plan together and assign a "captain" to take notes.
   - Turn the notes into the Management Plan that gets officially filed and distributed to the entire team, including parents.

3. The team knows how to motivate the child to start self monitoring and *wanting* to change his/her way of reacting/performing (Remember: start by establishing a good working relationship with the student. It will help facilitate the rapport, which itself acts as an intrinsic reinforcer. The student can then try to tolerate being challenged.)

4. The team is prepared to facilitate skill acquisition through ongoing collaboration.

5. The team is prepared to facilitate generalization of learned skills to class, home and community using pre-assigned materials that will be used across domains/locations.

6. The team agrees to re-evaluate needs and outcomes on a regular basis and teach the child to evaluate his/her own performance and behavior.

Setting the Stage for Student Success: Is the Child's Social Profile Represented?

I have found it extremely helpful to assemble an actual box of materials to use to teach the targeted social skill. These materials are supposed to correspond to:

- The child's level of play/cognition, learning style and personal preference (TOM).

- The documentation from the child's completed Social Skills Assessment Protocol and Social Skills Management Plan.

The kit of materials is meant to be used during Circle Time and scripted play schemas. The kit should contain an inventory form -, so that materials can be tracked, replaced, fixed and/or duplicated for the child's parents and therapists. Finally, the social skills kits of materials need to be multi-sensory and "user friendly" to encourage use. The child should be interested in using the materials in the kits. Remember: Learning needs to be both fun *and* motivating! Also, the lesson is only as much fun as the person who is giving it! Be creative! Try and think "outside the box"!

The Socially Speaking™ Social Skills Kits - Nuts and Bolts

Social Skills Protocols Are Needed for Specific Lessons On:
Feelings
Verbal Rejection
Initiating Social Contact and Conversations
Turn Taking and Respecting Boundaries
Problem Solving

Rules of Engagement re: Assembly, Distribution and Implementation

1. Each kit targets specific behaviors which need to be modified and/or fostered and shaped in a collaborative and pre-planned manner.

2. The kits are kept in one location, usually in the classroom, to be used as part of the teacher's lesson plan for the week.

3. The teacher sets aside a portion of every day to use the kit, with support from the speech therapist, such as Circle Time. The kit can also be used in therapy.

4. The parents are notified about what social skills will be targeted that week and/or month/year and how the lesson will be implemented.

5. The child's team leader keeps a Master Kit so that lost items can be replaced or duplicated and everyone knows what is going on.

6. The Protocols in each kit are determined by the data gleaned from The Social Skills Assessment Protocol and Management Plan.

7. <u>Social Skills Kits and Protocols Are Needed for Specific and Scaffolded Lessons On:</u>

- Feelings
- Verbal Rejection
- Initiating Social Contact and Conversations
- Turn Taking and Respecting Boundaries
- Problem Solving

Social Skills Kit: Sample Inventory Form to Include
Teacher's Name
Curriculum Content
Date Given
Consulting Therapist(s)
Inventory Listing Upon Distribution
Inventory Listing Upon Return
Special Alerts
Comments

The Socially Speaking™ Social Skills Management Plan Template

I designed the *Socially Speaking™ Social Skills Management Plan i.e. Lesson Plan Template (see Chapter 12)* to plot starting points for remediation, based on the information from the *Socially Speaking™ Social Skills Assessment Protocol Checklists*. Goal planning <u>must</u> be a collaborative team effort to document, file, and distribute a specific course of action to pursue/target:
- What behavior the child needs to "tone down."
- What behavior the child needs to increase.

- Where to teach the targeted skill? (individual versus group therapy session, therapy office versus classroom).
- What are the determining criteria to establish mastery and carryover of targeted skill(s)?
  - ★ <u>What</u> is the timeline re: learning to master the targeted skill?
  - ★ <u>When</u> will you decide that the skill has been mastered? When will you have a new meeting for closure purposes, or to discuss why the child is having difficulty mastering?
  - ★ <u>Where</u> will the skill have to be demonstrated to be deemed mastered?

The answers to these questions will determine the size and content of each kit, the purpose of each kit and the length of time the team will spend on a particular kit. Here are more questions to consider when attempting to bridge gaps between readiness to learn and actual performance.

NOTE
Changes in Thinking Can Yield Results! Remember to:

- ☑ Have fun and decrease passivity in the child (action/reaction)
- ☑ Be developmental and sequential about goal planning and delivery
- ☑ Be multi-sensory, to creatively appeal to child's interests/learning style
- ☑ Give a common language and ground for child's IEP team to work from!

The Result? All of this will have a cascade effect on the child's ability to:
1. Establish and maintain rapport with you
2. Sustain attention and increase Time on Task (TOT)
3. Improve episodic memory and carryover, and decrease "situation specific" performance

The Socially Speaking™ Management Plan Template: Questions to Consider
What is your long term goal?
What is your short term goal?
What materials will you present?
How will you present them? (Which visual format? Which manner--structured versus free style?)
How will you ensure attention and compliance? (choose reinforcers and decide how many trials)
How will you cater to student's specific learning style? (auditory-visual-tactile)
How will you judge performance and determine criteria for progress?
How will you generalize this learned skill to other situations and environments?

The answers to these questions can be found in the documentation I mentioned previously; the Functional Behavioral Assessment and the ABC Chart, the *Four Crisis Intervention Questions,* the *Socially Speaking™ Social Skills Assessment Protocol*, the *Socially Speaking™ Play Stages Formula* and standardized test results. The team will have to cross reference everything so that it can carry out practical, functional and sequential goal planning.

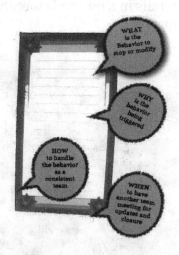

CRISIS INTERVENTION: THE 4 QUESTIONS TO ASK

Again, you can find my *Socially Speaking™ Social Skills Management Plan* in Chapter 12 with my other reproducible forms, and also as part of my Socially Speaking™ iPad® App.

Social Skills Kits: Cooking Up Lessons and Staging "Teachable Moments"

As stated previously, all the kits will be premeditated, pre-assembled and pre-approved by the entire team. These social communication goals will be targeted, as they are all related to orientation to person/place/time and the corresponding goals to improve Body Awareness, Expressing Feelings and Problem Solving-- my trifecta encompassing:

- Feelings
- Verbal Rejection
- Initiating Social Contact and Conversations
- Turn Taking and Respecting Boundaries
- Problem Solving

As stated previously, when targeting social skills for remediation, it is best to do it in a structured, developmentally linear and methodical manner. The above list is merely a starting point, from which other goals can be chosen and interspersed along the continuum. I have found that I can work on the first two protocols with children with ASD as young as three years old. As always, it is crucial to keep in mind the child's socio-emotional and developmental age, rather than his or her chronological age. The protocols of materials need to be assembled and put in the social skills kit, as stated previously. It is helpful to put the materials in a box and store them in one place for organization and time management purposes.

I have been repeatedly asked for "cookbook style" tips that are practical, easy to understand and easy to implement when planning a social skills curriculum. I will now share my suggestions with you. I usually start off implementing these lesson plans in a 1:1 setting, such as a speech therapy session. Once the skill is achieved in a structured, elicited, situation specific activity, I can move on to practicing this skill in:

❖ Another environment such as an empty classroom, the bathroom, or on the bus and

❖ Another setting such as group play time during recess or in the middle of lunch. It is important to spend as much time as needed on reviewing the skill in a 1:1 setting.

Generalization of learned skills and the ability to retain learned information takes time. It usually takes more time for children with ASD to internalize and carryover what they learn to a social situation that is usually noisy, novel and fast paced. These are exacerbating factors, which are usually hard for these children to deal with. I therefore caution a child's team to plan accordingly, and allow for much time and practice to gradually introduce, teach and generalize the skill.

You can start by teaching the child to first express basic feelings such as anger and happiness, excitement and sadness, fear and fatigue and of course hunger and/or thirst, as well as the need to use the bathroom. Then move on to using words to express displeasure, such as "no" or "stop". Begin targeting conversational skills which include eye contact, turn taking and respecting boundaries. Finally, when the child has mastered these initial skills, you can move on to the most challenging yet necessary social skill of all-- problem solving.

Suggested Guidelines for Using Social Skills Kits Effectively

Here are my "cook book style" therapy tips, as requested. These tips are in no way all-inclusive. They are meant as an opening salvo, to draw ideas from and to think about. The reader is encouraged to tailor these suggestions to the child in need. Let's start by reviewing some targeted vocabulary on feelings. You can introduce them as a color coordinated art project, or as a picture photo identification task. You should ensure that the child has developed Self Concept and comprehension of the underlying language concepts needed before learning about expressing feelings, and then moving on to problem solving. Remember, we want to integrate elements of Verbal Behavioral Therapy and Floortime™ when using these kits in treatment! We thus want to methodically and sequentially "pack" specific materials and techniques to achieve goals.

The Socially Speaking™ Social Skills Kits: *Four Elements of Floortime™ to Consider*
Does it encourage joint attention and emotional engagement?
Does it encourage two way communication?
Does it encourage expression of feelings?
Does it encourage logical thought and problem solving?
* Source: *The Child with Special Needs*, page 125

The Socially Speaking™ Social Skills Kits: Penina's Hierarchy and Formula
Materials to Foster Compliance/Rapport & Enhance Cognition/Readiness
Materials to Foster Orientation & Enhance Language/Sensory Processing
Materials to Foster General Social Skills: Self Regulation, Play, and Theory of Mind
Materials to Foster Body Awareness
Materials to Foster Expressing Feelings/Communication of Feelings
Materials to Foster Problem Solving, Resiliency, and Executive Functioning

Protocols for Promoting the Expression of Feelings:

1. Make sure that the child can identify body parts in self and in others (pictures). Make sure the child understands the concept of, and the function of The Five Senses. Make sure that the child has developed a "sense of self".

2. Identify facial expressions in photos and in a mirror. Use a camera to take photos of the child and create a pairs "memory" style game of various facial expressions. When matching the photos is mastered, use those digital photos to match to icons of facial expressions using clip art and/or the Boardmaker™ CD. Make each child a book about him or her self and his or her feelings that they can view and you can elaborate on during specific activities targeting social skills (Show&Tell, Arts&Crafts, Circle Time style group discussion) where you discuss how child feels today.

3. Create a photo "bingo" or "lotto" style game card using facial expression digital photos and/or icons within a group of 6-9 to promote mastery and visual scanning of emotion. This can function first as a structured 1:1 task and then used in a "free style" group play activity such as Musical Chairs, or music time i.e. "Match the music you hear to your present mood" while hearing instruments of various volumes/tempos.

4. Ask questions to promote understanding the "why?" of feelings using classic language stimulation photo cue cards from educational and therapeutic catalogs usually seen in a special education setting. I really like materials from the Super Duper™ Inc. and Great Ideas for Teaching™ catalogs, along with The Speech Bin™ catalog. Most of these catalogs are now online, and contain toll free numbers to call and request one by mail. Your child's speech therapist is also a great resource on where to find and how to use these kinds of materials to foster comprehension of Causality and the vocabulary of feelings.

A BASIC FEELINGS WHEEL

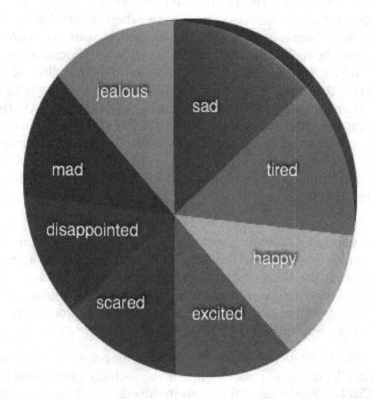

Remember to Consider Lessons Using Music and Art to Teach
Target Vocabulary and Foster Self Expression and Carryover!

Protocols for Promoting Ability to Request/Reject Verbally:

1. Promote the child's understanding of his own wants/needs and the importance of expressing them appropriately. Also, foster the child's ability to "tune in" to him or her self when he or she is upset. Help him or her understand, recognize and express their own sadness, anger, fear, disappointment etc. when things don't go his or her way, and/or when an outburst has occurred. In higher functioning, more verbal children, you can use the technique that Jed Baker calls the "Social Autopsy". You can review the event and its trigger, discuss how it was handled and discuss how it could have been handled better. You can also use the REPLAYS™ technique to role play with puppets, dolls and/or with "little people" and a dollhouse, etc. Another technique I like to use is giving the child an opportunity to discuss and digest his or her feelings by playing a version of "fifteen seconds of fame" when the announcer asks the Super Bowl winner what he plans to do and holds a microphone near his face. You can empower the child, letting him or her know that his or her wants/needs count and that you want him or her to acknowledge their feelings verbally, into the microphone or tape recorder.

2. Teach the child to express displeasure verbally, using gestures (head shake "no", the universal hand sign for "stop")Social Stories and "Task Organizers" using visual supports to break down the steps (see my Verbal Rejection Template in the forms section of this book). You can also role play by creating mock problem situations that provide an opportunity for the child to practice using the new vocabulary such as "Stop this now!" or "I want to do this later".

3. Teach the child to deal with teasing/bullying without an outburst. You can break down the steps visually using a "Task Organizer" or verbally in conversation, during a group lesson or Circle Time to teach the steps involved:

• "Put the blinders on" hand motions or a scarf pretend play game to teach ignoring.

• "Keep the face blank" activity with mirror and digital camera to teach staying calm.

• Initiate eye contact with the bully and wait quietly until you have his or her attention.

• Express your feelings to the bully calmly and clearly.

• Tell the bully what you want from him or her instead of acting out and/or reacting physically

Protocols to Promote Better Initiation of Conversations with Others:

1. Provide "real time" opportunities to observe and imitate others engaged in saying hello and starting a conversation. Use video footage of that child or his family members. Plan out specific routines such as getting on the school bus or entering class each morning to model and practice greetings. You can also role play with puppets and/or dolls, and make telephone calls, imaginary and then real, to carryover this skill.

1. Teach the child to initiate and maintain eye contact when hearing his or her name called, when spoken to and when he or she wants to ask for something. Start with building concrete awareness using "hands on" materials such as arts & crafts tasks with "googly eyes", and talking to self in mirror and then to others in the mirror. You can then move on to a more abstract understanding of the need to have good eye contact. Once the child grasps this, and performs for elicited, structured activities, generalize this to scripted but less structured opportunities. For example, set up a situation where the child can make requests of a parent/teacher/therapist and then a peer, and then several peers, by playing a board game, ball, "Store" or "House". (Note: it will be more fun and realistic with a "dress up" component!)

Protocols for Increasing Sharing/Turn taking/Respecting Boundaries:

1. This is usually best taught by action instead of by passive observation. You can provide simple scripted opportunities such as playing concrete games like "Gears", "Memory," "Chutes&Ladders" and "Connect Four" to teach sharing and turn taking "live" and "in the moment". You can assign snack duty to different children who then bring in and share various food items with peers. You can use Circle Time to foster taking turns and respecting each other's "personal space". You can play physical games such as "Twister", "Mother May I" and "Red Light, Green Light" to facilitate understanding of these skills. You can video tape the child "in action", engaging in these skills or not, and then show and discuss.

2. You can collaborate with the child's team to create personalized Social Stories about "boundaries". You can set this as a goal during the child's Team Meeting, and then review the story in class, speech therapy and home.

3. You can lead a group discussion in Circle Time, on the idea of boundaries and what it means. You can review body parts and discuss "personal space". You can do a group activity and play with gears and/or make a collage from maps of the United States or the world. You can do an art project where the child creates a map leading to his house or bedroom etc. You can create a contrived, scripted, structured play activity for a small group with toy cars etc. Create highways with different lanes, construction zones and toll booths to enter a different state, by using a bridge. Finally, use videotaping in "real time" and engage in a variation of "talk to the hand" in a group setting to further facilitate the understanding of "personal space".

Protocols to Foster Understanding the Hierarchy of Skills Development re: Problem Solving:

1. *Awareness that a problem exists and how to react:* Use contrived obstacles such as giving broken toys or toys with missing pieces to foster this awareness. Play dumb and hide things the child wants, or pretend to misunderstand. Use classic photo "what's missing/wrong?" picture games. Create a Social Story about a problematic event the child recently experienced and reenact it with photos and props. Use scripted role play when playing with dolls and Legos, etc. to create chaos and ask hypothetical questions such as "What would happen if.....".

2. *Verbalizing the problem to an adult:* Create mock problem situations/obstacles so that the child has opportunities to practice stereotypical phrases such as "help me do....", or "I can't do this....". Role play with puppets and dolls, first in a 1:1 activity, and then in a group setting such as free play and Circle Time. Videotape the child expressing the need for help and positively reinforce attempts and successful verbalization of the problem.

3. *Exploring solutions/outcomes/options:* For higher functioning, more verbal children, you can use arts & crafts tasks such as lanyard, beading and sequential patterns to teach the idea of a timeline of cause & effect. You can also plant seeds and discuss the outcomes. You can have the child look at problematic photos (refer to the educational catalogs) and predict outcomes and/or provide solutions. You can create a "do it yourself" comic strip from these pictures to send home for homework. You can take video footage of the child engaged in an inappropriate behavior and explore solutions. I have sometimes found it quite helpful to create, send home and discuss with the child and his or her parents, a Visual Outcome Flow Chart. I use Computer Assisted Instruction (CAI) such as Apple™'s Pages™, Kidspiration™, Boardmaker™, or Kidpix™ to literally draw and present this abstract concept I am trying to teach.

4. *Verbal Negotiation to come to an agreement or compromise:* This is the hardest step for children with special needs to master. I compare this to weaving a tapestry that looks smooth on one side, and has a definite pattern, while the other side is a mess of knots and shorter and longer threads. I use this analogy when explaining this goal to parents and educators. Negotiation is an art, much like weaving with a loom or painting with oil paints. It is learned through patience, creative thinking, a vision of the desired end result and the ability to be flexible. This skill requires much modeling and role play in a 1:1 setting, using materials I previously mentioned in this chapter. It also requires providing many scripted, contrived situations and much coaching in a group therapy session, to master this skill.

I have found that creating a Task Organizer using Boardmaker™ and Social Stories with real photos about the problematic situation fosters improved comprehension about the specific negotiation needed. Role play and videotaping is also invaluable to these children. I have found that these children can learn to negotiate with others whom they trust, feel safe with and have rapport with. Why? Because they know that they will come to a mutually satisfactory agreement with the familiar person. Sometimes certain things are not up for negotiation. The child with ASD has to learn that as well. Social Stories can really help the child internalize that, and clearly delineate what the target vocabulary is for the entire team to review.

5. *Conflict Resolution where both parties agree with outcome:* This is the final frontier of social skills building and having a social consciousness. All over the world, this is the last bastion of civilization, and the hardest skill to master. Senseless wars have been fought, and enmity has flourished, because of continued issues with conflict resolution and accepting undesirable outcomes graciously. At one time or another, it comes down to making a choice. It is both a privilege and a responsibility to teach our children, even children with special needs, how to resolve conflict and accept undesirable outcomes. The degree and frequency of acceptance varies, as does the individual situation and choices of how to handle it. Nonetheless, it is this particular skill that can make all the difference for a person who wants to make and keep friends, hold down a job and choose to emotionally connect to another person.

This is the most abstract concept to teach, and it requires a higher level of cognition and socio-emotional health to achieve and master. I work on this skill last, after seeing a child "climb the ladder" and master the previously discussed prerequisite skills. I first work on this skill in therapy, usually during an individual session. I create mock obstacles in "real time and model and role play the act of accepting the outcome, using exaggerated facial expressions and humor. I then use photos of the child's family and friends to discuss (with exaggerated intonation) a recent episode(s) that triggered the need to resolve a problem. I can either use the photos as individual teaching moments, or chain them together in a Social Story format, complete with scripted text and stereotypical phrases.

Once the child understands <u>what</u> he or she has to do to "fix" a problem, we can move on to practicing <u>how</u> to do it. I will usually videotape the facial expression of the child in "crisis" mode, and the facial expression and reaction of the adult to that child. I will then view it and discuss it later, with the child and possibly his teacher/parent. I will then recreate the trigger on a smaller scale, with other people, and immediately use positive reinforcement for agreeing with the outcome graciously and/or resolving the conflict.

Sometimes problems don't go away. The child with ASD needs to learn this too. Accepting life's unfairness is not easy for anyone, but it is especially difficult for children with ASD. I have found that providing visual supports reminding the child to be accepting and patient, and chaining it with an alternative choice, has proven very helpful. In the end, I sometimes use the almighty "because I said so". It should be invoked sparingly, and only when there is trust and rapport. I usually use this phrase as a last resort, for resolving the problem that arises from time constraints, not socially driven conflict with peers, arising from "social blindness" or difficulty with overall problem solving.

Sample Outcome Flow Chart
Awareness of the problem
Verbalization of the problem and offer of a solution
The provision of an option for the problem
Accepting the resolution and outcome of the problem

Example: The noisy vacuum cleaner triggers a tantrum. Here's a sample outcome flow chart:

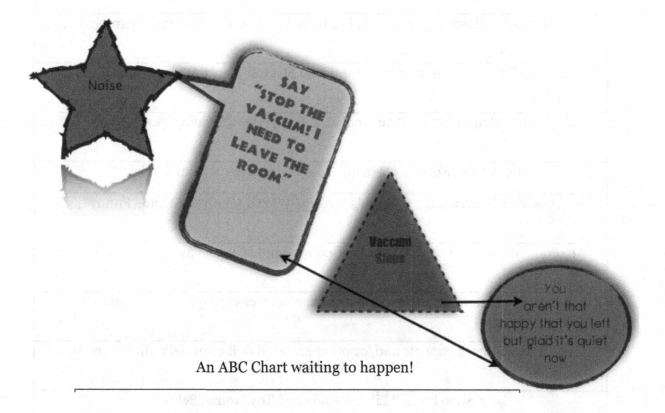

An ABC Chart waiting to happen!

What to Consider When Planning Social Skills Kits:
❖What the treatment plan's starting point(s) should be (goals based on assessment).
❖ How to implement change (a documented social skills management plan).
❖ Where specific skills will be practiced (inventory list, team collaboration).
❖ Why you are choosing specific materials and goals to start with, based on TOM

Social Skills Kits: Suggested Materials
The Socially Speaking™ Social Skills Management Plan Template
Inventory Form (copy in kit, master form in office)
One 8x10 mirror with a magnetic back for easy mounting when not in use
Tactile Toys: play dough, Mr. Potato™ Head, Alex™ String a Farm, a doctor's kit, block constructs toys, puzzles, Colorforms™ Silly Faces, a toy bowling set, toy musical instruments, Chutes & Ladders and other board games, lacing and bead toys
Feelings Lotto Matching Game and laminated digital photos of facial expressions
An iPad® and a digital camera for Social Stories, pictures, videos and apps
"The Verbal Rejection Boardmaker™ Template" © Penina Pearl Rybak
Customized worksheets using Google™ images or Boardmaker™
Assorted Picture Games: What's Wrong? What's Missing? What's Funny?
An iPod nano or iPod shuffle with headphones and speakers and pre-loaded music
Arts & Crafts items to make puppets and misc. faces (googly eyes, mouth etc.)
Melissa and Doug™ puppets and/or other assorted dolls, stuffed animals and farm animals
Fisher-Price™ Little People and Toy House/School
Donated used dishes and clothes for "dress up" and pretend play schemas

Final Words

"Social Skills Kits" are a developmental, playful, methodical and creative way to implement IEP goals targeting the "whole child". It facilitates overall social-communication, graphomotor and fine motor, cognitive and executive functioning skills in a more sequential, consistent manner. When done right, the kits can seamlessly help the team move from assessment to treatment mode, allowing collaborative goal-planning, implementation and carryover. The kits are designed for decreased situation specific performance, i.e. splintered skill acquisition and increased accountability on the educator and the student's part. Both need to self-evaluate progress and efficacy on an ongoing basis to ensure that the kits are doing what they are supposed to. Both need to understand that there are thus readiness indicators to its use:

- There is documentation on file providing insight into goals and a course of action.
- There is a "paper trail" about the child's behavior, Theory of Mind (inner landscape, preferences, learning style, perspective, rapport with others) and level of play development.
- There is consensus re: the kits' assembly based on these factors: storage space, budget, medical alerts/allergies and the assigning of a team leader to monitor inventory.

As stated previously, all the kits will be premeditated, pre-assembled and pre-approved by the entire team. These social communication goals will be targeted, as they are all related to orientation to person/place/time and the corresponding goals to improve Body Awareness, Expressing Feelings and Problem Solving--my trifecta.

- ♦ Feelings

- ♦ Verbal Rejection

- ♦ Initiating Social Contact and Conversations

- ♦ Turn Taking and Respecting Boundaries

- ♦ Problem Solving

To reiterate an important point, despite the team following protocol, some children may not respond positively to this structured approach. They may initially resist, especially in group learning situations/group therapy sessions--even if they have established rapport and routine with the educator and have a familiarity, i.e. working knowledge of the items in the kit. Like any tool, a person's physical and emotional status will affect performance and attention span. Some children with Autism will therefore need their emotional temperature taken before "setting the stage" for learning with a specific kit. Some children will require a review of previously learned material before transitioning them to a new kit with unfamiliar materials. It's all about making sure the train tracks (rapport, behavior management) are kept clean and smooth so that the social skills train (with the kits on board) can get to where it needs to go. Remember what I wrote in

Chapter 1? Building rapport means being vigilant in the driver's seat, especially when engaging the child in a "teachable moment" using the kit!

Materials for Your Toolbox

• <u>Key References</u>

Bader, Stephanie et al (2010). *Enhancing Communication in Children With Autism Spectrum Disorders: Practical Strategies Series in Autism Education.* Waco, TX: Prufrock Press Inc.

Baker, Jed (2003). *Social Skills Training for Children and Adolescents with Asperger Syndrome and Social Communication Problems.* Shawnee, KS: Autism Apserger Publishing.

Barbera, Mary Lynch, and Rassmussen, Tracy (2007). *The Verbal Behavior Approach: How to Teach Children with Autism and Related Disorders.* Philadelphia, PA: Jessica Kingsley Publishers.

Barekit, Rachael (2006). *Playing it Right! Social Skills Activities for Parents and Teachers of Young Children with Autism Spectrum Disorders, Including Asperger Syndrome and Autism.* Shawnee, KS: Autism Asperger Publishing.

Baron-Cohen, Simon (2002). *Targeting Autism: What We Know, Don't Know, and Can Do to Help Young Children with Autism and Related Disorders.* Berkeley, CA: University of California Press.

Basu, S. et al (2010). Measuring Collaborative Consultation Practices in Natural Environments. *Journal of Early Intervention,* 32(2), 127-150.

Beckerleg, Tracey (2008). *Fun with Messy Play: Ideas and Activities for Children with Special Needs.* Philadelphia, PA: Jessica Kingsley Publishers.

Beukelman, David and Mirenda, Pat (2006). *Augmentative and Alternative Communication: Supporting Children and Adults with Complex Communication Needs.* Baltimore, MD: Brookes Publishing.

Brady, Lois Jean, et al (2011). *Speak, Move, Play, and Learn with Children on the Autism Spectrum.* Philadelphia, PA: Jessica Kingsley Publishers.

Chiak, D.F., Wright, R., and Ayres, K.M. (2010). Use of Self-Modeling Static- Picture Prompts Via a Handheld Computer to Facilitate Self-Monitoring in the General Education Classroom. *Education and Training in Autism and Developmental Disabilities,* 45(1), 136-149.

Christie, Phil et al (2009). *First Steps in Intervention with Your Child with Autism: Frameworks for Communication.* Philadelphia, PA: Jessica Kingsley Publishers

Delaney, Tara (2009). *101 Games and Activities for Children with Autism, Asperger's, and Sensory Processing Disorders*. Europe: McGraw Hill.

Densmore, Ann (2007). *Helping Children with Autism Become More Social: 76 Ways to Use Narrative Play*. Westport, CT: Praeger Publishing.

Gallo-Lopez, Loretta, and Rubin, Lawrence (2012). *Play-Based Interventions for Children and Adolescents with Autism Spectrum Disorders*. New York, NY: Taylor and Francis Group.

Greenspan, Stanley, and Weider, Serena (1998). *The Child with Special Needs: Encouraging Intellectual and Emotional Growth*. Cambridge, MA: Perseus Books Group.

Kowalski, Timothy (2002). *The Source for Asperger's Syndrome*. East Moline, IL: Linguisystems.

Manela, Miriam. (2014). *The Parent-Child Dance: A Guide to Help You Understand and Shape Your Child's Behavior*. Passaic, NJ: OT Thrive Publishing.

Mannix, Darlene (2009). *Social Skills Activities for Special Children, Second Edition*. San Francisco, CA: Jossey-Bass/Wiley & Sons Inc.

Mannix, Darlene (2009). *Life Skills Activities for Special Children, Second Edition*. San Francisco, CA: Jossey-Bass/Wiley & Sons Inc.

Martin, Nicole (2009). *Art As an Early Intervention Tool for Children with Autism*. Philadelphia, PA: Jessica Kingsley Publishers.

Morgan, J.J. (2010) Social Networking Web Sites: Teaching Appropriate Social Competence to Students with Emotional and Behavioral Disorders. *Intervention in School and Clinic*, 45(3), 147-157.

Moor, Julia (2002). *Playing, Laughing, and Learning with Children on the AutismSpectrum: A Practical Resource of Play Ideas for Parents and Carers*. Philadelphia, PA: Jessica Kingsley Publishers.

Prelock, Patricia et al (2012). *Treatment of Autism Spectrum Disorders: Evidence-Based Intervention Strategies for Communication and Social Interactions*. Baltimore, MD: Paul H. Brookes Publishing Company.

Quill, Kathleen Ann (2000). *Do-Watch-Listen-Say: Social and Communication Intervention for Children with Autism*. Baltimore, MD: Paul H. Brookes Publishing.

Sher, Barbara (2009). *Early Intervention Games: Fun, Joyful Ways to Develop Social and Motor Skills in Children with Autism Spectrum or Sensory Processing Disorders*. San Francisco, CA: Jossey-Bass/ Wiley & Sons Inc.

Siegel, Bryna (2003). *Helping Children with Autism Learn: Treatment Approaches for Parents and Professionals*. New York, NY: Oxford University Press.

Weiss, Mary Jane and Harris, Sandra (2001). *Reaching Out, Joining In: Teaching Social Skills to Young Children with Autism*. Bethesda, MD: Woodbine House.

Weiss, Mary Jane and Demiri, Valbona (2011). *Jumpstarting Communication Skills in Children with Autism: A Parents' Guide to Applied Verbal Behavior*. Bethesda, MD: Woodbine House.

Willis, Clarissa (2006). *Teaching Young Children with Autism Spectrum Disorder*. Beltsville, MD: Gryphon House Inc.

- <u>Key Links to Peruse</u>

<u>http://bit.ly/1yKoBVv</u>

<u>http://bit.ly/1F7CK6o</u>

<u>http://bit.ly/1DfSsxm</u>

<u>http://bit.ly/1yK1kFZ</u>

<u>http://bit.ly/1zByeeB</u>

<u>http://bit.ly/1KeGohT</u>

<u>http://bit.ly/1xl71bK</u>

<u>http://edcate.co/1zSUtjs</u>

<u>http://bit.ly/1LNW11r</u>

<u>http://bit.ly/1F7Eb4I</u>

<u>http://bit.ly/1DfU8XL</u>

<u>http://bit.ly/1zaGHBZ</u>

- <u>Key Concepts to Address</u>

Play, Theory of Mind, Orientation, Self Regulation, Episodic Memory, Pre-Literacy and "Teachable Moment"

• <u>Key Toys to Use in Treatment</u>

❖ **Feelings and Verbal Rejection:** Fisher Price Classic Record Player, Puppets, dolls, mirrors, stop sign stickers, Melissa & Doug Stop Sign (Vehicles) Jumbo Puzzle, Melissa & Doug Deluxe Wooden Vehicles & Traffic Signs, Crayola™ Color Me a Song Toy, YouTube Clips of Harry from Sesame Street™ (vintage), digital camera to take selfies of facial expressions, Emotions by Colorcards, Webber Photo Cards- Emotions, by Super Duper, Faces and Feelings Lotto by Key Education, Carson Dellosa Key Education Emotions Learning Cards, Carson Dellosa Key Education Talk About A Child's Day Learning Cards, Melissa and Doug Band in a Box, VTech KidiBeats Drum Set, Winfun Step To Play Giant Piano Mat and Magic Mic by Toysmith.

❖ **Books:**

Carla's Sandwich by Debbie Herman and Sheila Bailey, *Alexander and the Horrible, No Good, Very Bad Day* by Judith Viorst and Ray Cruz, *Dot* by Randi Zuckerberg and Joe Berger, *Bread and Jam for Frances* by Russell Hoban and Lillian Hoban, *Today I Feel Silly* by Jamie Lee Curtis and Laura Cornell, *I'm Gonna Like Me* by Jamie Lee Curtis and Laura Cornell, *Chalk* by Bill Thomson, and *The Magic Rainbow Hug* by Janet Courtney.

❖ **Initiating Social Contact and Conversations:** Mirrors, Playskool Sesame Street Elmo's Cell Phone, VTech - Slide And Talk Smart Phone, Photo Conversation Cards for Children with Autism and Asperger's Learning Cards by Carson Dellosa, Mr. Potato Head™, arts and crafts items including dot paint and Googly Eyes, Guess Who? Game by Hasbro, Rory's Story Cubes, ThinkFun Roll and Play Board Game, Create-a-Scene Magnetic dollhouse, dolls, puppets and pretending to ignore or talk to the object the child wants (inanimate-reference).

❖ **Books:**

Touch and Feel Books by DK Publishing, *Brown Bear, Brown Bear, What Do You See?* by Bill Martin Jr. and Eric Carle, *Are You a Cow?* by Sandra Boynton, *Chicka Chicka Boom Boom* by Bill Martin Jr. et al, *Do Princesses Wear Hiking Boots?* by Carmela LaVigna Coyle et al, *Are You My Mother?* by P.D. Eastman, Go Dog Go! by P.D. Eastman, *Guess How Much I Love You* by Sam McBratney and Anita Jeram, *The Snowy Day* by Ezra Jack Keats, *Whistle for Willie* by Ezra Jack Keats, and *Caps for Sale* by Esphyr Slobodkina.

✤ **Turn Taking and Respecting Boundaries:** Trampoline, outdoor swing, slide, seesaw, Tire Swing, Earlyears Baby Farm Friends Bowling, Alex™ String a Farm, Hape String Along Shapes, Fisher-Price Brilliant Basics: Snap-Lock Beads - Vehicle Shapes, Tolo Toys Roller Ball Run, Easy-Grip Jumbo Pegs & Pegboard, Melissa and Doug Stamp Sets, TOMY Gearation Refrigerator Magnets Building Toy, Gizmos and Gears by Learning Resources, ThinkFun S'match Game, ThinkFun Zyngo, Qwirkle Board Game, HedBanz Game, Mindware Imaginets Magnet Game, High Ho Cherry-O, Giant Blocks, Magna Tiles , and Legos®.

✤ **Books:**

Open the Barn Door by Christopher Santoro, *The Very Hungry Caterpillar* by Eric Carle, *Hop on Pop* by Dr. Seuss, *Stone Soup* by Ann Mcgovern and Winslow Pinney Pels, *If You Give a Mouse a Cookie* by Laura Numeroff and Felicia Bond *If You Give a Dog a Donut* by Laura Numeroff and Felicia Bond, *Pinkalicious* by Victoria and Elizabeth Kann, *Click Clack Moo: Cows That Type* by Doreen Cronin and Betsy Lewin, *Press Here* by Herve Tullet, and *The Big Book of Berenstain Bears Beginner Books* by Stan and Jan Berenstain.

✤ **Problem Solving:** Broken toys, toys/games with missing pieces, Cause and Effect Toys like the Fisher Price Go Baby Go! Press and Crawl Turtle and the See n' Say Toy, *Where Does It Go?* by Margaret Miller, Alex™,Emotions and Photo What's Wrong? Flashcards, both by Colorcards, Carson Dellosa Key Education What's Wrong? Learning Cards, Smethport Mind Your Manners Language Cards, Mind Your Manners Game by Smethport, Consequences Game by TaliCor, Problem Solving Photo Lotto Game by Super Duper, Webber "What Are They Thinking?" Photo Card Deck by Super Duper, Learning Resources Pizza Mania, Yummy Tin Toy Tea Set, Don't Break the Ice, Chutes and Ladders, Quadrilla Marble Railway, Tinkertoys, Learning Resources Gears! Gears! Gears! Let's Go Fishin', Guidecraft Magneatos Master Builder (89 pieces) and Successful Kids Patch Products Blunders Board Game.

✤ **Books:**

Moo Baa La La by Sandra Boynton, *I Want My Hat Back* by Jon Klassen, *Wacky Wednesday* by Theo LeSieg and George Booth, *I Don't Want to Be a Frog* by Dev Petty and Mike Boldt, *Amelia Bedelia* by Peggy Parish and Fritz Siebel, *The Cat in the Hat* by Dr. Seuss, *Giraffes Can't Dance* by Giles Andreae and Guy Parker-Rees, *The Day the Crayons Quit* by Drew Daywait and Oliver Jeffers, *Sheep in a Jeep* by Nancy E. Shaw and Margot Apple™, *Where the Sidewalk Ends* by Shel Silverstein, and *The Mrs. Piggle Wiggle Series* by Betty MacDonald and Hilary Knight.

• Key iPad® Apps to Use in Treatment

☞ *For the Service Provider:* At this stage of social communication intervention I usually recommend focusing on specific goals using specific materials to facilitate carryover and mastery. The goal of iOS App integration into lessons at this phase of treatment is really to *supplement* your play materials in your proverbial toolbox for broader teachable moments re: actual social skills. I therefore recommend these particular apps which are uniquely designed and/or appropriate to address behavior/social communication needs:

☞ *Social Skills:* Socially Speaking™ iPad® App: The Management Plan Template Portion, Autism Emotions by Model Me Kids, Model Me Going Places 2, Let's Be Social! by Everyday Speech, Social Adventures, Social Skill Builder Lite and Full, SocialNorms, Little Star Learning Story Creator, Storybook Maker by Merge Mobile, 2Create a Story, 2Do It Yourself, MashCAM, OnceAppon, SonicPics, My Story, Chatterpix, Talking Train, Bag Game, Junganew: A Herd of Sounds "S", Comic Life, Comic Book!, Strip Designer, LifeSound, Doodlelicious, Shuttersong, AutisMate Lite and Paid and ABC Video Pro Lite.

☞ *For the Child:* Once the child has increased cognitive awareness of the need to achieve the goals listed below re: social communication, I can then introduce iOS apps into the therapy/educational regimen or homework assignment. I cannot stress enough how important it is to play with manipulatives in real time first, before integrating apps into lessons in these areas:

✤ **Feelings and Verbal Rejection:** Emotions Flashcards by I Can Do Apps, ABA Flashcards and Games- Emotions and Touch & Learn Emotions by Innovative Mobile Apps, Autism Emotions by Model Me Kids, Model Me Going Places 2, Meebie, Preschool Feelings by iTouchiLearn, Chatterpix, SonicPics, MashCAM, Pepi Doctor, Social Emotional Exchange-S.E.E. by Saym Basheer, EQ for Kids, Feel Electric, What's the Expression by Web Team Corporation, Feelings with Milo, Avokiddo Emotions, Emotions Collections by ItBook, Expressions for Autism, Discovering Emotions with Zeely, Recycling Workshop, Puppet Workshop, American Doctor, Ear Doctor, Sago Mini Doodlecast, Little Red Hen:Wordwinks, Autism and PDD: Concepts, Tellagami, Smiley Booth and Cartoon Builder Free.

✤ **Initiating Social Contact and Conversations:** Caillou 1, Drawp Edu, Strip Designer, Comic Life, Sago Mini Doodlecast, Comic Book!, My First Words- Flashcards by Alligator Apps, Knock Knock Family, Model Me Going Places 2, Describe It To Me by Smarty Ears Apps, Wh? Questions by Smarty Ears Apps, Story Creator, Story Builder, Sentence Builder, and Language Builder by Mobile Education Apps, Bag Game, Talking Train, StoryMaker Free, Build a Story and Glow Draw®.

✤ **Turn Taking and Respecting Boundaries:** Sound Touch Lite, Vocal Zoo, Memory King, Fun Flowers Lite, Sort It Out 1 & 2, Balls by iotic, Paint Sparkles, Draw in 3D, Draw, Music Sparkles, AnimalPiano, Feed Maxi, Photo Buttons, Little Fingers Lite, Glow Draw®, Draw in 3D, Music Group by Tiny Tap, Monsters, Furry Friend, Talking Ginger, Toca Tea Party, Cute Food, Lets Create, Little Patterns by Grasshopper Apps, Kids CARS by Pyjamas Apps, Preschool! All In One, Abby Monkey® Animated Puzzle Adventures Game, Preschool Toy Phone, Toca Builders, Toca Car, Kids Learning Puzzles- Build a House, Blocks Express, PuzzleFarm, Abby- Basic Skills Preschool: Puzzles and Patterns HD Free, Fiete (story book), Drawp Edu, Stick Around, Jigsaw Puzzle Free, Community Helpers Play & Learn and LEGO® DUPLO® Train.

❖**Verbal Problem Solving re: Social Communication & Humor:** Is That Silly? by Smarty Ears, Story Builder by Mobile Education Store, Sequencing Post Office, Making Sequences by Zorten, iSequences, Autism and PDD Reasoning and Problem Solving Lite and Paid, What Doesn't Belong? by Tiny Tap, Toca Hair Salon 1 & 2, Cat in the Hat by Dr. Seuss, Elephant's Bath, Princess Chocolate, You Doodle Plus, Alex the Handyman Free, Ear Doctor, American Doctor, Understanding Inferences Fun Deck, How Would You Feel If...Fun Deck, What Are They Asking? Fun Deck, What's Being Said? Fun Deck, What Would You Do At Home If...Fun Deck ,What Would You Do At School If...Fun Deck, Difficult Situations Fun Deck, Let's Predict Fun Deck, If....Then Fun Deck , Imagination Questions Fun Deck, Once Appon, Toontastic, Toontastic Jr., Old MacDonald by Duck Duck Moose, Five Little Monkeys Jumping on the Bed, Another Monster at the End of This Book, Grover's Number Special, Trixie and Jinx, Junganew: A Herd of Sounds "S", Faces iMake-Right Brain Creativity, Explain Everything, Haiku Deck, Comic Life, Comic Book!, Strip Designer, LifeSound, Doodlelicious, Educreations, Screen Chomp, and Between the Lines Level 1.

Penina's Pointers: Materials

Verbal Rejection Difficulty is a Self Regulation Issue, due to the EF "Emotional Control"!

- PECS: "no", "stop sign"
- ASL/signing: teach "bye"
- Verbal Speech: role play: "no", "don't want it", "later" etc.

Penina's Pointers: Materials

Social Initiation Difficulty is a Body Awareness Issue, due to SPD. Review Body Parts and Use Physical Humor, Including Exaggerated Affect!

- Greetings: toy phones, real cell phone calls
- Eye Contact: REPLAYS™, Mr. Potato Head™, arts&crafts
- Role play with sock puppets and googly eyes
- Inanimate Object Reference: Use Humor! Pretend to talk to the object child wants and is looking at, instead of you

SOCIAL SKILLS KITS

Penina's Pointers: Materials

Sharing & Turn Taking Difficulty is an Emotional Attunement Issue, due to Reduced Theory of Mind!

- One Toy with Physical Border: tire swing, slide
- "Part/Whole Toys": stringing bead toys, mini-bowling set
- Toys evoking Empathy: dolls, doll house

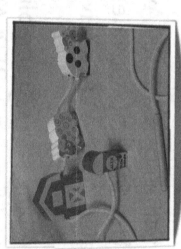

SOCIAL SKILLS KITS

181

Penina's Pointers: Materials

Respecting Boundaries Difficulty is a Body Awareness Issue, due to SPD and Reduced TOM. Use Physical Activities, Physical Humor, Visual Supports, and Exaggerated Affect When Giving Constructive Criticism!

- Physical Activities: climbing stairs, trampoline, building forts
- Physical Humor & Visual Supports: REPLAYS ™, YouTube ™, Social Stories ™ with correct/incorrect photos
- Construct Toys: Legos ™, Tinker Toys ™, peg & gear toys
- Inanimate Object Reference: Dycem ™ and duct tape (markers)

Penina's Pointers: Materials

Problem Solving Difficulty is an EF Issue With Flexibility and Metacognition. Move from Physical Humor to Linguistic, Using Visual Supports, Role Play, and the "Social Autopsy". Use Photos/Video Footage Correct/Incorrect Performance in Various Situations/Settings!

- Create Obstacles: give puzzles & shape sorter missing pieces, give broken toys, pretend to misunderstand/ignore requests
- Humor & Visual Supports: books, what's funny? what's wrong? games
- Cooperative Play Toys: pretend tea party, blocks, board games
- The Socially Speaking™ Problem Solving Hierarchy

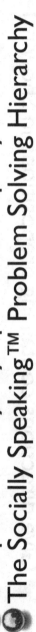

Penina's Pointers: Materials

Tips for Teaching Body Awareness and Spatial Awareness:

- Take digital photos while reenacting body positions in Real Time and make a story book and/or Memory Game to play with later on that same day

- Give directions containing prepositions in Show'n'Tell games

- Build a bridge from tissue boxes, blocks, plastic cups etc. Build a highway out of plastic train tracks, pieces of toilet paper or paper towel etc. Set the timer and play "driving" with mini cars

- Hide favorite toys and have a "treasure hunt" with visual map

- Use arts & crafts to glue various items "into position" on paper

Penina's Pointers: Materials

Tips for Teaching "Part/Whole Relationships"– Precursor to Learning About Numbers:

- Identify actual body parts on self, on doll, and on adults/peers in visual range or on video

- Identify photos of body parts and cut up to make a collage

- Make arts & crafts out of body parts (face with googly eyes, puppets with craft sticks/yarn)

- Play with toys that have pieces ex: different puzzles, Mr. Potato Head™, Colorforms™

- Build things with blocks and/or Lego™ pieces and take photos putting together/taking apart

- Take photographs or worksheets, cut them in half, paste back together to create "whole"

- Work on improving categorization of like/unalike objects/pictures using actual sorting bins

- Create thematic units and worksheets about seasons, holidays, community events etc.

- Work on 1:1 correspondence and counting skills using visual (picture games and books) cues and tactile cues (arts & crafts items and other manipulatives, including real life objects for tasks involving ADL such as getting dressed, setting table etc.)

Penina's Pointers: Materials

Tips to Teach Sequencing:

Go from maximum perceptual support (visual cues) to minimal or none, i.e. elicited learning ⇧ spontaneous ability, Also, use the numbers 1-3 in conjunction with your visual supports/"props" to reinforce the concept of things having "an order".

⬤ Identify "first and last" using actual numbers 1 & 2 and real objects such as: banana in peel, chocolate wafer or licorice wrapped and then unwrapped, a whole apple, and then just the core, an egg, and then crack it, a sock and then a shoe, putting cereal in bowl and then milk etc.

⬤ Identify "first and last" using #1 & 2 and real time photos of person in action such as: putting on shirt and then buttoning it, pouring juice and then drinking it, opening closet and taking out coat, hanging dress on hangar and putting it in closet, running bath water and then bathing etc.

⬤ Play pre-made interlocking puzzle games (and include the numbers 1-3) that have pictures that tell a "story" according to "first/middle/ last"

⬤ Create customized sequencing worksheets for the child using license free digital, stock, and/or clip art photos

⬤ Do an activity and break down the procedure into at least 3 steps to reinforce that there is "an order" to things such as making pizza, baking cookies etc. and take digital photos to review later and create a story using arts & crafts items or an iPad® story making App

⬤ Read story books with illustrations and discuss the pictures in sequence

⬤ Have child retell a familiar story in order, without any kind of perceptual support (i.e. pictures, books, props etc.) and audio record the story using an iPad® recorder App.

Penina's Pointers: Materials

The Socially Speaking™ Visual Presentation Protocol- A Suggested Hierarchy:

1. Use objects in a structured way to teach child to:
   - Identify it on command (label it, point to it)
   - Describe basic object function
   - Follow directives about it e.g. "give it to me" or "put in..." for social interaction purposes, not to teach prepositions (elicited learning vs. incidental learning)

2. Use real photos (digital camera etc.) such as cards and puzzle games

3. Use photos to create lotto boards to match to the already familiar objects and photos

4. Use a mixture of objects/photos/icons in an unstructured, play type of activity, to give the child "hands on practice" and opportunity for carryover, including motivating the child that learning is FUN!

5. Introduce worksheets to help the child:
   - Generalize previously learned skill to another medium
   - Understand the concept that time passes, i.e. everything in life basically has a beginning /middle/end (difficulty understanding this is why many of our kids "act out" and/or engage in repetitive behavior and "self-stim")
   - More accurately self evaluate (judge) performance which increases self awareness

Penina's Pointers: Materials

Tips For Using Visual Supports To Teach Vocabulary and Concepts:

◉ A child's level of visual acuity determines the size/nature of your visual stimuli and <u>how</u> you present it (table top/horizontal vs. velcro board/ vertical)

◉ Some lower functioning children may spend <u>much</u> time at the "object" phase, and may not be ready for visual supports for a while. Repetition and patience are key!

◉ Worksheets vary in visual complexity, so choose wisely or create your own!

◉ When teaching concepts, it is good to have an organized lesson plan that fluidly and seamlessly integrates structured learning with spontaneous play time i.e. Thematic Learning

◉ Use a multi-sensory approach where children are taught "hands on" in a group and get to "act it out" later that hour/day etc. in an individual symbolic play schema at their level, with incorporated visual stimuli corresponding to target vocabulary

◉ A child may have a large receptive lexicon, and may be great with photos/pictures, but still needs to be introduced to a new, unfamiliar concept <u>kinesthetically</u> (remember: developmentally, we all start out to be tactile learners, and many of our kids are "stuck" at this phase!)

SOCIAL SKILLS KITS

Chapter 10:
<u>Toilet Training:</u> What You Need to Know About Children With Autism

Anecdote

Dillon is a 3 year old placid, cheerful, easily distractible, lovable little boy with a diagnosis of Autism and Sensory Processing Disorder. He is about to be enrolled in a therapeutic preschool class for the first time with related services. His parents have requested that he be toilet trained as soon as possible, as Dillon is either unaware or uninterested. Dillon has recently started speaking in single words, currently wears pampers and needs supervision when dressing/undressing himself. He dislikes eating and touching certain textures, and likes movement. The kiddie pool and porch swing at home are his favorite hangouts. When Dillon is happy, he flaps his hands or rocks back and forth. When he's upset, he "shuts down" and tries to run away and hide. His parents have reportedly tried toilet training him for a few months now, but he manages to wriggle off the potty and run. According to his parents, he doesn't indicate wetness or seem concerned, although he is "not letting us change him as much as he used to".

Strategy and Technique

Readiness Indicators for Child to Learn Toileting

Any comprehensive social skills resource for children with ASD involves information on toilet training. In Western cultures, toilet training is usually done with children around age two. As discussed previously, one needs to account for the autistic child's mental and psycho-social age <u>instead</u> of the chronological age when addressing social skills development, even regarding toileting. As with any social skill, a child needs to be **ready** to learn. A child needs to have the groundwork done and the "stage set", especially for toileting. Toilet training children with ASD can be a real challenge. It requires a level of motivation *and* cognition on the part of the child, and a level of guidance and patience on the adult's part as well. Adherence to social mores endears one to another and helps an individual integrate with the social collective. This is especially true with children with ASD on many levels; the first being that an older child in diapers is no fun, at school and at home.

We want the child to endear himself to others, yet we need to remember that these children, with their unique "inner landscape" and neuro-motor functioning, may be "blocked" or on a different time table. That is not to say that we should not make toilet training our preschoolers with ASD a priority. We just need to go about doing so in a sequential, organized, methodical and consistent fashion. This will help the child understand and internalize what is expected of him or her. It will also help him generalize what he learns to all environments such as home, school and Grandma and Grandpa's house, etc.

Upon deciding to work on this important daily living skill, the child's entire team needs to get on board and make it a group effort. The child's success and mastery of this skill will certainly affect his or her future hygiene, socializations and overall behavior. One therefore needs to look at readiness indicators before starting to work on toileting.

A Child's Readiness Indicators-Prerequisites For Addressing Toilet Training:
- Joint Attention and rapport so that positive reinforcement is meaningful.
- Communicative Intent so that child can ask for toilet and/or indicate wetness.
- Understanding Causality (cause& effect, contingencies) so that child can make a connection between his action(s) and your reaction(s).
- Body Awareness so that child feels when he or she is wet and knows from where.
- Understanding Part-Whole Relationships so that child can follow the steps and make sense of the toileting process and the vocabulary involved.

One also needs to keep in mind factors that may "block" a child with ASD from being ready to be toilet trained. These factors can include:

1. *Sensory issues* such as partial or total lack of sensation in certain body parts leading to unawareness of being wet, reduced Sensory Integration resulting in decreased body awareness and proprioception and aversion to smells and/or hyper-sensitivity to smells.
2. *Behavioral issues* such as transitioning difficulty, inability to cope with changes in routine, disorientation to person/place/time and reduced ability to "tune in" and attend to the task at hand.
3. *Cognitive issues* affecting understanding of the sequence of events (e.g. "Get undressed, sit on the toilet, stand up, wipe up and flush.") and/or target vocabulary involving body parts, articles of clothing, oral directions containing verbs (e.g. "Flush the toilet, turn on the sink, take soap and wash hands.") and part-whole relationships (e.g. "Pick up the toilet seat.....Push down the handle to flush.")

It is therefore crucial to first determine readiness indicators and possible "blocks" that can impact the toilet training process. We want to help the child be successful, not set that child up for failure! It's not enough that the child knows what a toilet is. There needs to be an awareness and understanding of the items/vocabulary associated with that toilet. Think of the classic shape sorting toy we give toddlers. The same principles apply.

Readiness Indicators for Team to Address Toileting:

Once the team has decided that the child is ready to learn to be toilet trained, a protocol can be written, distributed and filed. It is important to note that sometimes parents want to start the process when the school staff feels that the child is not yet ready. It is important to hear the parents' concerns. It is equally important to have the school staff explain their concerns. If a child is deemed to be almost ready, then we need to work together to address the above three issues which may be contributing to the delay.

An OT and sometimes a pediatric neurologist can help address the sensory issues. A speech therapist and teacher can help address the behavioral and cognitive issues, with input from the psychologist and/or social worker who coordinates with the child's parents. We need to work collaboratively to ensure the child's readiness before embarking on this endeavor. We want to ensure success, not set the child up for failure. It is therefore imperative that a team meeting be held BEFORE starting the toilet training regimen in order to update baseline data about the child's overall level of functioning.

Once the baseline data and readiness for toileting has been documented, a toilet training regimen can commence in a systematic progression. The child's team members can all lend a hand and all play a role. The parents, teacher, speech therapist, psychologist, social worker, occupational therapist, teacher aide and even the bus driver, need to be kept "in the loop". Everyone needs to know <u>what</u> the child needs to do, <u>where</u> he or she will begin to do it, and <u>how</u> he or she will learn to do it. When I work with a team to toilet train a student, I am usually asked for the procedure and order.

The Socially Speaking™ Toilet Training Protocol

Toilet Training Protocol for Children with ASD: An Outline
Document Readiness Indicators at a team meeting.
If child is not ready, chart a course of action to facilitate readiness.
Document a plan of action, i.e the step by step procedure to improve independent toileting, using steps listed below: Note: I like to buy a box to store everything in one place. I then send home a duplicate box for parents and I label them both "The Toilet Training Kit for_____".
Organize the materials in the kit and make sure to include extra "pull ups", changes of clothing, several pairs of underwear, a kitchen digital timer that counts down and rings, photos of the child on the toilet, wet wipes and a roll of toilet paper.

THE PROCEDURE:

✓ *Collect data* on the child's bodily functions such as **what** kind of accidents are occurring (urine only? a combination?), **when** is he or she likely to relieve him or her self (after lunch, before going home?) and **how** does he or she respond to wetting him or her self (gets upset? doesn't notice? is indifferent?). Have each team member observe and document.

✓ *Make a joint decision on which positive reinforcement the child will get* for using the toilet successfully, and whether to reward unsuccessful attempts, based on the level of trust and cognition the child exhibits. Remember to use a reward based on the child's own preferences and designate it for this purpose. You may have to have several versions or copies of this reward to keep in different environments. Take a photo of the desired reinforcer and embed it and mount it on a 2-4 picture Visual Schedule, depending on the child's level of functioning re: behavior and cognition. This schedule is shown to the child before he or she goes to the bathroom *and* while he or she is in there. The actual reinforcer should also be made visible, but not reachable. Introduce the child to the reinforcer *and* the toilet simultaneously, and then take away the reward but keep it in the child's line of vision.

NOTE

In the beginning, the child may need to get rewarded for tolerating even sitting on the toilet for a few seconds, using a digital timer. You can slowly increase the time and use delayed gratification to get the child to stay motivated to sit on the toilet for longer periods of time, and then to eventually relieve him or her self. Make sure that the child knows that the reinforcer does not leave the bathroom! It is meant to be paired with the act of toileting and should not be given for completing any other task, even bathroom related tasks such as teeth brushing. The toileting reinforcer should thus be *very* differentiated from others. For example, if the team chooses to give music as the reinforcer, then choose a song that becomes 'The Toilet Theme' and is only heard **in** the bathroom. You can still use music etc. as a reward for a different task, just remember to pick a different theme song!

✓ *Create photo cards and worksheets (Topic Flash Cards) to teach the target vocabulary* during 1:1 time such as speech therapy sessions, getting ready to ride the bus to school, or reviewing them at home on the couch. Pair this activity with a pleasurable activity you know the child wants, such as watching a video or getting a drink. The child will then associate this new, unfamiliar activity with a familiar, desirable activity. The child's interest, motivation, attention and retention will all increase as a result. I usually use a digital camera to take actual photos of the child's own body parts and clothing, which are familiar and more motivating.

NOTE

I do *not* use these photos for academic learning tasks such as identification, matching and categorization, etc. These photos are *only* for instructional use re: toileting! They should *not* be kept with other materials meant for learning IEP goals. I also like to provide a sensory activity in therapy to teach adjectives such as "clean/dirty" and "wet/dry". I spend time in a speech therapy session having the child explore and discuss various textures, using real objects. I do art projects where the photo or worksheet becomes wet and/or dirty, etc. I use dolls and the REPLAYS™ technique to also increase awareness and understanding. All these multi-sensory "hands on" activities are easily duplicated and invaluable to the child with ASD!

✓ *Create a Social Story on toilet training and the steps involved.* This will help with motor planning, transitioning and the memory of his experience of the toileting process in general. Review the story before and after every time the child is taken to the bathroom. Since Social Stories are usually told in first person, with relevant photos, the entire process can become more personalized and meaningful to the child. It can also serve as an incidental reinforcer. Some children ask for the story when they are urinating on the toilet. If they were successful, this story can serve as a supplemental reinforcer *in addition* to the one previously chosen, based on the child's preferences. I prefer using Boardmaker™ to create these Social Stories that are copied and distributed to the entire team.

✓ *Videotape the child's experience and efforts,* including his or her compliance, success (zoom in on a shot of the toilet bowl) and a shot of him or her enjoying the Social Story being read with him *and* the subsequent reinforcer such as listening to music, etc. Send a copy of the clip to the entire team, to view and review with the child present to provide further positive reinforcement. In the interest of efficiency and time management, I really like using an iPhone or iPad®'s camera to take video footage, edit it, export it as a slideshow and/or a movie and show it to the child and the entire team.

✓ *Find relevant story books about children getting toilet trained and/or using the bathroom.* Read these books with the child in various settings and in conjunction with the other steps of the toileting procedure. The internet offers a wealth of information on this topic. I also like the library as a resource to obtain books such as those books listed on www.TEACCH.com by Susan Boswell and Debbie Gray.

<u>Going to the Potty</u> by Fred Rogers, Jim Judkis (Photographer)<u>Your New Potty</u> by Joanna Cole and Margaret Miller (Illustrator)
<u>The Toddler's Potty Book</u> by Alida Allison, Henri Parmentier (Illustrator)
<u>Potty Time</u> by Bettina Paterson (Illustrator)
<u>No More Diapers (Personalized Edition)</u> by Tina Dorman
<u>Once Upon a Potty (Boy)</u> by Alona Frankel
<u>Once Upon a Potty (Girl)</u> by Alona Frankel
<u>Bye Bye Diapers (Muppet Babies Big Steps)</u> by Ellen Weiss, Tom Cooke (Illustrator), W. Weiss
<u>Sam's Potty</u> by Barbo Lindgren, Eva Eriksson (Illustrator), Barbro Lindgrin
<u>What Do You Do With Potty? : An Important Pop-Up Book</u> by Marianne Borgardt, Maxie Chambliss (Illustrator)
<u>Have to Go (Sesame Street Toddler Books)</u> by Anna Ross, Norman Gorbaty (Illustrator)
<u>On Your Potty</u> by Virginia Miller
<u>Everyone Poops</u> by Taro Gomi, Amanda Mayer Stinchecum (Translator)
<u>Toilet Training in Less Than a Day</u> by Nathan H. Azrin, Richard M. Foxx It's Potty Time, SmartKidzMedia (with flushing sounds)

Final Words

A Word About Punishment........

While I do believe in consequences, I have found that punishing the child with ASD when an accident occurs is nonproductive. It does not facilitate faster understanding of the toileting process. It does not facilitate motivation and self control. It does not facilitate rapport and trust between you and the child. I have found that ignoring accidents and focusing on rewarding for compliance and attempts, and/or actual successes, goes a long way in helping the child internalize what is expected of him or her. Children with ASD need time, practice and patience to master this challenging skill. It behooves us to remember that they are having accidents not to cause trouble or to be disrespectful. They are either simply not yet in tune with their body, cognitively ready, or self motivated to change a familiar routine.

The use of *positive* reinforcement can help the child with ASD learn to act differently and try to please the adults in his or her life. The use of rewards for learning is not a new concept. From that first cup of coffee each morning upon waking to watching TV at night before sleeping, everyone rewards themselves for one thing or another. Some rewards are intrinsic and social based. This is not always useful to children with ASD. Their Theory of Mind and "inner landscape" make tangible, fixed intervals of positive reinforcement more productive, to enable them to stay focused on the present and try-- even when it's hard for them. We need to remember this when facilitating any type of social skill, including the ability to ask for and independently use the bathroom.

A Word About Boys vs. Girls......

In my experience, we special education professionals approach toilet training as a unisex endeavor when in reality, gender counts! There IS a difference between toileting intervention for boys and girls! We female service providers in particular do our *boys* a tremendous disservice by not teaching them to:

- Stand and aim from the get go. I myself have been guilty of teaching young boys to sit first and then wonder why they have difficulty in general education settings later on!
- Make sure there's space i.e. a urinal/ stall in between them and the next person so that privacy is maintained, not to mention etiquette! Respect the boundaries!
- Quietly and quickly concentrate on doing their business and moving on. The restroom is a social place for gals, not guys! While girls and women may use it to gab and catch up on the latest gossip, gregarious boys in the restroom will get raised eyebrows or worse! I once treated an 11 year old boy with HFA (Asperger's Syndrome) who had been toilet trained at age 3 by his mother, had 3 older sisters who babied him, had only seen female special education (self-contained) teachers/therapists until now and was considered a potential behavior issue. He was labeled "polite, gifted, but weird beyond belief" by his new regular education teacher/peers in his mainstreamed class in a new school. Why? Because while in the bathroom, he sidled up to other boys, standing quite close and proceeded to hang out and chat!! His classmates complained, and his teacher, concerned about possible bullying, requested an emergency meeting to request both a speech therapy and a psychological evaluation!

Materials for Your Toolbox

- <u>Key References</u>

Attwood, Tony (2004). *Exploring Feelings: Anxiety-Cognitive Behavior Therapy to Manage Anxiety*. Arlington, TX: Future Horizons

Baker, Jed (2008). *No More Meltdowns: Positive Strategies for Managing and Preventing Out of Control Behavior*. Arlington, TX: Future Horizons

Barbera, Mary Lynch, and Rassmussen, Tracy (2007). *The Verbal Behavior Approach: How to Teach Children with Autism and Related Disorders*. Philadelphia, PA: Jessica Kingsley Publishers

Biel, Lindsey, and Peske, Nancy (2005). *Raising a Sensory Smart Child: The Definitive Handbook for Helping Your Child with Sensory Integration Issues*. New York, NY: Penguin Books

Dunn Buron, Kari (2003). *Incredible Five Point Scale: Assisting Students with Autism Spectrum Disorder in Understanding Social Interactions and Controlling Their Emotional Responses*. Shawnee, KS: Autism Asperger Publishing

Greenspan, Stanley, and Weider, Serena (1998). *The Child with Special Needs: Encouraging Intellectual and Emotional Growth*. Cambridge, MA: Perseus Books Group

Greenspan, Stanley (2002). *The Secure Child: Helping Our Children Feel Safe and Confident in an Insecure World*. Cambridge, MA: Perseus Books Group

Greenspan, Stanley, and Weider, Serena (2006). *Engaging Autism: Using the Floortime Approach to Help Children Relate, Communicate, and Think*. Cambridge, MA: Da Capo Press/Perseus Books Group

Gray, Carol (2010). *The New Social Story Book: Revised and Expanded Tenth Anniversary Edition*. Arlington, TX: Future Horizons

Hodgdon, Linda (1995). *Visual Strategies for Improving Communication: Practical Supports for School and Home*. Troy, MI: Quirk Roberts Publishing

Levine, Karen, and Chedd, Naomi (2007). *REPLAYS: Using Play to Enhance Emotional and Behavioral Development for Children with Autism Spectrum Disorders*. Philadelphia, PA: Jessica Kingsley Publishers

Quill, Kathleen Ann (2000). *Do-Watch-Listen-Say: Social and Communication Intervention for Children with Autism*. Baltimore, MD: Paul H. Brookes Publishing Co.

Shellenberger, Sherry, and Williams, Mary Sue (2001). *How Does Your Engine Run? A Leader's Guide to the Alert Program, Take Five: Staying Alert at Home and School.* Albuquerque, NM: Therapy Works Inc.

Thompson, Thomas (2008). *Freedom From Meltdowns: Dr. Thompson's Solutions for Children with Autism.* Baltimore, MD: Paul H. Brookes Publishing

Volkmar, Fred, and Weisner, Lisa (2009). *A Practical Guide to Autism: What Every Parent, Family Member, and Teacher Needs to Know.* Hoboken, NJ: Wiley Press

Wheeler, Maria (2007). *Toilet Training for Individuals with Autism or Other Developmental Issues, Second Edition.* Arlington, TX: Future Horizons

• Key Links to Peruse

http://bit.ly/1zT18u3

http://bit.ly/1zT1aSN

http://bit.ly/1LO7YnI

http://bit.ly/1CwDDqZ

http://bit.ly/1BVOpSh

http://bit.ly/1zT1Jfj

http://bit.ly/1EHxOrB

http://bit.ly/1zT1YXA

http://bit.ly/1LO9upW

http://bit.ly/1EHy5L6

• Key Concepts to Address

Body Awareness, Self Regulation, Sensory Processing, If...Then Contingent, Reinforcement, Gender Differences, Readiness Indicators

• Key Toys to Use in Treatment

Toilet training children with Autism is all about facilitating comprehension of the related nouns/object function, adjectives/textures and verbs/actions that need to be demonstrated visually, kinesthetically, and auditorily and practiced. I therefore do not distinguish between toys for the service provider vs. the child's perspective because rapport, collaboration and readiness are the keys to success. So I recommend trying these suggested toys or ones similar to them: *Once Upon a Potty* Book and other related books, Melissa and Doug "Annie" Drink and Wet Doll, other life-like dolls with diapers who can get wet without damage, Mini-Potty Set, Fisher Price Ready for Potty Baby Dora and plastic or foam bath toys that can get wet/float to show what wet vs. dry means: nesting cups, Fisher-Price Little People® Noah's Ark, rubber ducks and Bright Starts Roll Shake and Spin Activity Balls.

• Key iPad® Apps to Use in Treatment

☞ **For the Service Provider:** It is recommended that a team approach be agreed upon and implemented to track progress. I therefore suggest using only one or two apps collaboratively at first. I believe that toilet training involves "whole body" learning and that specific readiness indicators must be present before proceeding. I also believe that one must be careful bringing the iPad® into contact with wet surfaces, and be careful about not using it as a timer, distraction or as a bribe to gain the child's cooperation. Body Awareness and overall comprehension must be addressed in a natural way! That's why I recommend only these specific apps:

☞ *Teaching Target Vocabulary/Routine:* Potty Training Time, iCan Toilet Training Program, Potty Training: Learning with Animals, See Me Go Potty English, My First Words- Flashcards by Alligator Apps, Potty Training Social Story, Talking Train, Adobe Voice- Show Your Story, SonicPics, My Story, Stories About Me, Art Maker, Chatterpix, Comic Life, Strip Designer, Pic Jointer, Talking Ginger and InnerVoice.

☞ **For the Child:** The key to toilet training children with Autism in particular is increasing self awareness and Body Awareness, not to mention comprehension of Causality. While I believe in honoring the child's inner landscape, i.e. learning style/ preferences, I do not believe in actively and exclusively using technology, i.e. the apps to teach the *steps* of the toileting process. That should be physically experienced in real time and perhaps recorded using the iPad® camera and made into a slideshow in the Photos App. I do also believe in using these specific apps (take your pick, depending on the child) as visual supports to increase the understanding of the *need* (and consequences) to engage in the toileting process:

☞ *Increasing Awareness:* The Potty Show, First & Then by Alisha Forrest, Picture Me Calm, Potty Training Game, Dino Bath & Dress Up and The New Potty-Little Critter.

Chapter 11:
<u>Digital Citizenship in the iEra</u>-What You Need to Know About the iPad®,
Ed-Tech, and Best Practices for Both

Anecdote

I've been a Mac Girl all my life, and an unofficial Mac Evangelist (the official title originally went to Guy Kawasaki; techie, author, and entrepreneur) since I was given my first addictive taste of the Apple™ Macintosh computer as a child. I was actually professionally trained by Apple™ Inc. in the late 90s. I remember being a newly minted speech therapist fresh out of graduate school, who was chosen as one of the few educators, let alone female ones, to learn Apple™ technology applications for special education curricula, under the auspices of the New York State TRAID Project. I got a good laugh in 1995 at our first meeting, when I recited the credo from the famous Apple™ commercial "Here's the the crazy ones" from 1984, narrated by Steve Jobs himself. I got much interest from people when I took my Mac Performa to the American Association of Mental Retardation (AAMR) Annual Conference of 1996 in Manhattan, and showed off software/materials I had created using Boardmaker™, KidPix™, Intellipics™, and HyperStudio™ for lesson plans.

Those lessons and worksheets would become the prototype for my copyrighted Socially Speaking™ Social Skills Curriculum years later. The late 90s were a time of "pushing the envelope" professionally, technologically and economically. Innovation was everywhere, and American special education visionaries were eager to herald in a new age and a new way of educating children with learning differences and behavioral challenges.

Mavericks such as Steve Jobs, Dr. Patty Slobogin at The Westchester Institute for Human Development overseeing The NY TRAID Project, Ben Lehmann, regional vendor at Mayer-Johnson Inc. for Boardmaker™ and Dynavox®, and Principal Susan Gartenberg, my very first boss and special education mentor (when I transitioned from being a special education teacher to a speech-language pathologist in the school system) all understood innovation. They understood and embraced the power and potential of innovation through digital citizenship (i.e. becoming media literate by using technology to foster learning, specific behaviors and membership in a global ecosystem) as a way of life, not just a way to harness technology to accomplish tasks for greater productivity. Their teachings, thought leadership and philosophy about technology had a profound influence on my own Theory of Mind and overall tech savvy, not to mention the design of my own social skills curriculum!

Each of them started me on my journey towards fully realized digital citizenship, which should be the professional development goal of every educator and service provider in the 21st century classroom and workplace. Being a seasoned Apple™ technology expert and subsequent iPad® Evangelist taught me the value of using digital visual supports to tap into the inner landscape of children with Autism and special needs. It also taught me the value of seeking out multi-sensory learning experiences and then providing them for others. That's why I advocate for the combining of toys and tech in treatment for a truly holistic approach to enhancing working and episodic memory. I learned that designing teachable moments that promote what we now refer to as digital citizenship must involve the synthesis of design, functionality and portability. I learned that digital citizenship is as much an attitude, a way of life, as it is a skill set in need of steady cultivation for future success, both professionally and personally.

Strategy and Technique:

The Rise of Digital Citizenship and Implications for Special Education

"Digital citizenship has a central place in teaching curricula. It is through educating kids on the appropriate ways to use, navigate, interact, create and share web content that they develop the skills necessary for thriving in a knowledge economy."

-- Med Kharbach, Educational Technology and Mobile Learning Blog, 7/15/14

http://bit.ly/1v3EWWB

When I was in graduate school, the buzzword everyone in special education used for children with Autism was Computer Assisted Instruction (CAI). It covered a broad range of Assistive Technology (AT) use within curricula from documentation to productivity, from "visual aid" to "teaching tool" and everything in between. Initially, being tech-savvy within the special education arena meant having a working knowledge of Augmentative Alternative Communication (AAC) devices from famous and obscure companies such as Dynavox®, Mayer-Johnson Inc., Parrot, and Zygo. It also meant being able to use software applications such as Word Perfect and Boardmaker™ to create materials for lesson plans . A tech-savvy person knew how to access Email and the Internet (before Web 2.0) and knew how to "game the system" to tweak and share files before social media and PDFs. The first wave of the Tech Revolution started in the late 90s when CDs hit the market and personal computers with floppy disk drives became the norm. It continued when Apple™ took a practical and widespread interest in partnering with educators, resulting in the global distribution of iMacs in classrooms across the United States.

Apple™ Macintosh computers were a real game changer, which forever changed the way many of us view personal "ownership" of technology. They forever changed the topography of the educational landscape-- especially for children with Autism who tend to be visual learners. The revisions to the IDEA in 2004, and subsequent revisions to the service delivery re: implementation of IEP goals within special education curricula, further paved the way for children with Autism to be educated with technology. When Apple™ removed the floppy disk drive and instead outfitted their iMac G3 desktop computers with the first USB port, I knew that this was an important precursor to digital citizenship. Why? Because for the first time, allowances were being made for wireless, portable and relatively inexpensive ways to design, store, and transfer data, especially visual data.

As one of the first people to be trained in the 90s by what is now one of the prototypes for the Apple™ Educators Program, I quickly grasped the power of technology and how to harness it for better educational outcomes. I understood that what was needed was a universal social communication curriculum that synthesized the integration of toys and tech in treatment. More importantly, the result of this integration would help lay the foundations for both students and educators to occupy a virtual space, adhering to certain rules and etiquette to maintain decorum. It would also culminate in helping children with Autism and/or special needs transition from Me to We, becoming part of the global community; now a reality, thanks to the Internet. I anticipated that technology advances will occur almost every day, and thus created lesson plans which synthesized toys and tech in treatment, to prepare teachable moments more effectively, safely, and easily.

I thus started toying around with the technological and collaborative components of my Socially Speaking™ Program in the late 90s and beyond, tweaking my visuals and my own vision with each new Apple™ product and tech incarnation I got. I guess I was a great guinea pig for the Apple™ R & D folks interested in getting people to use their computers to work hard, play hard and do something unique in special education that hadn't been done with any other computer.....personalize the user-interface and customize its output.

That is the real essence of authentic digital citizenship; something rather taken for granted today when mobile technology and smartphones allow anyone to customize app features. It's why I joke that I'm living in the iEra where it's all about Me. It's why my philosophy as both an educator and entrepreneur is to transition all of us, not just children with Autism, from Me to We. It's why I became a public iPad® Evangelist in 2011, a year after the iPad® hit the stores. I immediately saw the potential for Autism Intervention using the iPad®. I immediately saw that the iPad®, more than any other technology device to date, would be a tremendous game changer in special education. I also saw that the iPad® in particular was poised to become the harbinger of global digital citizenship for people in general, not just in the educational community.

The Rise of eLearning with An iPad® and Implications for Autism Intervention

The widespread use of the Internet these past 2 decades has created a shared space where shared ideas and lessons can be used as a springboard for greater communication, performance and overall professional development. Like many, I eagerly watched the rise of eLearning as cyber-space expanded to encompass the worlds of mobile technology, Web 2.0 and social media, which all enrich our lives but are still just tools-- weapons to be wielded wisely. There was initial widespread concern in education about the effect of technology use on a child's overall development, especially for a child with Autism and/or special needs. But it became clear that the proper use of technology can truly help "fill in the blanks" in unexpected, unforeseen and frequently unorthodox manners.

Special educators and parents alike have long been concerned about bridging the gap between readiness to learn and actual performance, which is crucial for social communication development. With the IDEA revisions of 2004, which federally mandated a Behavior Intervention Plan as part of each student's IEP, there is increasing interest in proactive intervention to foster self regulation. We must methodically document and facilitate social communication development for children with challenging behaviors, particularly Autism. Social skills development can be a slow, splintered and challenging process for young children with ASD. Service providers need to integrate social communication goals into treatment, for more developmentally appropriate, multi-sensory and functional "teachable moments".

Research shows that children with Autism tend to be "visual learners". A unified, collaborative, methodical team approach re: iOS App integration can prove very beneficial. Children with Autism can greatly benefit from iPad® based lesson plans to facilitate self regulation and language development, involving "whole body" learning, emphasizing the visual modality.

The iPad® is a singularly unique tool for today's special educators to wield when implementing IEP goals for children with ASD, no matter what the domain or the setting. The underlying features and the intrinsic iOS architecture support learning using multiple intelligences, support principals of Response to Intervention (RTI) and support the framework for Universal Design for Learning (UDL). An iPad® is visually accessible, adaptable, socially appealing and has an easy to navigate user interface. Its use is predicated on the execution of time sequenced movements, which facilitates both "muscle memory" and motor planning. Its user interface fosters comprehension of time passing and the If...Then Contingent, which is a cornerstone of self regulation. The ability to activate/deactivate/transition among apps, and the intrinsic reinforcer nature of "whole body learning" using these apps, all promote learning, episodic memory and attention span AKA Time on Task (TOT).

The use of an iPad® spurns a "teachable moment" or string of them, rife with opportunities. Opportunities for children with Autism to more naturally and sequentially learn target vocabulary/concepts, while simultaneously engaging in the repeated practice of behaviors, especially desirable behaviors-- specific behaviors which promote Attention, Causality and Problem Solving. These are all part of the umbrella of Executive Function Skills, which many of these children have difficulty with. It results in the social communication challenges so often seen at home or in school, especially when faced with unfamiliar or undesirable tasks.

So iPad® integration into eLearning experiences is not just about Alternative-Augmentative Communication (AAC) for non verbal or verbally limited students. It is also not just about "going green" i.e. sustainability, or behavior management, i.e. reinforcement. Developmental integration of iOS apps into treatment is about methodically filling, and later tapping into, the child's episodic memory banks, using the five senses, with emphasis on the visual modality, to teach these children how to learn and how to actually help themselves. It teaches them how to recall vocabulary associated with specific events (that is essentially the definition of episodic memory), and how to adapt and self regulate, when organic, i.e. biological and/or environmental triggers cause disorientation to person/place/time.

Setting the Stage for Integrating iOS Apps into Lessons

Like any tool or toy, an understanding of developmental milestones and language development helps the special education service provider know which app to use when. Understanding the child's inner landscape and potential "triggers" are needed to set the stage for maximum impact. What is also needed before introducing an iPad® into lesson plans is:

☑ A universal way to assess which iOS App is actually worth buying

☑ A developmental hierarchy to consider, when introducing specific iOS apps into treatment at specific junctures in time

To that end, I have developed the *Socially Speaking™ Framework for iOS App Integration*, which are suggested guidelines that I have created for curriculum development. It is based upon the clinical research I have read, the extensive treatment I have provided to a diverse population of special education students with Autism/special needs for twenty years and the informal research I have conducted through a myriad of conversations with my varied, educated, professional and technologically inclined seminar audiences around North America these past four years. I have seen that there are a plethora of special education service providers and parents of children with Autism and ASD trying to make sense of emerging technology trends, new service delivery regulations and new information re: best practices for assessment and treatment, using educational technology.

I have found that it is crucial to keep in mind both play and pre-literacy milestones and cross reference them with psycho-social milestones, to gain a clearer picture of baseline data and which materials will cognitively and emotionally resonate with a child when implementing IEP goals and specific lesson plans. The way a child interacts with a toy, an App, or even the adult engineering the "teachable moment", speaks volumes. It provides a window into the child's "inner landscape," i.e. Theory of Mind and Executive Functioning, especially when treating a young child with Autism. These two metacognitive, neuropsychological processes are often underdeveloped in youngsters with Autism and are often at the root of their behavioral issues and reduced self regulation. These two areas are required for social communication proficiency, especially in these domains: Body Awareness, Expressing Feelings and Problem Solving. Keeping in mind developmental norms and my Socially Speaking™ Trifecta, I have developed these 2 formulas for knowing when to:

- ☑ Introduce specific iOS apps into lessons at specific times
- ☑ Introduce specific social communication goals into overall "teachable moments" using iOS apps

Socially Speaking™ App Formula:

Visual Support Apps + Real Time Play= Increased Theory of Mind + Self Regulation
Pre-Literacy Apps + Social Communication Apps= Increased Executive Functioning

The iPad® is more than a viable AAC device, or a plaything to be used for reinforcement, or a live demo of target vocabulary. iOS apps, by the way they operate, go beyond simple social communication and into the realm of Executive Functioning and Theory of Mind. These are two neuro-cognitive processes which are needed, in order for people to transition from being a Me to a We in different settings.

A developmental approach to iPad® integration must be carefully considered. Best practices do not include a haphazard activation of an iOS App to hit a point home at the end of a lesson, or to provide a reward or respite between lessons. It is crucial for special educators to treat the iPad® as another tool, albeit a versatile, multifaceted one, in the toolbox of instruments for best practices, by truly knowing which App to use when. That's what makes the iPad® so unique-- but dangerous in the wrong hands, or in the hands of someone with the wrong mindset. As Dr. Temple Grandin says, "People are always looking for the single magic bullet that will totally change everything. There is no single magic bullet". The iPad® experience for children with Autism in particular, can be as educational, meaningful, and magical as an informed educator and/or parent makes it to be. It is up to you, even when the iPad® is no longer in your hands.

At the end of the day, we want children with Autism/special needs to integrate into family and community life as much as possible, given their individual status. We want to provide intervention, whether concrete or abstract, whether physical or digital, to help these children better orient to person/place/time and transition from being a Me to a We as needed. Structured teaching provides a predictable environment for children with Autism to increase social communication proficiency, and decrease the frequency and duration of tantrums i.e. outbursts, not following directions and stereotypical behaviors (Blubaugh & Kohlmann, 2006; Savner & Myles, 2000). Best practices today involve structured teaching, which can implement both visual supports, (which was previously discussed) and eLearning with an iPad®. That's why I created the framework of guidelines below, in keeping with current research re: visual learning, behavior management and language development in children with Autism in particular.

Socially Speaking™ Framework for iOS App Integration

Facilitation of Behavior Management: Visual Supports Hierarchy
Photo Apps
Flashcard Apps
Drawing Apps
Social Story Apps
Facilitation of Orientation to Person/Place/Time
Person:
Body Awareness, Theory of Mind & Emotional Attunement: Photo, Flashcard & Drawing Apps, Farm/Animal Apps
Place:
Self Regulation: Visual Schedules created from Camera/Photo Apps & Social Story Apps
Spatial Relationships: virtual worksheets created from Drawing Apps, and specific iOS Apps teaching prepositions
Time:
Language Development and AAC Apps to teach Executive Functioning, pre-literacy concepts & communication skills
Expressing Feelings Apps (labeling feelings, story books, and wh? questions)
Transitioning Tasks Apps (sequencing, turn taking, fast moving games)
Problem Solving Apps (wh? questions, games, categorization, building/puzzle Apps)
Multimedia Apps (camera/photo, story and music based) to foster episodic memory

Setting the Stage for Integrating Toys and Tech in Treatment- Clinical Implications

"You can learn more about a person in an hour of play than in a year of conversation."

--Plato

Exposure to structured, repetitive, and creative interaction using toys and tech in treatment, can really benefit children with Autism. This integration can foster a child's ability to access episodic memory and retain learned skills/generalize learned social communication skills using the following:

😊 Cues appealing to a child's learning style (auditory/visual/tactile), such as visual supports

😊 "Wh" questions that facilitate the development of problem solving and Executive Functioning

😊 Visual supports such as schedules and outlines containing target vocabulary, to facilitate the access of semantic memory, development of time management skills and overall pre-literacy and later reading comprehension skills

The process of eLearning involves active student participation, is usually self-motivating, and immerses the student in multi-sensory learning experiences engaging one or more of the five senses. It is no wonder that I advocate for more play and have embraced integration of iPad® apps into individual and group instruction and classroom learning! Also, the flexibility that the iPad® promotes is inherent in its user interface, which, by nature, is individualized and flexible, especially when dovetailed with the student's curriculum.

Furthermore, the very repetitive nature of play, whether it be with toys or tech, provides intrinsic reinforcement and practice trials for all children. Every child with Autism, no matter what the level of instruction, can thus develop better attention spans and better self esteem, as well as retention of learned material over time. These are all byproducts of a good social communication treatment plan, which we educators strive for on a daily basis with our students, *no matter what their challenges!*

Implementation of behavioral strategies into special education strategies which many of us already use, (such as visual supports and positive behavioral support), allows for an even more seamless integration of toys and tech in treatment. This, in turn, facilitates Self Concept and overall social and academic performance in today's rapidly changing , globally connected, tech-driven world. Careful, customized and creative content curation for lesson plans while remaining mindful of the steady evolution of technology is the best practice for today's educator to implement, no matter where the lesson plan is taking place and for whom it is intended.

Why Use the iPad® in Autism Intervention for Social Communication Skills?

FAQ: Why Use the iPad®? Wording for Grants:

- eLearning is a preferable, sustainable option for students today.
- Research shows many children with Autism are "visual learners."
- iPad® use involves "whole body" learning, building "muscle memory" and emphasizing the visual modality, to foster episodic memory.
- iPad® is a creative, customized, intuitive and fun educational tool to add to your arsenal, to foster social communication.
- The iPad® facilitates implementation of lessons in a motivational manner.
- It addresses IEP goals methodically and consistently.
- It utilizes behavioral strategies to foster self-regulation.

Fostering Orientation to Person and Body Awareness:

1. **Drawing Apps** facilitate Body Awareness through building muscle memory, which then facilitates episodic memory and Theory of Mind (TOM). They also help introduce topics, practice behavior, reinforce performance and build self esteem.

You can use *Drawing Apps and/or Documentation Apps* with child participation during a "teachable moment". You can start with "clean slate" apps that let you fill the page, like Paint Sparkles Draw. You can increase visual complexity by introducing several visual stimuli at once, such as Drawing Box Free. For more advanced, "teachable moments", use mind mapping and/or photo+drawing capable apps together, such as Simple Mind +, Grafio, Comic Life, and Turbo Collage.

2. **Farm/ Animal Apps** facilitate Self Concept and Theory of Mind (TOM) through triggering episodic memory, empathy and motoric imitation. They foster comprehension of Causality through the action/reaction set up and user interface. You can start teaching the If...Then Contingent and reinforcing behavior, with simple apps that feature one realistic photo/drawing of one animal per page, such as Peekaboo Barn. You can increase complexity by introducing an auditory processing component such as Vocal Zoo, or a visual processing component such as matching animals, photo to drawing such as Farm Flip.

Fostering Orientation to Place and Expressing Feelings:

1. *Social Story Apps* foster self regulation and attention skills. You can export/Email Photos of completed work as a strategy to increase Time on Task (TOT). You can share your work with family and other providers to provide practice in other settings (homework, carryover and episodic memory). Some Social Story Apps like Pictello can be shared as a PDF, while others like Stories About Me have Drop Box Integration. Some are more scripted like Carol Gray's StoryMaker, while other "free style" multimedia apps like ComicBook! 2 allow for an unorthodox yet effective Social Story.

2. *Photo Sharing Apps* foster both expressing feelings and and orientation to place. Use them to take snapshots of the child's facial expressions and draw on them, while creating scripted conversations and maybe even a montage for a later arts & crafts project. Just remember to print out the photos! Use Photo Apps to take snapshots of the child's likes/dislikes for your visual support (Reinforcer Roster) and for later practice with verbal rejection (set the stage for the child to be given choices and have the opportunity to express feelings about them). Use the "**screen capture**" mode with the child during lessons to create object function tasks for later recall, an on-the-spot reinforcer break and/or a homework worksheet that's meaningful to the child. Remember that the Photo Sharing Apps can only work if you previously uploaded photos to the iPad® or took some on the fly with the Camera App. Orientation to place means preparing and planning for the "teachable moment" which will help the child learn target vocabulary and stay anchored to the present. So it's important for educators and parents to realize that:

- Picture/Photo Apps can be used to create instant *Visual Schedules* to anchor child.
- Photo Apps can be used to create instant *Social Stories* for behavior management.
- Both Photo Sharing and Social Story Apps are intrinsically self motivating.
- Social Story and Photo Apps provide user-friendly, customizable "teachable moments."
- Photo Sharing Apps can facilitate team collaboration, team correspondence, parent advocacy and participation and the child's own episodic memor,y i.e. recall of past events he/she experienced (later recall fosters carryover and self regulation).

FAQ: How Do Pictures Get in the iPad®? How Should I Store/View Them?

- Camera Roll
- iTunes > Photo Library
- Email as attachment > save image
- Photos App: Folders, Albums, Slideshows
- Peripherals: Apple™ Camera Kit, SD Card Reader
- Take screen capture > Camera Roll

When to Use Photo Apps
To teach target vocabulary and prepare child for Social Story activity
To record/share "teachable" moment(s)
To reinforce performance
To help child tap into "inner landscape" i.e. preferences/creativity

3. *Puzzle and Prepositions Apps* are appropriate for children with an eye for detail and readiness to develop graphomotor skills. I usually use these kinds of apps with children who need to learn target vocabulary in a more spatial, multi-sensory, methodical and structured manner: Make a Scene: Farmyard, Wood Puzzles Vehicles (Free), Labo Car Designer, PrepositionBuilder™, Speech with Milo: Prepositions, Preposition Remix, Preposition Pets and misc. drawing apps for following directions.

Fostering Orientation to Time and Problem Solving:

1. *Pre-Literacy and Language Apps* foster comprehension of Causality, categorization of like/unalike items and sequencing of directions and narratives. These are all prerequisite skills to learning problem solving-- the pinnacle of any effective social skills curriculum. That's why I don't address problem solving digitally until the child has mastered specific skills (previously mentioned) in real time using manipulatives and natural contexts within a play schema first. The *Socially Speaking™ Program* adopts a developmental approach to iOS App integration into treatment which begins with first addressing orientation to person and place and corresponding play and pre-literacy stages of development before moving on to orientation to time and problem solving.

Once the child is deemed ready to be engaged with an iPad® to teach pre-literacy and language apps correlating to social communication goals and performance, I like to use these types of apps to develop skills and carryover:

2. *Audio, Music Creation and Video-recording Apps* with a mic feature and customizable recordable interface: Use them to enhance self monitoring, Theory of Mind (TOM) and overall social skills building by recording the child's speech and even tantrums (Social Autopsy), discussing recorded facial expressions, the feelings evoked at that time and how they were handled/should be handled next time (remember the 5 step problem solving hierarchy) and provide "teachable moments" re: perspective and empathy. These apps basically help me cement the child's skills re: level 2 of my curriculum (Expressing Feelings) so that I can more seamlessly address level 3 (Problem Solving).

3. ***Early Childhood Language and Social Skills Apps:*** The App Store seems to lump all pre-literacy, early literacy and and social communication apps under "Autism Apps" or "Language Apps". We know the truth about special education students--that the child's learning style, preference, cognitive level and motoric dexterity will determine readiness to use these apps to learn. I therefore only access them in treatment when I can plug them into my Socially Speaking™ Paradigm, which provides me with a clear way to cross reference play, pre-literacy, social communication and assistive technology needs simultaneously. That means that I will only use sequencing and storybook apps during the final phase of treatment.

4. ***Critical Thinking and Problem Solving Apps:*** Once the child has engaged in my *Socially Speaking™ Program* and learned all the readiness skills and precursors to achieving Causality and sequencing in real time, the iPad® can be used to teach critical thinking and problem solving. Both are needed to generalize overall social communication proficiency and executive functioning. It is at this juncture in treatment where I let the child more freely use the iPad®. It is at this point in my ongoing lesson plan where I encourage the child to move away from pre-made games/pictures/ templates and independently create projects where he/she is in the "driver's seat". The result? An opportunity to troubleshoot within context and in a more natural way, while creating individualized, multimedia (audio, visual, exportable) activities that encourage critical thinking and inferencing, which I list elsewhere.

Lining Up Your Ducks in a Row: The Socially Speaking™ Developmental Integration Hierarchy of iOS Apps

⊌ **Drawing Apps:** Address Theory of Mind and orientation to person. Start the child's iPad® Experience using Drawing Apps as a Reinforcer for performing a task in real time. Start with "clean slate" apps like Paint Sparkles Draw, move on to prearranged pictures like Drawing Box Free and other intermediate level apps, and end with importing target vocabulary photos like Doodlelicious and other advance apps.

⊌ **Animal Gaming Apps**: Foster Self Concept and early language skills such as Joint Attention, communicative intent, labeling, matching, imitation and auditory localization/closure skills.

🌑 **Language Apps:** Use a variety of educational apps to develop language and social skills while being mindful of the child's learning style and visual needs (photos vs. icons) so that episodic memory increases gradually. Start with apps that resonate with the child's inner landscape and then slowly increase the visual complexity and demands. For instance, start with Peekaboo Barn, continue with Injini and move on to Question Sleuth or Story Builder. Don't address sequencing and problem solving using apps until the child has mastered categorization (inclusion and exclusion) and expressing feelings using toys during play activities.

 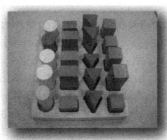 

Suggested Best Practices re: iOS App Integration in Social Communication Lessons

My Basic Formula When Using Apps:

🌑 Start with the introductory one that speaks to the child's learning style, continue with an intermediate one that offers choices and increased opportunity for honing pre-literacy and pre-graphomotor skills; then use an advanced App that utilizes/bombards the child's senses (auditory, visual and tactile) and offers generalization of learned skills to situations involving complex directions re: recall, problem solving and having conversations.

🌑 Gradually move from using the iPad® primarily as a reinforcer to using it in conjunction with real time toys, to provide "teachable moments" and *new* experiences.

🌑 Constantly update baseline data and observe performance as a team! Cross reference the child's level of functioning re: cognition, play, visuo-motor and sensory processing skills!

🌑 Keep in mind developmental norms! Start with apps containing a "memory" and/or "cause and effect" format to counteract situation specific learning and splintered skill acquisition. We must facilitate sequential learning and retention (episodic memory).

🌑 iPad® integration *must* be cross-referenced with *Pre-Reading Readiness Hierarchy*!

A child's level of *play* is the determining factor re: cognition and which apps to use when! Cross reference baseline data with the *Socially Speaking™ Play Stages Formula*!

A child's Multiple Intelligences, i.e. *learning style* and overall personality drive the level of motivation/successful interaction with the App's "user interface"!

Use the Socially Speaking™ iOS App Assessment Rubric (also in Chapter 12) to determine which ones are worthy of purchase, based on specific educational features.

Basic App Toolbar Features to Look For:

1.

   = change of the order of listed text

2.

   = export to Email, Home Screens, or Camera Roll etc.

3.

   = add "new" text, folder, photo, or album etc.

4.

   = find info on this App, including Developer Contact Info etc.

If I see it, I understand it.....

- Dr. Temple Grandin

Desirable Features	Play Skills	Motor Skills	Language Skills	Social Skills	Cognitive Skills
Dynamic/ interactive					
Teaches causality through intrinsic use					
Has sound, motivates & reinforces auditory learners					
User friendly: easy to navigate, is intuitive & flexible					
Easy to share results: Exports to PDF; Email end products for provider or child					
Fosters creativity and problem solving					
Targets visual learners: customizes photos					
Encourages carryover of ideas and language concepts					
Promotes solutions for targeted behaviors					
Enhances collaboration and cooperation among providers/ peers					

The Socially Speaking™ iOS App Assessment Rubric by Penina Rybak MA/CCC-SLP, TSHH
© 2012 Socially Speaking LLC, All Rights Reserved
Score: (25 or higher makes it a worthy purchase)

Suggested Best Practices for Storing Data and Finding Worthy Apps for Treatment:

Free App Helpers
App Miner (new, free for the moment, and free paid; 2 kinds)
Kindertown
Autism Apps
Edutecher
Geek SLP
App Free HD

Websites To Find Apps
appymall.com
teacherswithapps.com
thespeechguy.com
bridgingapps.org
smartappsforkids.com
iPad®insights.com
iOSnoops.com
Educational Technology and Mobile Learning http://www.educatorstechnology.com
Pinterest-Lauren Enders http://www.pinterest.com/lasenders/
teachthought.com

How Documents Get Transferred/Shared on An iPad®
Email them to yourself as a PDF and open them/save them in a PDF App
iCloud Drive (for Pages documents)
Google™ Drive AKA Google Docs (universal access-docs of all types are stored in Google™ format)
Dropbox.com
SugarSync.com
iTunes > My Apps > manually insert them into PDF Apps

Cloud Based Storage for the Data You Back Up/ Need to Access
iCloud for Apple™ (gives 5 GB free to start) multimedia
DropBox (free) documents, photos, PDFs
Evernote (free) documents, photos, PDFs
Google™ Drive (free) documents, PDFs
SugarSync (free) documents, music, videos, photos, PDFs
Amazon Cloud Drive (free) documents, music, photos
Microsoft SkyDrive for PC access
Zip Cloud
Backup Genie

NOTE

You must connect your iPad® to iTunes on your desktop for extra storage and group/ batch uploading and downloading of photos/music/PDFs, etc. Use iCloud as your main back up system. You can even buy more than the initially allotted 5 GB of storage in iCloud for a fee. It's crucial to regularly back up your photos, music, documents, drawings (exported as a JPG or PDF file) to your laptop/desktop, an external hard drive *and* the "Cloud"! Why?

Redundancy is the key to troubleshooting and smooth data organization! Basic "Toolbox" Apps are constantly evolving and can usually be found in the App Store under these categories: productivity and utilities. It is therefore *crucial* to monitor the App Store bimonthly, your folder configurations and your backup workflow. Also, take screen captures of your toolbox folder(s) at least once every other month and update your folder(s) as needed to get the most out of your "iPad® Experience"! One of the common complaints of people using my *Socially Speaking™ Program* is that due to all the planning and creation of pre-made activities and templates, iCloud storage becomes immediately full.

It is beyond the scope of this book to delve into the care and feeding of your iPad®. But I want to share this Infographic I created. It will help you understand how to manually manage your iCloud backups by turning on/off specific apps that don't need to store the data every time you used it to create a birthday cake, sing a song, color a picture, or draw a car etc. The reading list at the end of this chapter can provide more information.

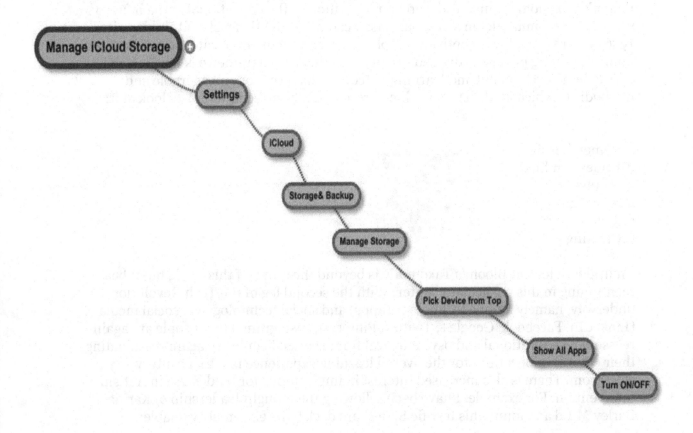

Infographic created with Simple Mind+ for iPad
by Penina Rybak MA/CCC-SLP

Bloom's Taxonomy and Implications for iOS App Integration

When asked to explain what Bloom's Taxonomy is in simple terms, I usually refer people to this funny Seinfeld video on YouTube:

http://bit.ly/1zmNkpn

I also refer people to this link, The Glossary of Education Reform, for this good working definition:

http://bit.ly/1DFmlor

"A classification system used to define and distinguish different levels of human cognition, i.e. thinking, learning, and understanding."

Bloom's Taxonomy gained widespread recognition in the educational arena in 2001 when Dr. Benjamin Bloom's original classification (of the six levels of thinking circa 1956) was revised. It's deceptively simple, logical and sequential categorization of the human learning process is divided up into 6 sections. This framework lends itself to curriculum development and learning outcomes that are more measurable and methodical, which is why special educators, especially speech therapists look at it:

1. Remembering
2. Understanding
3. Applying
4. Analyzing
5. Evaluating
6. Creating

An in-depth look at Bloom's Taxonomy is beyond the scope of this book, but it bears mentioning in this particular chapter. With the second leg of the Tech Revolution underway, namely mobile technology (apps) and social technology i.e. social media (LinkedIn, Facebook, Google+, Twitter, Pinterest, Instagram, etc.), people are again reassessing educational and psychological frameworks. People are again reevaluating their clinical implications for the overall learning experience in a 21st century classroom. There is also increased interest in implications for iPad® use in Autism intervention. For example, I have been following the thought leadership of Karina Barley M.Ed and found this terrific Slideshare deck to be extremely valuable:

http://slidesha.re/1D4oxVo

The advent of new, rapid advances in easily accessible and ever evolving technology has made us all rethink these frameworks, which are still relevant today. Best practices in special education today require a familiarity with frameworks re: behavior management, thanks to The Individual with Disabilities Education Act (IDEA, revised in 2004), and The No Child Left Behind Act (NCLB, 2002). They also require familiarity with various paradigms re: cognitive and psychological hierarchies such as Bloom's Revised Taxonomy (2001) and Maslow's Hierarchy of Needs (1943).

Both Bloom's Taxonomy and Maslow's Hierarchy have gained real traction in the educational and special education arena with the introduction of iPad®s into eLearning best practices. They are also impacting our learning process within a socially connected world. An in-depth look at Maslow's hierarchy is also beyond the scope of this book, which is why I recommend reading these two posts for further information:

http://bit.ly/1Kmo6bl

http://bit.ly/1vzoLTq

I also recommend that readers look at the list of suggested links I've compiled re: **Bloom's Taxonomy Application for iPad® Integration Best Practices** below, under Key References. It provides an overview of current thought leadership to ponder.

Let me briefly explain why understanding Bloom's Taxonomy, its terminology and its ramifications all matter in overall Autism Intervention. Basically, if we examine those six levels of learning, we will understand the importance of collaboratively and developmentally addressing specific areas of "social thinking" and social communication. Both of these areas can be difficult for young children with Autism, especially if they are slated for inclusion, i.e. mainstreamed regular education settings where literacy and social communication are paramount to the average curriculum. We will then better understand how the *Socially Speaking™ Program* targets goals that are aligned with both Bloom's Taxonomy and the child's overall IEP:

• *Remembering* learned material and rules (self regulation and behavior management, orientation to person/place/time: how the world "works") and accessing it in new, unfamiliar situations with (visual supports) or without perceptual support. (nouns/verbs/adjectives, prepositions)
• *Understanding* target vocabulary (matching, verbal description) and the rules of conversation: body language/respecting boundaries/Body Awareness, Theory of Mind, grammar/verb tense, topic maintenance and other listener needs, repairing communication breakdowns and turn taking.
• *Applying* learned skills to new situations: honing self regulation and episodic memory through play, fostering carryover of verbal language skills, especially Expressing Feelings, decreasing situation specific learning and splintered skill acquisition.
• *Analyzing* and sizing up situations and/or language concepts and making associations based on knowledge of Causality and object function: same/different sorting, categorizing like/unalike objects with verbal rationales, Why? questions, making inferences, drawing conclusions, verbal reasoning.

- *Evaluating* one's own performance in real time: self-monitoring behavior, beginner sequencing and narratives, Social Autopsy, first 3 steps of the Problem Solving Hierarchy, justifying actions verbally.
- *Creating* possible solutions and inventing new outcomes by using concepts/items differently: advanced sequencing and storytelling, making verbal predictions, actively differentiating between physical and linguistic humor and knowing which one to use when, the last 2 steps of the Problem Solving Hierarchy-- negotiation and accepting undesirable outcomes, being flexible with disappointment and setbacks/failure, and being resilient/overcoming obstacles.

Response to Intervention (RTI) and Learning in the iEra

There is another framework special education uses, with regard to both Autism Intervention and iPad® integration, known as Response to Intervention. The RTI Model was officially recognized in 2004, upon the reauthorization of the IDEA, and the prominent implementation of the No Child Left Behind Act of 2001. It is an educational strategy that has slowly gained momentum in schools across the country. Professional development and methodical accountability are becoming more widespread, with the advent of recent technological advances. We are also seeing an increase in integration of Assistive Technology (AT) into classrooms for a variety of students. It is becoming more routine for teachers to use lessons involving *Smart Boards* and computer tablets such as the iPad®. It is hoped that the future synthesis of AT use and RTI will help children progress. Parents are a crucial part of the child's team! Check out these articles online:

⦿ "Response to Intervention Guidelines" by James Hale: http://bit.ly/1zmNZXU

⦿ Response to Intervention-A Primer for Parents" by Mary Beth Klotz and Andrea Canter: http://bit.ly/1CzODnF

⦿ National Center for Learning Disabilities (NCLD) eBook/PDF, "A Parents' Guide to RTI": http://u.org/1Kx7Gya

RTI is a proactive, collaborative approach among parents, teachers, related service providers and administrators, to foster learning and target students who are "falling through the cracks" academically. The RTI framework has been adopted by many educators. It emphasizes the importance of early detection/intervention, monitoring progress and structured teaching that caters to the child's interests and specific needs. This three-tiered instructional model is geared towards identifying students at risk for learning difficulties, addressing the evaluated student's specific learning style, strengths and learning differences, in addition to implementing a collaborative approach to treatment.

Five Outcomes of the Use of RTI in Schools:

1. It promotes early detection through screenings at least 3 times a year.

2. It promotes teacher designed differentiated instruction (lessons) targeting the specific student's strengths and weaknesses.

3. It promotes "assessment driven instruction;" i.e. collaborative teamwork provides a "checks & balances" approach where techniques that aren't working are analyzed, discussed and dropped from that particular student's Management Plan.

4. It promotes ongoing staff professional development for the entire team, so that curriculum trends and teaching methods stay current and of high quality.

5. It promotes positive student interactions based upon personal learning styles, preferences, interests and strengths; i.e. lessons are geared to the student's unique "inner landscape" to enhance motivation, self esteem and mutual respect.

Principals of Learning and RTI Implementation

1. Personalized student assessment and management plans/lessons help cater to the child's interests, determine specific goals and methods for intervention and build camaraderie and optimism in class.

2. Learning styles in children tend to fall into 3 main categories: visual/auditory/tactile.

3. Learning in children tends to stem from either *Analytic* or *Global* (gestalt) Thinking.

4. Multiple Intelligence has 8 categories where student abilities can be tapped:

   - Verbal/linguistic

   - Logical/mathematical

   - Visual/spatial

   - Tactile/kinesthetic (Body Awareness)

   - Musical/rhythmic

   - Interpersonal (Pragmatics, Social skills)

   - Intrapersonal (Executive Functioning, Metacognition, Introspection)

   - Naturalist (diverse environments, outdoors preferred)

Basic Principals of RTI
All children can learn and "tap into" their potential.
Quality assessment drives instruction.
Quality teaching drives differentiated instruction.
Positive Behavioral Support enhances learning and peer relationships in class.
Team collaboration is crucial for the student's academic success.

The RTI framework hinges on the idea that when providing lessons in school, purposeful grouping yields results; academically, socially and emotionally. At tier 1, purposeful grouping is done in the "least restrictive environment;" i.e. the teacher uses information gleaned through screenings and informal assessments to plan lessons for everyone around the children's learning style, interests, strengths and weaknesses. A "buddy system" (AKA peer pairing) and other Positive Behavioral Supports are put in place, to help the students develop their own self reliance, self monitoring and Executive Functioning skills. Grouping students according to deficit/need/ability in a tier 1 setting has been shown to be less effective because: a) it negatively impacts the student's self esteem b) it causes parental concern about the social stigma their child may experience and c) it doesn't always allow the student to vary his/her interests and learning style, leading to a lack of diversity within the lesson and the group. At tier one, the two most important team members are the teacher and the parent(s).

The RTI framework mandates that smaller, more intensive grouping be conducted for tier 2 students as a "pullout service" within the school day. That is usually because tier 2 students have been found to have deficits in specific academic areas such as reading or math. They therefore need to be provided with group instruction that caters to the specific deficit while appealing to the child's multiple intelligence, learning style, interests and behavioral/pragmatic (social) needs. At tier 2, the team expands to include the reading specialist, possibly the school psychologist, speech-language pathologis, and occupational therapist, just to name a few.

The RTI Model intersects with the standard special education model and the implementation of the Individualized Education Program (IEP) at tier 3. Students in tier 3 are usually given intensive 1:1 learning opportunities to "fill in the gaps", such as individual speech therapy on a weekly basis. They may attend smaller classes with a smaller teacher-student ratio. They may still be given group instruction over the course of the school day, but the group dynamics and goals may differ between tier 1 and 2. For example, the concepts of "Circle Time" and "Centers" have been cherished times of the day in special education, self contained classrooms for decades.

These are 2 sacred times of the day when the child with special needs is introduced to purposeful grouping, given the opportunity to start developing specific academic and social skills that will enable the gradual transition from a Me to a We. As with all tiers, RTI has 3 elements that have become the responsibility of the team, through ongoing collaboration and professional development.

Elements of RTI
High Quality Instruction
Frequent Progress Monitoring
Data-Based Decision Making

Clinical Application of RTI and iOS App Integration

The clinical application of RTI within eLearning, such as integrating iPad® use into lesson plans, can be broken down into 2 categories:

1. Collaborative Goal Setting (include student input if applicable)

2. "Activating Prior Knowledge," AKA accessing episodic memory, using:

❖ *Cues* appealing to child's learning style (auditory-visual-tactile) ex: visual supports

❖ *Wh? Questions* that facilitate development of problem solving and Executive Functioning

❖ *Advanced Organizers,* i.e. outlines containing target vocabulary to facilitate access of semantic memory, development of Time Management skills and overall reading comprehension skills

In reality, eLearning involves active student participation, is usually self motivating and immerses the student in multi-sensory learning experiences engaging one or more of the Five Senses. It is no wonder that advocates of the RTI model have embraced integration of Assistive Technology (AT) into group instruction and classroom learning! Also, the flexibility that RTI promotes is inherent in the very use of AT, which by nature is individualized and flexible when dovetailed with the student's curriculum.

Furthermore, the very nature of the iPad®'s "user interface," i.e. the way the home screen operates, allows the RTI team to seamlessly transition between lesson plan apps for the student and note-taking and assessment apps to document progress, etc. This is all done while simultaneously empowering the tier 1 & 2 student to have a say in his/her goals, have students from all 3 tiers access episodic memory to use the AT and have students from all 3 tiers problem solve how to successfully navigate the "user interface" of the iPad®, etc. Aren't these the very outcomes we advocate through the RTI approach?

Finally, the very repetitive nature of AT devices such as the iPad® provide intrinsic reinforcement and practice trials so that students in every tier of RTI instruction develop better attention spans, retention of learned material over time and self esteem. These are all byproducts of RTI implementation, which we educators strive for on a daily basis with our students, no matter what their challenges are!

The long term ramifications of RTI implementation in special education need to be further studied and documented. The benefits of AT integration into IEP lesson plans, in special education in particular, have already been documented extensively. It is only a matter of time before we see journal articles on the efficacy of treatment and overall learning outcomes of the most famous yet recent "new kid on the block" AT device, the iPad® from Apple™. Dr. Dave Edyburn wrote about the value of using AT to enhance learning before the iPad® was even a household name.

"When a task is too hard to be completed successfully, students get frustrated and disengage. When a task is too easy, students get bored. Learning occurs when the challenge level of a task is 'just right.' I refer to this phenomena as "The Goldilocks Effect."

Edyburn, D.L. (2006). Failure is not an option: Collecting, reviewing, and acting on evidence for using technology to enhance academic performance. *Learning and Leading with Technology*, 34 (1): 20-23.

A critical function of teaching is to find the level of challenge that is "just right" for each student. I maintain that integrating the iPad® into lesson plans does just that. Implementation of the RTI model into special education strategies many of us already use, such as Visual Supports and Positive Behavioral Support, allows for an even more seamless integration of AT and eLearning. This in turn facilitates a child's Self Concept and overall academic performance in today's rapidly changing world.

A Word About RTI, Assessment Driven Instruction, and the Socially Speaking™ App

Assistive Technology integration into educational curriculums has become pretty much a standard practice in special education settings across the country. Integration of AT such as the iPad®, in those settings already using RTI, begins with the service provider first becoming more comfortable about using technology, and then implementing it while thinking "outside the box" and what the Big Picture is re: the student's behavioral, academic, and AT needs. To that end, I designed my *Socially Speaking™ App for iPad®* to be an interactive App, that gives AT a "human touch" by tailoring it to both the user and the child being documented. My App was designed with the principals of RTI in mind, including best practices re: AT. It caters to the service provider's varied caseload, need for "assessment driven instruction" and need for positive interactions based upon the child's interests and individual learning style. The Socially Speaking™ App thus gives the user opportunities to use the iPad®'s multi-App interface, to customize lesson plans with goals and personal photos/graphics, giving the child's team common ground/ language, better perspective and an easier time documenting future IEP goals. My Socially Speaking™ App is both an assessment protocol/screening tool re: social skills development and a lesson plan template to help track the young child with Autism and other special needs. This is the very essence of RTI--updating baseline data, determining starting points for remediation and succinctly documenting the team's approach re: materials and techniques.

Final Words

Digital citizenship today is a customizable, individualized and rapidly evolving virtual playground-- one where tech-savvy adults and diverse children meet, and critical thinking and social communication abound. This is where different frameworks of learning intersect to implement best practices and generalization of learned skills across environments. The focus of a good digital citizenship protocol implementing educational technology, especially iOS apps, lies in elegantly scaffolding the tech; i.e. building upon previous design and features of "old school" curricula targeting language, literacy, graphomotor and social skills. The Apple™ Inc. odyssey has laid the groundwork for unprecedented advances in technology which will impact our personal and professional lives for years to come. It's no wonder the iPad® has become the "It Product" of the new millennium!

It's important to remember that best practices in overall education, not just educational technology, involve assembling a meaningful toolbox of specific materials to implement change. It begins with assessing where the student is at cognitively and behaviorally so that developmentally relevant goals can be planned accordingly. As a result, the toolbox is handled with care and sensitivity re: budget constraints and cultural differences. The materials being used for the "teachable moment" get packaged properly for the "train ride" the student is embarking on. It's something that every educator considers carefully, which is why I am grateful for these two trailblazing speech therapists and fellow iPad® Evangelists. Two women who have helped us all pack for our ride: Lois Jean Brady MA/CCC-SLP and Lauren S. Enders MA/CCC-SLP.

Digital citizenship in the iEra is therefore as much about mindset as it is about performance. It's more than being a card carrying Mac user, a brilliant gadget-geek, or an ardent space- age pioneer in attitude. It goes beyond knowing how to intuitively navigate the user-interface for the iPad®. It means truly understanding that the whole really is greater than the sum of its parts. It involves understanding the inner landscape of the human mind, which is sculpted by exposure to technology in all its mediums, where one walks that tightrope of order and chaos.

A true digital citizen both acts upon the technology around him/her and reacts to it as well. A true digital citizen displays behavior and etiquette online and offline that showcases the ability to communicate and problem solve-- both which are the results of transformation from Me to We. That is the pinnacle of a human being's education and of my social skills curriculum. Dr. Maslow's Hierarchy of Needs has self-actualization as the highest level a person can achieve. In today's iEra, many would argue that attaining digital citizenship and having a useful, helpful and positive digital footprint is part of that achievement.

"True digital citizenship requires a degree of morality, accountability and responsibility."

True digital citizenship requires a degree of morality, accountability and responsibility that goes beyond the current chatter about fair use, cyber-security and safety and cyber-bullying. There needs to be more dialogue and effort in setting universal standards of performance and a unified protocol of best practices. We need regulations and rules which are developed by staying current re: best practices in AT and ed-tech trends. Being an authentic digital citizen means understanding, implementing and troubleshooting the tech, so that we can achieve better work/life balance and humanity/technology balance . The outcome: our collective dream of Computer Assisted Instruction (CAI) in special education, which started in the 1990's, becomes fully realized.

The increased use of mobile technology, especially iOS devices, is helping us make global digital citizenship a reality. But there is still work to be done by educators and parents everywhere, so that we can harness technology to be actually productive, not just busy. So that we can both "think differently" (the Apple™ credo) and "just do it" (the Nike mantra) with regard to educational, economical and social reform world-wide.

That is why I am an iPad® Evangelist who publicly advocates for its use in special education curricula, especially those geared for children with Autism. I passionately believe that we need to more fully, developmentally and creatively integrate iOS apps into treatment plans for children with Autism and/or special needs with social communication challenges. The customizable features of each iOS App, the ability to use iOS apps to generalize an individualized blue print (drawing, photo, audio-recording, etc.) of that child's Theory of Mind status and the social stature and ease of portability associated with this learning tool, all align with some unexpected results. While the child with Autism is engaged in learning in Real Time, and processing visual information more efficiently, given his/her learning style, the activity's (beginning/middle/end) execution provides collectible data for the behaviorist in every special educator to analyze and document: backwards chaining, fading, physical prompts and shaping/generalization.

Research shows that children with special needs, particularly Autism, appear to be "visual learners" who can have real challenges developing self regulation and social communication skills. They can greatly benefit from a methodical, collaborative and eclectic approach to behavior management so that we can more effectively bridge the gap between readiness to learn and actual performance. They can then truly benefit from the developmental, sequential and creative integration of toys and tech in lessons involving "whole body" learning, emphasizing the visual modality.

Word of mouth and popularity of eLearning, using the iPad® in particular, is growing rapidly. The app industry is one of the fastest growing forms of commerce in the world today. Parents, children and special educators/service providers are all increasingly lauding and using the iPad® as a creative, customized, intuitive and fun educational tool. It is being used more and more frequently at homes and in schools to implement lesson plans, address goals and utilize behavioral strategies to foster self regulation and social communication skills. It's why we need more great thought leadership about this and why I appreciate the teachings and writings of Med Kharbach and Tony Vincent.

Isn't it time you added this terrific technology to your toolbox? Isn't it time you joined the ranks of true digital citizens who can, and will, induct others into its ranks?

Materials for Your Toolbox

• Key References

☛ **For Autism Intervention Incorporating Assistive and Mobile Technology**

Brady, Lois Jean (2015). *Apps for Autism, 2nd Edition*. Arlington, TX: Future Horizons.

Chiak, D.F., Wright, R., and Ayres, K.M. (2010). Use of self-modeling static-picture prompts via a handheld computer to facilitate self-monitoring in the general education classroom. *Education and Training in Autism and Developmental Disabilities*, 45(1), 136-149.

Edyburn, D.L. (2005). Technology-enhanced performance. *Special Education Technology Practice*, 7 (2): 16-25.

Edyburn, D.L. (2006). Failure is not an option: Collecting, reviewing, and acting on evidence for using technology to enhance academic performance. *Learning and Leading with Technology*, 34 (1): 20-23.

Flores, M., et al (2012). A comparison of communication using the Apple™ iPad® and a picture-based system. *Augmentative and Alternative Communication*, 1-11. DOI: 10.3109/07434618.2011.644579.

Hodgdon, Linda (2012). *Special Report: Identifying Key Uses and Benefits From Apps for iPad®s for Autism Spectrum Disorders*. Troy, MI: Quirk Roberts Publishing.

Johnston, S., et al (2003). The use of visual supports in teaching children with autism spectrum disorder to initiate interactions. *Augmentative and Alternative Communication*, 19 (2), 86–104.

Maione, L., & Mirenda, P. (2006). Effect of video modeling and video feedback on peer directed social language skills of a child with autism. *Journal of Positive Behavior Interventions*, 8(2), 106–118.

Morgan, J.J. (2010) Social networking web sites: Teaching appropriate social competence to students with emotional and behavioral disorders. *Intervention in School and Clinic*, 45(3), 147-157.

Prest, J. M., Mirenda, P., and Mercier D. (2010). Using symbol-supported writing software with students with Down Syndrome: An exploratory study. *Journal of Special Education Technology*, 25(2), 1-12.

Rao, S. M., & Gagie, B. (2006). Learning through seeing and doing: Visual supports for children with autism. *TEACHING Exceptional Children*, 38 (6), 26-33.

Shepard, I., & Reeves, B. (2011). *iPad® or iFad – The reality of a paperless classroom.* Abilene Christian University, PDF.

Whitten, Elizabeth, Esteves, Kelli, and Woodrow, Alice (2009). *RTI Success: Proven Tools and Strategies for Schools and Classrooms.* Minneapolis, MN: Free Spirit Publishing Inc.

☛ For iPad® User Interface and Navigation Best Practices

Baig, Edward, and LeVitus, Bob (2014). *iPad® for Dummies.* Hoboken, NJ: John Wiley & Sons Inc.

Biersdorfer, J.D. (2014). *iPad®: The Missing Manual.* Sebastopol, CA: O'Reilly Media

Carlson, Jeff (2013). *The iPad® Air and iPad® Mini Pocket Guide: Fifth Edition.* Berkeley, CA: Peach Pit Press.

Hess, Alan (2012). *The New iPad® Fully Loaded.* Indianapolis, IN: Wiley Publishing.

Negrino, Tom (2013). *iCloud: Visual Quick Start Guide: Second Edition.* Berkeley, CA: Peach Pit Press.

Rosenzweig, Gary (2014). *My iPad®: Seventh Edition.* Indianapolis, IN: Que Publishing.

Rich, Jason R. (2013). *Your iPad® At Work: Fourth Edition.* Indianapolis, IN: Que Publishing.

Rich, Jason R. (2014). *How to Do Everything iCloud: Second Edition.* New York, NY: McGraw Hill.

Rich, Jason R. (2014). *iPad® and iPhone®: Tips & Tricks: Fourth Edition.* Indianapolis, IN: Que Publishing.

Rybak, Penina (2014). *The NICE Reboot: A Guide to Becoming a Better Female Entrepreneur.* Palmyra, VA: Maven House Press

• Key Links to Peruse

☛ **For iPad® Integration into Autism Intervention Best Practices**

http://bit.ly/1DasjzK

http://bit.ly/1yK0BVv

http://bit.ly/16HLrZf

http://bit.ly/1usX8Ov

http://bit.ly/1vbBZmS

http://bit.ly/1A33eaX

http://bit.ly/1C7TrLH

http://bit.ly/1A7mOBi

http://bit.ly/1IxuFxn

http://bit.ly/1vzdSVb

http://bit.ly/1A37mHZ

http://bit.ly/1C8V26t

http://bit.ly/1AKUhmm

http://bit.ly/1xRPTe2

http://bit.ly/1C7VpvI

http://bit.ly/1KDMYN8

http://bit.ly/1FsQJTX

http://bit.ly/1A3xcLI

http://bit.ly/1zMFrc1

http://bit.ly/1yJJW0g

☛ **For Bloom's Taxonomy Application for iPad® Integration Best Practices**

http://slidesha.re/1D4oxVo

http://slidesha.re/1zyqJGF

http://bit.ly/1DS4XNB

http://bit.ly/1zMmlCN

http://bit.ly/1zmrwpe

http://bit.ly/1A7rDdT

http://bit.ly/1FnhroR

http://bit.ly/1yXWwwY

http://bit.ly/19oeokz

http://bit.ly/1DupI44

http://bit.ly/1M3IpPI

http://bit.ly/1vzfJJs

http://bit.ly/19oflto

http://bit.ly/1A7tdwc

http://bit.ly/1zMk5eL

http://bit.ly/1DS6K5r

http://bit.ly/1wYrep2

http://bit.ly/1CJ8TmX

http://bit.ly/1EQMZ1P

http://bit.ly/1yXWlSq

☞ For Educational Technology Best Practices

http://bit.ly/1zmuYAg

http://bit.ly/16HYCJQ

http://bit.ly/1KxPoPj

http://bit.ly/1M9zf1q

http://bit.ly/1xSfkMH

http://bit.ly/1FnoyXc

http://bit.ly/19Oiauu

http://bit.ly/1A7zkko

http://bit.ly/1M3Sa0a

http://bit.ly/1A7EdKo

http://bit.ly/1utahap

http://bit.ly/1DaDecH

http://bit.ly/1KxVcIx

http://bit.ly/1vbKGhf

http://bit.ly/1DuzLGh

http://bit.ly/1DUouK6

☞ For Digital Citizenship Best Practices

http://bit.ly/1CJhQwu

http://bit.ly/1CJgP7t

http://bit.ly/16ZvqyG

http://bit.ly/1KE2etl

http://bit.ly/1CJjr5h

http://bit.ly/1DuG5h2

http://bit.ly/1M3WnkK

http://bit.ly/1C86JYF

http://bit.ly/1KxWLpT

http://bit.ly/16Cua3o

http://bit.ly/16ZAqDr

http://bit.ly/1EQQOEc

http://bit.ly/1zmBpDk

http://bit.ly/16Zzb7l

http://bit.ly/1KxTVRR

http://bit.ly/1CJgdil

☛ **For Response to Intervention Resources**

http://bit.ly/1DUi9RR

http://bit.ly/1vbQYog

http://bit.ly/1zmNZXU

http://bit.ly/1zmIbJt

http://bit.ly/1FnCekV

http://bit.ly/1CJo2o3

http://bit.ly/1M4oJrS

http://bit.ly/1EQZ473

http://bit.ly/1KE7NrM

http://bit.ly/1DUncSe

http://bit.ly/1KE8CB1

• <u>Key Concepts to Address</u>

iOS Apps, iPad®, educational technology, digital citizenship, best practices, user-interface, multiple intelligences, and rubric.

• <u>Key Toys to Use in Treatment</u>

☞ *For Cognitive Development:*

We can prepare children for digital citizenship and the use of mobile technology by introducing Cause and Effect Toys such as the Sassy Pop n' Push Car, Playskool Busy Poppin' Pals Toy, Earlyears Pound n' Play and Chicco Butterfly Spinner Toy.

☞ *For Fine Motor Development:*

We can prepare younger children for digital citizenship and the use of mobile technology by introducing toys that facilitate finger isolation and fine motor skills such as bubble play (pop with finger) and toy pianos, etc. We can also use other "pointing toys" such as the Fisher Price Toddlerz Chatter Phone, Fisher Price Laugh and Learn Click n' Learn Remote, VTech Spin and Learn Color Flashlight and The Learning Journey Shop and Learn Cash Register.

• <u>Key iPad® Apps to Use in Treatment</u>

☞ **For the Service Provider:** The ability to customize apps are a hallmark of digital citizenship whether one is using them for cloud storage or lesson plan creation purposes. Productivity and documentation apps are also getting more individualized, and were partially mentioned at in the app listing at the end of Chapter 1. Here's a suggested sampling to try:

☞ *Cloud Storage:* Dropbox, Evernote Premium, Pocket, Sugar Sync, Google Drive, Copy, Cubby, Box for iPad®, Shoebox - Photo Backup and Cloud Storage, iFile Browser & Download Manager, File Hub, Cloud Player, Cloud Mail.Ru, StreamNation and OneDrive by Microsoft.

☞ *Lesson Plan Creators:* Bitsboard, SonicPics, Doodlelicious, Kids Rainbow, Sago Mini Doodlecast, Art Maker, Photo Collage HD Pro, Keynote by Apple™, iPhoto by Apple™, Haiku Deck, Educreations, Screen Chomp, Explain Everything, Final Argument, Stick Around, ShowMe, Adobe Voice-Show Your Story, StoryMaker Free, SlideNotes by Anson Li, Air Sketch, Prezi, SlideShark, Doceri, Presentation Viewer for PowerPoint, Notability, Corkulous Pro, lino Sticky and Photo Sharing, Splashtop Whiteboard, Jot! Free and Whiteboard.

☞ *Mind Maps and Flow Charts:* Popplet and Popplet Lite, MindNode, Grafio, Canva, SimpleMind+, Mind Tree, Final Argument, iMindQ Lite, MagicalPad HD, BigMind Pro- Mind Mapping, Mindly, Connected Mind, Pearltrees, Mindomo, MindMapper, Connected Mind Classroom Edition, LearnDiscovery Map of Human Knowledge,

ToDo Maps with iCloud Integration Across Devices and Thought Cloud with Email Integration.

☞ *PDF Readers and Editors:* Notability, Adobe Reader, PDFree, iAnnotate PDF,, PDFPen, Easy Annotate, UPad Lite and Paid, Documents 5 by Reedle, Paperport Notes, Documents Free by Savy Soda, Memeo Connect Reader for Google Docs, PDF Reader, GoodReader4, Genius Scan- PDF Scanner, SignNow, Sign Easy, HelloSign, DocuSign, TinyScan Pro, WEB to PDF by Darsoft, PDF Printer by Darsoft, Scribd, To PDF, PDF2Office Free, Doc Scan HD, PDF Cabinet 2.0, PDF Slicer Free, Briefcase Pro, My Document for PC Users, PDF to Word, Type on PDF Free, Notes HD Free, Fast Scanner, CamScanner HD, Camera to PDF, Air Transfer, Voice Dream Reader Lite, Cortado Workplace, Inkflow and PDF Converter Pro and Free by Pradeep Singh.

☞ *Honorable Mention:*

◉ iPad® Mirroring Options, by Tony Vincent: http://bit.ly/16xGX08

◉ The Tile App for Inventory and Tracking Items in Real Time: http://bit.ly/1CJqdbm

◉ Zite App for Content Curation: http://bit.ly/1CJqlHW

◉ Desensitizing Children to Background Noise: http://bit.ly/1vbUdV

For the Child: Ed-tech best practices involves teaching children to harness their executive functioning and social communication skills by using multimedia/multi-sensory apps *under supervision.* Apps that teach creativity and critical thinking, as well as those that reinforce fine motor skills (grasp, pointing, tracing, pinching, etc.) and digital literacy are all crucial to 21st century curricula, especially in our globally connected society and shared economy. Here's a suggested sampling to try:

☞ *Creativity and Critical Thinking:* Sago Mini Doodlecast, Tiny Tap Maker: Make & Play Educational Games and Interactive Lessons, Toca Car, Toca Hair Salon, iCreate by Dewen Liu, Art Maker, My Story, Stick Around, Disney Creativity Studio, Comic Life, Strip Designer, Book Creator, Little Minds, Flashcards Deluxe, Amazing Alex, Build and Play 3D, Kids Trains Boats and Cars, ScratchJr., Superzaic- Kids' Mosaic Activities, Crayola Lights, Camera, Color!, Canvastic, Drawing with Carl Free, Little Star Learning Story Creator, Storybook Maker by Merge Mobile, 2Create a Story, 2Do It Yourself, MashCAM, My Story, Adobe Voice, Puppet Pal, Scribble Press, Doodle Buddy, Doodlelicious, OnceAppon, Easy Blogger Jr., Cracks the Books App, Explain Everything and Final Argument.

☞ *Motor Dexterity:* Fun Bubbles, Monster Chorus, MovePaint, Draw in 3D, Photo Buttons, ZoLO Lite and Paid, Injini Lite and Paid, DialSafe Pro, Felt Board, Make a Scene: Farmyard, MyPlayHome, Cake Doodle, SandyStories, Sago Mini Doodlecast, You Doodle Plus, Dexteria Jr., Stanza, Labo Car Designer, Snap Type for Occupational Therapy, Doodle Critter Math Shapes, Bug Art App, Toca Mini, Voice

Dream Reader, AbiliPad®, Bag Game, Talking Train, Starfall ABCs, Word Mover, Storia by Scholastic, LearnDiscovery, Geo Walk, WeirdButTrue and Little House Decorator Lite and Paid.

Chapter 12:

Conclusion and Reproducible Forms

Anecdote

When I was a child attending summer camp, the burgeoning educator in me breathlessly awaited two rites of passage. One was The Field Day Scavenger Hunt, where we looked for items posted on old fashioned "wanted posters" on the tree barks and cabin doors. The other was the Awards Banquet, where certificates of various achievement, big or small, were handed out with pomp and circumstance. I adored the signs helping me navigate the campgrounds, searching for clues and miscellaneous items. I enjoyed the anticipation and hoopla surrounding the awards ceremony. Those camp counselors knew a thing or two about "teachable moments"! They used multi-sensory, fun experiences as a motivator to engage in a specific behavior. They also used peer pressure and public verbal praise, to reinforce desirable, socially appropriate behaviors and actions. At the end of the day, we all want to know where things "stand" so that we can prepare for the next day's challenges and new opportunities. We also want appreciation and recognition for our accomplishments, and look to our inner circle for this validation. If I had to summarize the content of my book, I would divide it up into two categories; Wanted Poster for students and Certificate of Achievement for educators:

WANTED: YOUR SOCIALLY APPROPRIATE YOUNGSTER!
Who is able to orient to person/place/time
Who is able to get wants/needs met, and self regulate
Who has Body Awareness and respects boundaries
Who has an emerging sense of self, humor and TOM
Who can initiate and maintain eye contact, turn taking and sharing during conversation and play activities
Who can express feelings verbally, without tantrums
Who can problem solve and negotiate verbally, and accept outcomes graciously

CERTIFICATE OF ACHIEVEMENT

EXCELLENT SOCIAL SKILLS TREATMENT

★Fostering compliance in children with ASD through establishing rapport and routine, using knowledge gleaned from their "inner landscape"

★ Using indirect and direct behavior management strategies to bridge the gap between readiness to learn and actual performance by providing a) proactive attention, b) clear expectations and activities with a clearly defined beginning/middle/end, c) environmental modifications to facilitate learning and d) documenting behavioral triggers, replacements and consequences for the entire "team" to understand.

★ Knowing the prerequisite skills children need before developing social skills.

★ Understanding the role of The Five Senses and its effect on learning language and emotional attunement.

★ Understanding the role of Causality and humor in facilitating improved problem solving skills.

★ Implementing specific protocols to promote specific social skills (such as verbally expressing feelings and problem solving), based upon data collected from The Social Skills Check List and documented at a team meeting in the Social Skills Management Plan.

★ Implementing social skills goals into your multi–sensory lesson plans during specific portions of your day (Circle Time, meal time, free play, therapy sessions and dismissal)

★ Maintaining an optimistic, humorous and respectful outlook when teaching your students, documenting their progress and attending IEP meetings

Final Words

"I am never afraid of what I know."

-- Anna Sewell, *Black Beauty*

The pursuit of learning, whether it involves language or social skills, is a lifelong process for all human beings. We are all on the journey together, and are all generally heading in the same direction. We need to include everyone on the train ride, even young children with Autism and special needs. Many are unaware that there is a train. Many are often fearful to board it and take a ride with us into the unknown. We therefore need to understand their "inner landscape" and how it affects their perceptions and feelings about the world and those in it. We need to gently steer these children towards expanding their horizons and new views of their surroundings.

We need to methodically help these children climb the developmental ladder, so to speak; in a structured, linear manner, to maximize learning and carryover. We must patiently wait for the moment of transition from a Me to a We which is the goal of every parent and educator. We can then take great satisfaction in seeing these children blossom and grow. I hope I have shared some of the lessons I have learned on my own journey. I have enclosed reproducible forms, to help others on their own journey into the world of educating young children with ASD and other special needs. Understanding the value of teamwork is crucial in any arena, but especially so in targeting social skills building for these children.

It is a worthy endeavor, whose fruit can be harvested over time and practice......and enjoyed for years to come.

"All I ever needed to know I learned in kindergarten."

-- Robert Fulghum

I read a powerful essay many years ago, which I have since shared with others-- in my mentorship and supervision of students, in my parent meetings, in my IEP meetings, in my Socially Speaking™ Seminars and most recently in my 2014 book on female entrepreneurship, *The NICE Reboot- A Guide to Becoming a Better Female Entrepreneur: How to Balance Your Cravings for Humanity and Technology in Today's Startup Culture.*

Robert Fulghum's deceptively simple recipe for improving social consciousness and interpersonal relationships offers cookbook style therapy tips at their finest. Allow me to partially share his brilliant essay with you; it will really stop and make you think......

All I Ever Really Needed to Know I Learned in Kindergarten

by Robert Fulghum

"These are the things I learned: Share everything. Play fair. Don't hit people. Put things back where you found them. Clean up your own mess. Don't take things that aren't yours. Say you're sorry when you hurt somebody. Live a balanced life. Learn some and think some and draw and paint and sing and dance and play and work some every day.

And then remember the book about Dick and Jane and the first word you learned, the biggest word of all: LOOK .

Think of what a better world it would be if we.... clean up our own messes. And it is still true, no matter how old you are, when you go out into the world, it is best to hold hands and stick together."

If I could extrapolate his main idea it would be **look** around you and try to see those around you with new eyes. Take a closer look at the world we live in and really take a good look at the young child with Autism that you know.....and see what he or she is looking at. We now know that children with ASD see the world and its details differently. The Theory of Mind (TOM) and Mirror Neuron Hypothesis lend credence to this assumption. Robert Fulghum's essay should be required reading for all human beings out there-- for parents, for educators, for caregivers, or for friends.

In their early years, children have ample opportunity to look around and experience **wonder** as they learn about the exciting things this world has to offer. Their senses are bombarded and encouraged to explore, compare, experiment and process incoming stimuli-through the vehicle of play. Sometimes the pace of the activities presented can be overwhelming for the student with Autism/special needs. Their "inner landscape" gets flooded with too much, too quickly, resulting in sensory overload and the subsequent tantrums.

It is our job to help these children find the right balance and still find a way to "learn some and think some and draw and paint and sing and dance and play and work some every day". I have shared some ideas and tools from my Socially Speaking™ Toolbox to help you start. The rest is up to you! Let me know how I can help! You can be in touch and find additional resources by checking out my digital footprint and seeing what's on my radar.

"Alone we can do so little; together we can do so much."

-- Helen Keller

The above quote has been my motto throughout my career. "Join the Journey for Change!" and "Try the Socially Speaking™ Experience!" have been my company tag-lines since 2010. It's time to join the journey and change the way we do things. Change the way we all think about social communication development and the integration of toys and tech in treatment. It's time to change the way we educate ourselves and those special children in our care-- so that we can all move towards a more collaborative, bright future. Let's create a future where these children can more easily transition from Me to We, making the world a better place, one precious soul at a time. Who's in?

I respectfully leave you with some reproducible forms from my *Socially Speaking™ Program*. These forms have been curated, created, and copyrighted by me, but may be used for educational purposes. These forms are meant to be used in conjunction with the treatment goal, treatment plan and social skill kits, all of which were previously discussed in prior chapters. Please visit my website and/or social media sites to learn more, and access more helpful forms. Isn't it time to rethink intervention? Good luck!

Again, here is my digital footprint for my *Socially Speaking™ Program*:

Website: http://sociallyspeakingLLC.com

Email: Penina.SociallySpeaking@gmail.com

LinkedIn: Penina Rybak, http://www.linkedin.com/pub/penina-rybak/37/900/191

Facebook: Socially Speaking LLC

YouTube Channel: socialslp or Penina Rybak

Google+: Socially Speaking LLC

Pinterest: Penina Rybak

Twitter: @PopGoesPenina

About.Me Page: http://about.me/sociallyspeakingwithpenina

Success? There's an App for That..... APPLY Yourself and See Change Happen. Change Happens to You and Because of You.
- Penina Rybak

These are questions to ask at team meetings for data collection

When?
a) Doing a Functional Behavioral Analysis
b) Formulating goals for the Behavior Plan
c) Formulating Social Skills Goals

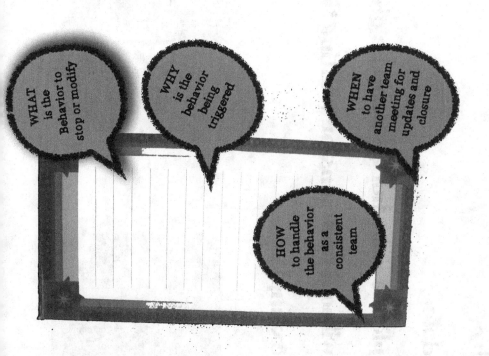

CRISIS INTERVENTION: THE 4 QUESTIONS TO ASK

detective in the house!

investigating likes/dislikes for behavior management for:

to build a reinforcer roster for class/therapy/home use:

by:

date:

please list what else can be given as a reward for completing work

without tantrums or wasting time..........

examples:

Rules in School:

Name:

Date:

sit nicely with
your feet on the floor

ask for what you want

talk quietly, no shouting

wait for your turn, even
if you don't want to

now

then

Visual Schedule in Class

Reinforcers to Choose (upon completing your work):

get a drink

ball

computer

swing

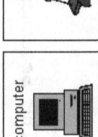

Visual Strategies created by Penina Rybak MA/CCC-SLP, using Boardmaker

How To Do This Sequencing Worksheet

Name:

Date:

1. Cut out the pictures in each row and place on the table

2. Look at each picture and decide where it goes

3. Paste the picture in the correct order first-middle-last

4. Tell me the "story" in order while coloring each picture

* Remember to ASK for help if you get "stuck"

Visual Supports-Task Organizer created by Penina Rybak MA/CCC-SLP, using Boardmaker

-This work was completed in class/speech therapy today (circle one) under the supervision of _____
-With assistance/sporadic assistance/no assistance by the teacher/speech therapist (circle one)

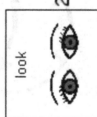

cut

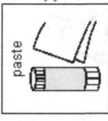

look

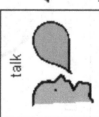

paste

talk

Prosody: A Social Skills Training Prerequisite Skill..... The Importance of Intonation When Talking

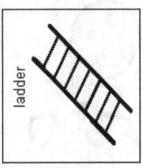

slide

_____'s voice tends to go down, like a slide. This is not good because it makes it hard to hear what he/she says, especially at the end of a sentence. Also, _____ needs to remember to speak long sentences, like a long slide.

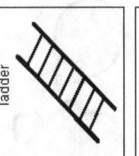

see-saw

Usually, when people talk, their voices go up and down, like a seesaw. This is good, because it makes the speech sound clearer. We can then understand each other better!

ladder

_____ needs to remember to raise his/her voice upward, when asking questions, like a ladder that starts off below, and goes up above. This lets us know when a question is being asked.

airplane

_____ needs to remember that talking is like an airplane flying. Sometimes the voice is steady/straight, and other times the voice dips below, or goes up high. Talking this way helps us show the other person our feelings AND what we are thinking and trying to say.

created by Penina Rybak MA/CCC-SLP using Boardmaker

Problem Solving When Teased: Social Skills Protocol on Bullying

What should you do when someone...

created by Penina Rybak MA/CCC-SLP using Boardmaker

 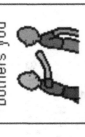

bothers you

tell a teacher

tell the person to

STOP

tell the person don't

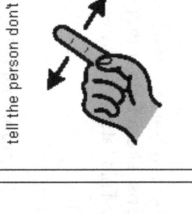

tell the person that you feel sad

Instead.........tell the person........

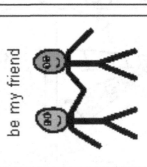

be my friend

I like you

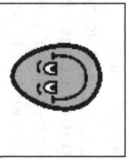 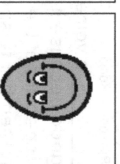

I have no one to play with....will you?

why are you doing that?

Dear Parents and Teachers:

Today in Speech Therapy with

paste your photo here	

To get better at.......

talking

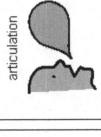

listening

oral motor skills

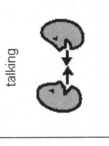

articulation

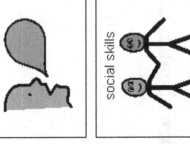

play skills

social skills

I played with the........

doll house	paints&worksheets
horn	computer
ball	

Name:
Date:
Comments:

Please write/call (circle one)

Visual Strategies-Communication from the Trenches: created by Penina Rybak MA/CCC-SLP, Using Boardmaker

The Five Senses Template

My name is _____ and I have 5 senses to learn about myself. I can tell you about...

What I like to hear:
What I am not supposed to hear:

What I like to see:
What I am not supposed to look at:

What I like to feel and touch:
What I am not supposed to touch:

What I like to smell:
What I am not supposed to sniff:

What I like to taste:
What I am not supposed to eat:

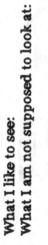

why is he happy?

why is he sad?

why is he mad?

Expressing Feelings and Verbal Rejection: Social Skills Task Organizer

created by Penina Rybak MA/CCC-SLP using Boardmaker V6+

Name:
Therapist/Teacher:
Date:

hurt

When something hurts me, I don't just cry. Instead, I can tell you where it hurts:

tongue	hand	mouth	eyes	finger

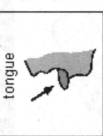  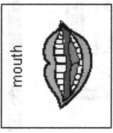 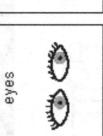

foot

Today I felt pain in my _____

Today I did not want to _____. Instead, I was able to use my _____ to say that. I was able to say it differently!

I don't want to

When I don't want to do something I can tell you this instead:

I don't want to	I want that	no	a little	later	take that away

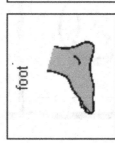 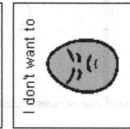 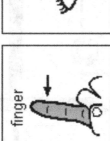 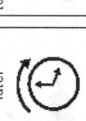  

Social Skills Curriculum: Task Organizer for The Problem Solving Hierarchy
created by Penina Rybak MA/CCC-SLP Speech-Language Pathologist

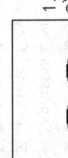

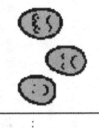

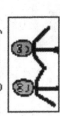
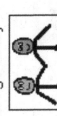
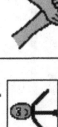
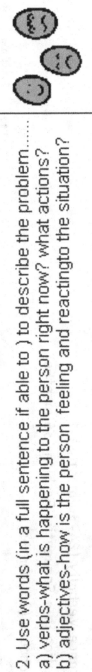

1. Look at the picture or person with the problem and notice......
   a) how does he/she feel?
   b) what's wrong?funny? missing?

2. Use words (in a full sentence if able to) to describe the problem......
   a) verbs-what is happening to the person right now? what actions?
   b) adjectives-how is the person feeling and reactingto the situation?

3. Think of possible solutions for the problem and......
   a) offer advice what to do
   b) talk about what NOT to do

4. VERBALLY negotiate and decide together how to try and fix things......
   a) come to an agreement of how to solve the problem, and admit to mistakes
   b) accept undesirable/unwanted outcomes graciously-no tantrums/whining!
   c) realize that some problems take longer to fix and/or don't go away
   d) decide that the outcome is OK and move on, even if
      you feel that it was unfair

Socially Speaking™ Social Skills Checklist for EI, © 2010 Penina Pearl Rybak MA/CCC-SLP

Early Cognitive Based Social Skills

	Rarely	Sometimes	Usually
1. Active Listening re: change in prosody/vocal inflection (3-6 months)	☐	☐	☐
2. Auditory Localization re: environmental sounds (6 months)	☐	☐	☐
3. Joint Attention with Eye Contact (7 months)	☐	☐	☐
4. Communicative Intent to get needs met (7-12 months)	☐	☐	☐
5. Babbles with Rising Intonation for Questions (12-18 months)	☐	☐	☐

Early Communication Based Social Skills

	Rarely	Sometimes	Usually
1. Initiates Greetings and Termination of Verbal Exchange-hi & bye (12-18 months)	☐	☐	☐
2. Verbal Rejection (protesting) emerges spontaneously (15-18 months)	☐	☐	☐
3. Theory of Mind (TOM) emerges: hands toy to adult for assistance (15 months)	☐	☐	☐
4. Body Awareness emerges: can identify basic body parts on self (18 months)	☐	☐	☐
5. Verbal Imitation emerges (18-24 months)	☐	☐	☐
6. Orientation (person/place): answers what/who/where questions (24-30 months)	☐	☐	☐
7. Requests Assistance Verbally (24-36 months)	☐	☐	☐
8. Relates Information in a Sequential Fashion (36 months)	☐	☐	☐
9. Understands Pronouns (36 months)	☐	☐	☐

Early Play Based Social Skills

	Rarely	Sometimes	Usually
1. Demonstrates a Social Smile (6 months)	☐	☐	☐
2. Demonstrates Object Permanence (9 months)	☐	☐	☐
3. Understands Symbolic Use of Objects (12-15 months)	☐	☐	☐
4. Expresses Environmental Awareness: explores toys (12-15 months)	☐	☐	☐
5. "Pretend" Play emerges (18-21 months)	☐	☐	☐
6. Problem Solving (the Physical Plane) starts:attempts to repair toys (24 months)	☐	☐	☐
7. Shares toys with others- "Parallel Play" starts emerging (30 months)	☐	☐	☐
8. Engages in Novel Play Schemas & "Associative Play" (36 months)	☐	☐	☐

The Socially Speaking™ Social Skills Preschool Checklist, ©2010 Penina Pearl Rybak MA/CCC–SLP

Child's Name _____ Teacher/Class _____

Date _____ Completed by _____ Speech Therapist _____

(to be filled out before the team meeting, IEP meeting, and /or before a behavior plan is drafted)

Introductory Social Skills

	Rarely	Sometimes	Usually
1. Active Listening (attention with eye contact)	☐	☐	☐
2. Making Requests	☐	☐	☐
3. Asking for Help	☐	☐	☐
4. Expressing Feelings Verbally	☐	☐	☐
5. Verbal Rejection (expressing dislikes and displeasure with task etc. using words)	☐	☐	☐

Intermediate Level Social Skills

	Rarely	Sometimes	Usually
1. Following Directions Promptly (response time, cooperation)	☐	☐	☐
2. Asking Questions (for clarification and social conversation reasons)	☐	☐	☐
3. Not Getting Discouraged (not giving up, trying when it's hard)	☐	☐	☐
4. Turn Taking in Group Activities	☐	☐	☐
5. Greeting Appropriately (verbal vs. gesture, adult vs. peer)	☐	☐	☐
6. Sharing with Others	☐	☐	☐
7. Transitioning/Bouncing Back	☐	☐	☐

Advanced Level Social Skills

	Rarely	Sometimes	Usually
1. Reading Body Language in Others (reading inflection, humor)	☐	☐	☐
2. Offering Assistance to Others (being kind, helpful, empathetic)	☐	☐	☐
3. Understanding Boundaries/Dealing with Feelings (ex:knowing who/when to hug)	☐	☐	☐
4. Problem Solving (The 5 Step Hierarchy © Penina Pearl Rybak MA/CCC–SLP)	☐	☐	☐
5. Stress Management (Self Soothing/Self Regulation re: mood– relaxing)	☐	☐	☐
6. Dealing with Losing During Play with Others	☐	☐	☐
7. Admitting Wrong Doing and Dealing with Mistakes	☐	☐	☐
8. Accepting Unfairness	☐	☐	☐

SOCIALLY SPEAKING™ LESSON MANAGEMENT PLAN

FOR_____ BY_____

LONG TERM GOAL: Date:_____

SHORT TERM GOAL: Date:_____

MATERIAL(S) TO BE USED AND RATIONALE :
Which AT is needed to ensure compliance? (ex: Visual Schedule, digital timer, "linked clips" attached to _____)

Note: Which visual format (objects vs. pictures etc.) and learning style (auditory-visual-tactile) is addressed?

Note: Is this a structured/elicited response type activity, or non structured/free style/spontaneous play task?

REINFORCERS BASED ON STUDENT'S PREFERENCES:
* food based (ex: piece of pretzel or licorice):
* toy based (ex: musical piano):
* social based (ex: discussing topic child chooses, clapping, singing, tickling etc.):

JUDGING PERFORMANCE AND DETERMINING PROGRESS:
* How many trials will be presented and counted?(ex: perform 3 out of 4 times)
* When will you consider a skill to have been "achieved"? (ex: when student completes a worksheet himself)
* How many repeated cycles will it take to teach the targeted skill? (ex: twice a day for 5 days)

FACILITATING CARRYOVER/GENERALIZATION TO OTHER ENVIRONMENTS:
Which activity can you present, in a free style way, to judge carryover? (ex: conversation with peer, obstacle course, playground time, playing "house", letting student be "the teacher" for a few minutes etc.)
Note: Carryover involves the student's verbal use of the targeted concept, spontaneously, in an attempt to self correct/modify his/her own behavior/performance, if child is capable of speech

Top 10 Features	Yes	No
I can both type and write (stylus) text		
I can create To Do lists and longer documents		
I can type using different fonts		
I can export via Email, Dropbox etc.		
I can draw/sketch with different colors		
I can annotate and export PDFs		
I can intuitively launch/ navigate the User Interface in timely manner		
I can create folders & tags for filing		
I can clip/attach photos, web content and URL links		
Online Support & Guides Available		

Documentation iPad® Apps Assessment Rubric by Penina Rybak MA/CCC-SLP
© 2013, Socially Speaking LLC, All Rights Reserved

Name of App:
Price:
Score out of 10:

Special Education iPad® Apps Assessment Rubric by Penina Rybak MA/CCC-SLP
© 2013, Socially Speaking LLC, All Rights Reserved

Desirable Features	Play Skills	Motor Skills	Language Skills	Social Skills	Cognitive Skills
Dynamic/ interactive					
Teaches causality through intrinsic use					
Has sound, motivates & reinforces auditory learners					
User friendly: easy to navigate, is intuitive & flexible					
Easy to share results: Exports to PDF; Email					
Fosters creativity and problem solving					
Targets visual learners: customizes photos					
Encourages carryover of ideas and language concepts					
Promotes solutions for targeted behaviors					
Enhances collaboration & cooperation					

Name of App:

Note: A score of 25 + makes the App worth purchasing

Socially Speaking™ Framework for iOS App Integration for Social Communication Proficiency in Early Childhood Special Education:

Visual Support Apps + Real Time Play= Increased Theory of Mind + Self Regulation

Pre-Literacy Apps + Social Communication Apps= Increased Executive Functioning

Facilitation of Behavior Management: Visual Supports Hierarchy
Photo Apps
Flashcard Apps
Drawing Apps
Social Story Apps
Facilitation of Orientation to Person/Place/Time
Person:
Body Awareness, Theory of Mind & Emotional Attunement: Photo, Flashcard, & Drawing Apps, Farm/Animal Apps
Place:
Self Regulation: Visual Schedules created from Camera/Photo Apps & Social Story Apps
Spatial Relationships: virtual worksheets created from Drawing Apps, and specific iOS Apps teaching prepositions
Time:
Language Development and AAC Apps to teach Executive Functioning, pre-literacy concepts, & communication skills
Expressing Feelings Apps (labeling feelings, story books, and wh? questions)
Transitioning Tasks Apps (sequencing, turn taking, fast moving games)
Problem Solving Apps (wh? questions, games, categorization, building/puzzle Apps)
Multimedia Apps (camera/photo, story, and music based) to foster episodic memory

COUNTERACTING SOCIAL BLINDNESS:
THE FOUR CORNERSTONES OF SOCIAL AWARENESS

From *Unwritten Rules of Social Relationships*, page 115
By Temple Grandin and Sean Barron © 2005
Edited by Penina Rybak MA/CCC-SLP

The Four Cornerstones of Social Awareness:	Definitions and Implications About Behavior and Pragmatic Skills	Correlations to the Socially Speaking™ Curriculum Areas	Suggested Speech Therapy Goals Based on the Socially Speaking™ Program
Perspective Taking	Putting oneself in another's shoes (TOM)	Body Awareness	1. Increase body parts vocabulary 2. Increase recognition of facial expressions in self/ others 3. Increase understanding of part-whole relationships 4. Increase inferencing skills
Flexible Thinking	Accepting change, adapting to the environment, and being responsive to changes in routine and alternative outcomes	Orientation to person/place/time	1. Increase understanding of pronouns, spatial relationships, and time concepts (receptive language skills) 2. Increase understanding & use of wh? questions 3. Increase sequencing skills (will also help with transitioning)
Positive Self Esteem	Having a "can do" attitude based upon having experienced repeated successes that start out small and concrete and becomes less tangible over time....forming the basis for accepting responsibility for one's actions, taking risks, and being resilient (not contingent on verbal praise)	Expressing Feelings	1. Increase ability to express feelings more age appropriately 2. Increase verbal rejection skills 3. Increase ability to verbally self monitor and self evaluate performance 4. Increase understanding and use of humor (physical and linguistic) 5. Increase facial affect through imitation and oral-motor exercises
Motivation:	Having sustained interest in exploring the environment, overcoming internal and external obstacles to work towards goals, broadening your "horizons" to learn new things and develop new interests about the world around you so that you can transition between being a "Me" and a "We"	Problem Solving	1. Increase ability to problem solve using The Five Step Hierarchy 2. Increase ability to initiate verbal greetings more age appropriately 3. Increase ability to maintain topic of conversation 4. Increase ability to ask questions more age appropriately re: prosody (intonation) 5. Increase Executive Functioning Skills (TBA)

Printed in the United States
By Bookmasters